W9-BVW-071

Historical Studies
in the
Physical Sciences
**4**

## Notice to Contributors

*Historical Studies in the Physical Sciences,* an annual publication issued by Princeton University Press, is devoted to articles on the history of the physical sciences from the eighteenth century to the present. The modern period has been selected since it holds especially challenging and timely problems, problems that so far have been little explored. An effort is made to bring together articles that expose new directions and methods of research in the history of the modern physical sciences. Consideration is given to the professional communities of physical scientists, to the internal developments and interrelationships of the physical sciences, to the relations of the physical to the biological and social sciences, and to the institutional settings and the cultural and social contexts of the physical sciences. Historiographic articles, essay reviews, and survey articles on the current state of scholarship are welcome in addition to the more customary types of articles.

All manuscripts should be accompanied by an additional carbon- or photocopy. Manuscripts should be typewritten and double-spaced on 8½" × 11" bond paper; wide margins should be allowed. No limit has been set on the length of manuscripts. Articles may include illustrations; these may be either glossy prints or directly reproducible line drawings. Articles may be submitted in foreign languages; if accepted, they will be published in English translation. Footnotes are to be double-spaced, numbered sequentially, and collected at the end of the manuscript. Contributors are referred to the *MLA Style Sheet* for detailed instructions on documentation and other stylistic matters. (*Historical Studies* departs from the MLA rules in setting book and journal volume numbers in italicized Arabic rather than Roman numerals.) All correspondence concerning editorial matters should be addressed to Russell McCormmach, Department of History of Science, Johns Hopkins University, Baltimore, Md. 21218.

Fifty free reprints accompany each article.

*Historical Studies in the Physical Sciences* incorporates *Chymia,* the history of chemistry annual.

*Editor*
RUSSELL McCORMMACH, *Johns Hopkins University*

*Editorial Board*
JOAN BROMBERG, *Simmons College*
CLAUDE K. DEISCHER, *University of Pennsylvania*
STANLEY GOLDBERG, *Hampshire College*
OWEN HANNAWAY, *Johns Hopkins University*
JOHN L. HEILBRON, *University of California, Berkeley*
ARMIN HERMANN, *University of Stuttgart*
TETU HIROSIGE, *Nihon University, Tokyo*
GERALD HOLTON, *Harvard University*
ROBERT H. KARGON, *Johns Hopkins University*
MARTIN J. KLEIN, *Yale University*
HERBERT S. KLICKSTEIN, *Albert Einstein Medical Center, Philadelphia*
BORIS KUZNETSOV, *Institute for the History of Science, Moscow*
THOMAS S. KUHN, *Princeton University*
HENRY M. LEICESTER, *University of the Pacific*
JEROME R. RAVETZ, *University of Leeds*
NATHAN REINGOLD, *Smithsonian Institution*
LÉON ROSENFELD,[†] *Nordic Institute for Theoretical Atomic Physics, Copenhagen*
ROBERT E. SCHOFIELD, *Case Western Reserve University*
ROBERT SIEGFRIED, *University of Wisconsin*
ARNOLD THACKRAY, *University of Pennsylvania*
HARRY WOOLF, *Johns Hopkins University*

# Historical Studies
## in the
# Physical Sciences

RUSSELL McCORMMACH, *Editor*
*Fourth Annual Volume*

PRINCETON UNIVERSITY PRESS
PRINCETON, NEW JERSEY

Copyright © 1974 by Princeton University Press

All Rights Reserved

LCC: 77-75220

ISBN: 0-691-08133-6

This book has been composed in IBM Selectric Aldine

Printed in the United States of America by Princeton University Press,
Princeton, New Jersey

# Contents

# Historical Studies
## in the
## Physical Sciences
# 4

# German Biophysics, Objective Knowledge, and Romanticism

## BY CHARLES A. CULOTTA*

In 1798 Friedrich Schelling said that life is the tendency toward individuation.[1] Over two generations later in 1897 Ernst Mach described death as the release from individuality.[2] The similar thought and phraseology in two works a century apart are not fortuitous; they express a cultural ideal common to one of Germany's greatest romantics and to one of Germany's most renowned champions of the critical method in science. The historiography of science has reached a stage in which it is no longer heretical to say the name of a romantic philosopher in the same breath with that of a physicist and critical philosopher.[3] To suggest that affinities exist between early nineteenth century romantics and rigorous scientists and philosophers of science later in the century should not be considered a semantic exercise in pairing similar phraseology.[4]

In the main, historians of science have looked at change in science as discontinuity, revolution, watershed, and generational chasm. They have

*Department of History, Bryn Mawr College, Bryn Mawr, Pennsylvania 19010. An earlier version of this paper was read before the Fifth Joint Atlantic Seminar on the History of Biology, Washington, D.C., March 1969. Requests for reprints of this article should be addressed to the editor of this series, Russell McCormmach, Dept. of History of Science, The Johns Hopkins University, Baltimore, Md. 21218.

[1] As quoted by Herbert Spencer, *The Principles of Biology*, 2 vols. (New York, 1898), *1*, 60; "Von der Weltseele" (1798), *Schellings Werke*, 3 vols. (Leipzig, 1902), *1*, 663.

[2] Ernst Mach, *Analysis of Sensations and the Relation of the Physical to the Psychical*, trans. 5th German ed. by C.M. Williams (1897; reprint New York, 1959), p. 5.

[3] The terms "romantic" and "romanticism" are used in a loose sense to permit a discussion of the similarities between them and other "labeled" forms of thought. Strict definition often serves only the academic purpose of dividing to conquer; the meanings of "romanticism," "Naturphilosophie," and "Wissenschaftslehre" are not so far apart at a general level of analysis. Each reveals the German concern for epistemological problems and for attitudes toward the subject matter of science. For a discussion of the problems of defining "romanticism," see John B. Halsted, ed., *Romanticism. Definition, Explanation*, and *Evaluation* (Lexington, Mass., 1965).

[4] Phillip Ritterbush, *The Art of Organic Forms* (Washington, D.C., 1968), p. 32: "Because the mechanist and vitalist positions are ultimately reducible to attitudes toward what has not yet been discovered, they are unsatisfactory as classifiers of scientific accomplishment. The label tells us not what a scientist actually discovered or stated but only where he was looking when he did it and what he made of it."

3

sensed the excitement and sometimes revolutionary mood accompanying scientific innovation. Yet they have also been troubled by their preoccupation with precipitous change; accordingly they have searched for precursors of the innovative scientist or for scientific anomalies antecedent to the innovation. They have not, however, devoted sufficient attention to the influence of cultural continuities on the scientist and to the continuity of problems he faces as a practitioner of his discipline.

In this study I will try to provide a cultural matrix for a scientific event that traditionally has been treated as a revolution: the rise of biophysics in opposition to the scientifically sterile romanticism of an earlier era. The preoccupation of historians with the materialist spokesmen for biophysics has obscured the influence of cultural and scientific continuity in the practice of biophysical science. Biophysics loses none of its scientific significance if we examine more fully its goals and limitations in relation to German cultural traditions of the 1830's and 1840's. The traditions that influenced biophysics include romantic views on nature and concern for unity of knowledge, national unity, the status of natural law, human freedom and consciousness, and epistemology.

I will demonstrate first that German biophysicists saw and practiced their science as a limited rather than as a universal program for the physical understanding of the animate world; second, that the limited program bears a stronger resemblance to romantic than to materialist philosophies; and third, that romantic concerns, having become deeply entrenched in Germany's political ethos, were the probable origin of the psychological views of the biophysicists.

By studying science within the rising German nation of the nineteenth century, the historian has a good opportunity to measure the interaction of general with scientific thought within a newly patterned social setting. The nationalistic drive of Germans for political unity, their politically planned industrial revolution,[5] their educational reforms and political intervention in academic science, and their eventual dominance of the scientific world all belong to the first three quarters of the nineteenth century.

Before Germans were concerned with political unity, they were concerned with unity of thought; since the time of Leibniz, German thinkers

---

[5] See William O. Henderson, *The State and the Industrial Revolution in Prussia, 1740–1870* (Liverpool, 1958), and Eugene N. and Pauline R. Anderson, *Political Institutions and Social Change in Continental Europe in the Nineteenth Century* (Berkeley, 1967).

agonized over philosophical unity, while the English worried little about it and the French presumed they had it. Germans felt compelled to affirm that unity and to demonstrate it whenever and wherever possible. Their concern with the unity of knowledge—with the unity of the humanities, arts, and sciences—found an institutional home in the German universities of the nineteenth century.[6]

The word "unity" appears so frequently in all genres of German writing that its importance cannot be doubted; the desire for unity was expressed by political reformers, by philosophical idealists, and by the rank and file of the romantic movement.[7] The German romantics' introspective search

[6]Throughout this paper the broad cultural basis of many of the ideas discussed are indicated by a series of references in a single footnote, preventing unnecessary repetition of names in the test. John T. Merz, *A History of European Thought in the Nineteenth Century,* 4 vols. (1904–1912; reprint New York, 1965), *2,* 241: "By far the most important psychological question with which Kant dealt was the problem of the unity of thought as it appears in the exact knowledge which we possess in the sciences." See also George G. Iggers, *The German Conception of History: The National Tradition of Historical Thought from Herder to the Present* (Middletown, Conn., 1968), pp. 51ff.; F. Schelling, *Of Human Freedom,* trans. James Gutman (Chicago, 1936), and *Vorlesungen über die Methode des academischen Studiums* (Tübingen, 1803); and Bruno Gebhardt, *Handbuch der deutschen Geschichte,* 8th ed., 4 vols. (Stuttgart, 1954–1960), *3,* 69.

[7]For general discussions of the importance of the unity of knowledge for the romantics, see Morse Peckham, *Beyond the Tragic Vision* (New York, 1962), p. 229, and Oskar Walzel, *German Romanticism,* trans. from the 5th German ed. of 1923 by A. Lussky (New York, 1932), p. 15. Kant also suggested that unity lies outside nature; see C. Meredith's introduction to his translation of *Kant's Critique of Teleological Judgement* (Oxford, 1928), p. xiii. For the similar concern for unity and psychology in other philosophers, see Martial Gueroult, *L'Evolution et la structure de la science chez Fichte,* 2 vols. (Paris, 1930), *1,* 48, 161, and Richard Brandt, *The Philosophy of Schleiermacher* (New York, 1941), p. 46. Novalis and the Schlegel brothers were equally concerned with unity; see Walzel, *op. cit.,* p. 63. Schelling made the problem of unity closely allied with but subservient to human consciousness; see his *Ages of the World,* trans. F. Bolman (New York, 1942), pp. 4–5. Hegel continued to be preoccupied with unity; see Gueroult, *op. cit.,* pp. 7–8, and J. van der Meulen, "Hegel's Lehre von Leib, Seele und Geist," *Hegel-Studien, 2* (1963), 251. Subsequent influential philosophers also stressed the unity of all forms of knowledge; e.g., after receiving his theological degree and after his conversion to Hegel, Ludwig Feuerbach studied science at Erlangen in order to grasp the whole of man. Arthur Schopenhauer struggled with unity in his *The World as Will and Idea,* trans. R.B. Haldane and J. Kemp, 3 vols. (London, 1893–1896), *2,* 378–379. Hermann Lotze insisted upon unity in his *Metaphysic* (1841), trans. B. Bosanquet (Oxford, 1884), pp. 169, 323, 373, 442–443. Iggers, *op. cit.* (note 6), p. 96, found that German historians were concerned with unity. Karl Rothschuh found the same for German physiologists; see his "Ansteckende Ideen in der Wissenschaftsgeschichte, gezeigt an der Entstehung und Ausbreitung der romantischen Physiologie," *Dtsch. Med. Wochenschr., 86* (1961), 396–402.

for a fulfilling cosmology derived from their rejection of the Enlightenment worldview. Like the idealists, they sought a unity of man and cosmos, but not from the idealist premise of ontological universals. For them, man was to be the measure of all things. From man's individual existence and his participation in and intuitive grasp of the cosmos, unity could be achieved rather than abstractly mandated. The romantics were not lost in whimsical speculation, but were deeply concerned that their introspection related to the world about them. Although their world was sensual and anthropomorphic, it included, besides science, human freedom and moral choice.[8] They sought universal order not in eighteenth century natural law, but in individual consciousness and, eventually, in the historical reality of the nation's collective consciousness.[9]

Romantics did not regard science as an unacceptable route to knowledge. They did, however, reject the godless, mechanistic science of the late eighteenth century in favor of a science in which man could feel secure.[10] I will examine the underlying role of romantic epistemology, regarded as a cultural influence, surviving in the work of scientists who had been exposed to romanticism in their youth. Although there are precedents for my approach,[11] there is a tendency among historians to dismiss romantic notions as having had no bearing on the experimental sciences.

Although the link between the history and the philosophy of science has been sometimes productive, it has had at least one deleterious effect on

[8]Peckham, *op. cit.* (note 7), p. 81, and Helmuth Plessner, *Die verspätete Nation. Ueber die politische Verführbarkeit bürgerlichen Geistes* (Stuttgart, 1959), p. 81.

[9]For Schelling's view of natural law, see *op. cit.* (note 7), p. 94; for Hegel's, see M. Riedel, "Hegel's Kritik des Naturrechts," *Hegel-Studien, 4* (1967), 177-204; on the general dislike of natural law concepts on the part of intellectuals, see Iggers, *op. cit.* (note 6), pp. 5-9, 35, 39, 94.

[10]Walter Wetzel, *Johann Wilhelm Ritter: Physik im Wirkungsfeld der deutschen Romantik*, unpublished doctoral dissertation (Princeton, 1968), pp. 1-27; Rudolf Haym, *Die romantische Schule* (1870; reprint Hildesheim, 1961), pp. 580ff.; Iggers, *op. cit.* (note 6), p. 59; Brandt, *op. cit.* (note 7), p. 55.

[11]See R.C. Stauffer, "Persistent Errors Regarding Oersted's Discovery of Electromagnetism," *Isis, 44* (1953), 307-310, and "Speculation and Experiment in the Background of Oersted's Discovery of Electromagnetism," *Isis, 48* (1957), 33-50; T.S. Kuhn, "Energy Conservation as an Example of Simultaneous Discovery," in M. Clagett, ed., *Critical Problems in the History of Science* (Madison, 1962), pp. 321-356; O. Temkin, "Basic Science, Medicine, and the Romantic Era," *Bull. Hist. Med., 37* (1963), 97-129; C. Probst, "Johann Wilbrand (1779-1846) und die Physiologie der Romantik," *Sudhoffs Archiv, 50* (1966), 157-178; H.A.M. Snelders, "Romanticism and Naturphilosophie and the Inorganic Natural Sciences, 1797-1840," *Stud. Roman., 9* (1970), 193-215; and John H. Randall, *The Career of Philosophy*, 2 vols. (New York, 1962-1965), *2*, 207.

the historiography of nineteenth century German science. Historians and philosophers have tended to associate epistemology exclusively with the scientific method. This association has not only forced epistemology to bear a greater scientific burden than is historically justified, but it has also obscured the powerful influence of romantic epistemology on science. Since there is little within romanticism from which one can build a respectable scientific method, historians have slighted its influence on modern science.[12] Whereas even the most conservative historians of the Renaissance and the Scientific Revolution take seriously mystical and alchemical worldviews as sources of scientific attitudes toward nature, historians of modern science have failed to explore fully the relations of romanticism and the dynamics of scientific change.

Too great a reliance on the generalization that Kant and Hegel were opposite philosophical poles toward which all subsequent German thinkers were attracted, or from which they were repelled, also has hampered a cultural approach to the history of nineteenth century German science. Although this generalization is certainly more true than false, the full implication of the magnetic pole analogy must be taken into account: lines of magnetic force imply that meaningful orientations lie between the polar extremes, and hence, following the analogy, the historian should look at more than just the poles to grasp the intellectual patterns of nineteenth century Germany.[13] Many of the generation of romantics and idealists succeeding Kant—such as J. G. Fichte (1762–1814), A.

[12] See, for example, Emile Meyerson, *Identity and Reality*, trans. from the 3rd French ed. in 1926 by Kate Loewenberg (London, 1930), pp. 288–289. While not exacting on scientific methodology, Schelling, for example, did make statements that profoundly affected one's outlook toward science; see Schelling, *op. cit.* (note 7), p. 94: "Propositions which are unconditioned, that is valid once [and] for all, are antagonistic to the nature of true science, which consists in progress." The confusion between epistemology and scientific method is pointed out in L. Laudan, "Theories of Scientific Method from Plato to Mach," *Hist. Sci.,* 7 (1968), 56, 79.

[13] J.H. Randall has shown that after 1806 German romantics followed Schelling in becoming more interested than their predecessors in empirical studies, yet he has felt it necessary to say that romanticism was harmful to science, even though science did not exist according to our modern understanding. See Randall, *op. cit.* (note 11), pp. 249, 250, 256; in contrast Richard Shryock, *The Development of Modern Medicine* (New York, 1947), p. 200, noted that: "To understand the whole sweep of German thought that was involved with particular reference to medicine and biology, one should begin by reading Schelling and end with Ernst Haeckel." It should not be forgotten that Schelling received special attention and royal favor at the Bavarian Academy; see Aloys Wenzel, "Die Vertreter der Philosophie in der bayerischen Akademie der Wissenschaften vom deutschen Idealismus bis zum kritischen Real-

Schopenhauer (1788–1860), F. W. Schelling (1775–1854), and H. Lotze (1817–1881)—were indirect but potent influences on the formation of scientific concepts; although they used Kant's terminology and definition of causality, their philosophies were far from rigid copies of Kantian idealism.[14] In addition, Kant's writings influenced several currents of thought in the nineteenth century that admitted no indebtedness, an eclectic plagiarism described by T. M. Greene.[15] It was only after a group of neo-Kantians had assessed Kant's legacy as *Erkenntnisstheorie* that his full impact could be seen. If Kant's ideas had an ambivalent and diverse influence on the nineteenth century, so had Hegel's; the endless stream of histories dealing with the Hegelian origins of socialism, communism, the political left, orthodox German historiography, and nationalism are well known. Although historians have acknowledged that romanticism had an impact on Hegel as well as on Kant, they have little appreciated that Hegel sought to preserve a major goal of *Naturphilosophie*. That goal was a unified science of nature, attained through greater rigor and massive reliance upon empirical investigation.[16] If the historian were forced, as he is not, to chose between the polar extremes of Kant and Hegel in locating epistemological mainstreams in Germany, Hegel would appear to him the more important of the two; however, the historian would do more justice to the rich complexity of nineteenth century German thought by recognizing that the mainstream was Kant as understood and disseminated by the Hegelians who dominated university posts in philosophy.[17]

An important aspect of the myriad philosophical reactions to the

ismus," in *Geist und Gestalt. Biographische Beiträge zur Geschichte der Bayerischen Akademie der Wissenschaften, vornehmlich im zweiten Jahrhundert ihres Bestehens. Erster Band. Geisteswissenschaften* (München, 1959), p. 50.

[14] For an excellent critical review, see G. Buchdahl, "Causality, Causal Laws and Scientific Theory and Philosophy in Kant," *Brit. J. Phil. Sci.*, *16* (1965), 187–208.

[15] "Introduction," *Kant Selections*, ed. T.M. Greene (New York, 1929), pp. xvii–lxxi.

[16] See A.V. Miller's translation of *Hegel's Philosophy of Nature Being Part Two of the Encyclopaedia of the Philosophical Sciences (1830). Translated from Nicolin and Poggeler's Edition (1859) and from the Zusätze in Michelet's Text (1847)* (Oxford, 1970), pp. 1, 6, 8, 10, 11–12, 273, 353.

[17] H. Gollwitzer, "Altenstein, Karl Sigmond Franz Frhr. vom Stein," *N.D.B.*, *1*, 216–217; Rudolf Virchow's 1893 address on "Die Gründung der berliner Universität und der Uebergang aus dem philosophischen in das naturwissenschaftliche Zeitalter," *Idee und Wirklichkeit einer Universität. Documente zur Geschichte der Friedrich-Wilhelms-Universität zu Berlin*, ed. Wilhelm Weischedel, 2 vols. (Berlin, 1960), *2*, 420; and Eden and Cedar Paul, *Treitschke's History of Germany in the Nineteenth Century*, 4 vols. (London, 1918), *4*, 568–569.

Enlightenment in Germany was a reorientation toward non-Lockean theories of epistemology.[18] Foreshadowed by Hume, they were cultivated by idealists, romantics, and biologists.[19] The quest for a learning theory and psychology that was simultaneously anthropocentric, pragmatically mechanistic, and proximate to classical idealism provided the common ground for humanistic and scientific scholarship in the period.[20]

It is therefore the sympathies and concerns of the romantic movement rather than its content that guide the historian in seeking an understanding of early biophysical science in Germany. The romantic concerns that survived in the culture of Germany in the 1830's and 1840's are man's uniqueness and freedom of moral choice, consciousness, epistemology, and the representation of the physical universe by the laws of matter and of motion. The presence of these concerns in the writings of biophysicists is evidence of their scientific relevancy or, at least, of their failure to prevent the growth of science. In either case the romantic concerns of German biophysicists place them within the cultural environment of their time.

In order to lay the groundwork for evaluating the role of romantic con-

[18]The common analogy in political thought between the growth of a plant and the growth of the state is just as indicative of an organismic outlook as vitalism in biology; and organicism goes hand in hand with descriptions of mental processes as more than the summation of sensations. See Peckham, *op. cit.* (note 7), p. 97: "Organicism, an Enlightenment idea in its origin, became a dominating mode of nineteenth century thinking." Eduard von Hartmann complained about Hegel's legacy of an unending stream of epistemological publications, yet admitting that "the theory of knowledge is the true *philosophia prima*" (*Philosophy of the Unconscious: Speculative Results according to the Inductive Method of the Physical Sciences*, trans. of the 9th German ed. of 1884 by William Coupland [New York, 1931], p. xxxiii).

[19]For the general significance of epistemology, see Merz, *op. cit.* (note 6), *3*, 197; on Hegel's epistemology, see Miller, *op. cit.* (note 16), p. 8; on Schelling, see *op. cit.* (note 7), pp. 90–91, and Walzel, *op. cit.* (note 7), p. 63. Schopenhauer, *op. cit.* (note 7), *2*, 383, 387, held the same opinion as Schelling. Lotze introduced this epistemological position as basic to physiology in his famous article "Seele" in Rudolf Wagner's *Handwörterbuch der Physiologie*, 4 vols. (Braunschweig, 1846), *3*, 143. Consciousness-based epistemology was already integrated into the work of physiologists a generation earlier; see Georg Prochaska, *Physiologie oder Lehre von der Natur des Menschen* (Wien, 1820), p. iii.

[20]This is not a case study of Karl Popper's thesis on the role of epistemology and falsification in the philosophy of science. All I wish to suggest is that at this point in time in Germany epistemology was a significant component of culture, and that therefore the epistemology of Hegel, Schelling, and the Humboldts did not have to disappear to permit the rise of science. For Popper's position, see his introduction to *Conjectures and Refutations: The Growth of Scientific Knowledge* (New York, 1962).

cerns in biophysics, it is necessary to clear away common misconceptions about the "revolutionary" program of the "biophysicists." They are usually pictured as the avant garde of the 1848 revolution, as if it were only natural that there be a direct link between two such contemporaneous, dramatic, and secular events. The link is made by identifying the revolutionaries as crass political materialists and by regarding the biophysicists as their militant counterparts in science. The political side of the stereotype has been shown to be woefully inadequate;[21] moderate political reformers were greater in number than the militants, and they experienced the greatest success, however shortlived.[22] So, too, were the moderate biophysicists more successful in their careers and more numerous than their extremist scientific counterparts.

Historians of science have generally regarded the biophysicists as extremists advocating the complete reduction of living phenomena to matter and motion,[23] as champions of the revolution and total enemies of *Naturphilosophie*.[24] The image of the biophysicists thus takes on an artificial clarity. Although biophysicists frequently made statements on behalf of their empirical science and against the speculative science of the *Naturphilosophen,* we may not conclude from this that the latter's philosophy was all speculation and that the biophysicists wholly rejected the previous generation's ideals.[25] There is a similarity between scientific, political, and philosophical attitudes in German society, but their similarity lies on the middle ground of thought and not on its extreme

[21] The theme of moderate liberalism runs through the works of several historians; see R. Hinton Thomas, *Liberalism, Nationalism and the German Intellectuals (1822-1847). An Analysis of the Academic and Scientific Conferences of the Period* (Cambridge, 1951); Theodore S. Hamerow, *Restoration, Revolution, Reaction. Economics and Politics in Germany 1815-1871* (Princeton, 1958); and Frank Eyck, *Frankfort Parliament 1848-1849* (New York, 1968).

[22] Hamerow, *ibid.,* pp. 187-192.

[23] E. Mendelsohn, "Physical Models and Physiological Concepts: Explanation in Nineteenth Century Biology," *Brit. J. Hist. Sci.,* 2 (1965), 1; P. Cranefield, "The Organic Physics of 1847 and the Biophysics of Today," *J. Hist. Med. and Allied Sci.,* 12 (1957), 408-409.

[24] E. Mendelsohn has pointed out that the attempt must be made to explain the transition from *Naturphilosophie* to biophysics ("The Biological Sciences in the Nineteenth Century: Some Problems and Sources," *Hist. Sci., 3* [1964], 42-43). I differ in that I view the origin of biophysics in diverse cultural, political, and intellectual forces rather than in the rejection of *Naturphilosophie*.

[25] P. Cranefield has recognized the influence of romanticism in a partial revision of his "Organic Physics of 1847" (note 23), entitled "The Philosophical and Cultural Interests of the Biophysics Movement of 1847," *J. Hist. Med. and Allied Sci.,* 21 (1966), 1, 5.

periphery. Although great tensions were created in German society by the reluctance of the classic estates to recognize the existence of, let alone relinquish political power to, the middle class,[26] German science (especially medicine), politics, and industry were forging their common links during the biophysics period and finding an ally in the upper middle class.[27] Historians of art and literature use the term "bourgeois" realism to describe the second half of the nineteenth century;[28] I propose extending the term to include a "bourgeois" biophysics as well.[29] The worldview of the scientist warrants more detailed study than it has received in the past, and until this subject can be explored more fully, the present essay is but a prolegomenon to the task.

The biophysicists best known to historians are five men all of whom worked for a time in Berlin before their careers separated them. Carl Ludwig (1816–1895), who later moved to Leipzig, Ernst Brücke (1818–1896), who later moved to Vienna, Hermann Helmholtz (1821–1895), Emil DuBois-Reymond (1818–1896), and Gustav Magnus (1802–1870) are usually referred to as the Berlin group. It is unfortunate that these men have received more attention than other biophysicists; none of the five can be classified as a typical, pioneer practitioner of biophysics or spokesman for the biophysical cause. Aside from his early years, Ludwig's role in the biophysics movement was closest to that of the typical practitioner. Helmholtz is a poor choice as an example of the typical biophysicist. His strong Kantian and Fichtean views were not shared by the others, and the physiological topics and methods he selected were not the specific organ and systemic approaches of the others who were in closer touch with the role of physiology in its typical medical school setting. Brücke was most famous for his researches in biochemistry, not biophysics, and he was a staunch opponent of the materialist theory of cell formation.[30] He used physical and chemical methods, which usually set biophysicists apart from

[26]Anderson, *op. cit.* (note 5), pp. 2–3, 9, 125–126, 182ff.

[27]Fritz Ringer, *The Decline of the German Mandarins: The German Academic Community, 1890–1933* (Cambridge, Mass., 1969), p. 11; J. Conrad, *The German Universities for the Last Fifty Years*, trans. John Hutchison (Glasgow, 1885), Chapter VI.

[28]Hermann Boechenstein, *German Literature of the Nineteenth Century* (London, 1969), p. 2. The theme of "bourgeois realism" was made famous by Arnold Hauser, *The Social History of Art*, trans. Stanley Goodman, 4 vols. (New York, 1957–1958).

[29]Eyck, *op. cit.* (note 21), p. 15.

[30]Erna Lesky, "Brücke, Ernst Wilhelm von," *D.S.B.*, *2*, 530–532.

other physiologists, but he couched his results in a far from typical teleological philosophy.[31] In assessing Brücke's impact on biophysics, one must keep in mind his close association with Ludwig during the latter's Vienna years and his practice after 1855 of sending his better students to Ludwig in Leipzig for further training. DuBois-Reymond was both a spokesman for and a practitioner of biophysics. His influence was more generally intellectual than scientific; in particular, he never completed his programmatic electrophysiological researches.[32] Magnus was highly influential as a source of biophysical methods for the Berlin group. However, his use of these methods, acquired in Paris and in Berzelius' laboratory, was not wholly successful, and physiology was not his life's work.

I have found it useful to examine a broader sample of biophysical spokesmen and practitioners than the traditional five. Equally involved in the biophysical movement were Hermann Lotze (1817–1881), Jacob Moleschott (1822–1893), Carl Vogt (1817–1895), Ernst Heinrich Weber (1795–1878), Karl Vierordt (1818–1884), and Gabriel Gustav Valentin (1810–1883). Their work first appeared in the 1830's and 1840's, *before* the Revolution of 1848. Although the enlarged group of eleven is not exhaustive, it is more representative than the traditional five usually discussed in secondary works. The members of the group differ in conceptualization, research interest, and degree of scientific success, but their common concerns characterize the early state of biophysics.

In defining the common attitudes of the biophysicists, it is essential to distinguish between the practitioners of and the spokesmen for biophysics, even in cases where both hats were worn by the same individual. The spokesmen were concerned with destroying vitalism and *Naturphilosophie,* the practitioners with applying physical methods to biological problems. Attacking vitalism and elucidating biophysical mechanisms may appear to have had the same purpose, but they were different activities when viewed from the standpoint of individual psychology, ability, and motivation. The former was destructive and polemical; the latter was constructive and required imaginative experimental skill and rigorous standards of proof.

Spokesmen were also distinguished from practitioners by their attitudes toward politics, biochemistry, and the nature of thought. I will discuss each of these attitudes in turn, beginning with the political. In general, the practitioners were blandly liberal and quiescent in political outlook,

[31] Karl Rothschuh, *Geschichte der Physiologie* (Berlin, 1953), p. 140.
[32] Cranefield, *op. cit.* (note 23), pp. 417–418.

occasionally having had radical leanings in their youth. The ardent spokes-men were more radical and often more political. Weber[33] and Ludwig[34] were practitioners who had given up their youthful political activities. DuBois-Reymond on the right and Moleschott,[35] Vogt,[36] and Büchner on the left maintained both their political militancy and a good part of their scientific militancy throughout their lives; they are best described as the spokesmen for biophysics. For the most part their political positions were similar to those of radical reformers in other walks of life; they sought a rational basis for government outside the natural law arguments for authority of the conservative politicians.[37] The spokesmen's outlook toward science had similar antiauthoritarian and anti-natural law over-tones. To the spokesmen, a science of descriptive laws such as those of polarity or vital force was nothing more than speculation from principles. They sought instead to explain all animate phenomena by the rules and facts known about matter and motion, relying on experimentation, not on authority. It is this antiauthoritarian position that has led historians to associate the extremist spokesmen with the spirit of 1848. However, there were other justifications for doing biophysics, ones typical of the practi-tioners rather than of the politically motivated spokesmen.

The political ideas of the biophysical spokesmen were not those that were a major force in German society at midcentury; neither were their scientific ideologies and achievements a major force in biophysical research. Moleschott was popular with university science students, perhaps more because of his politics than his biology. He believed that under the political conditions of Germany, the fruits of scientific labor were being consumed by priests, nobles, and businessmen—by the nonproductive elements in society.[38] For him knowledge was the key to power, and since knowledge was gained by scientific means the political prescription

[33]P. Hoffmann, "Ernst Heinrich Webers 'Annotationes anatomicae et physiolo-gicae'," *Med. Klinik*, 1934, Pt. 2, Nr. 37, pp. 1250–1251; C. Ludwig, *Rede zum Gedächtniss an Ernst Heinrich Weber* (Leipzig, 1878), p. 16.

[34]Heinz Schröer, *Carl Ludwig, Begründer der messenden Experimentalphysiologie 1816–1895* (Stuttgart, 1967), pp. 31–32.

[35]Walter Moser, *Der Physiologe Jacob Moleschott (1822–1893) und seine Philo-sophie* (Zürich, 1967), pp. 15, 21.

[36]O. Temkin, "Materialism in French and German Physiology of the Early Nine-teenth Century," *Bull. Hist. Med.*, 20 (1946), 324.

[37]Natural law was anathema to literary and historical reformers as well; see Iggers, *op. cit.* (note 6), p. 5, and Ralph Flenley, *Modern German History* (London, 1953), p. 138.

[38]Jakob Moleschott, *Der Kreislauf des Lebens. Physiologische Antworten auf Liebig's Chemische Briefe*, 3rd ed. (Mainz, 1857), p. 12.

was obvious: the reins of political power should be held by men of science.[39] He and other extremists associated political and theological conservatism with the *Naturphilosophie* they despised.[40] Moleschott's vision of a political role for scientists was not typical of the nationalistic and social thought behind the German revolution of 1848. Traditional authority survived the revolution, as it survived unification in 1870;[41] scientists were poorly represented in the Frankfurt Parliament of 1848 and in the Reichstag membership throughout the century.[42] Nor does Moleschott's vision correspond to the subsequent self-image of the professorial *Geheimrath*;[43] German scientists did not seek political power but complacently subsisted on government support after 1848.[44]

Vogt alone of the biophysicists sought and won a seat in the Frankfurt Parliament; he did so as Berlin's representative from the radical party. Berlin was one of the more radical German cities because of a higher percentage of enfranchised lower classes, not because the professors at Prussia's largest university were radical.[45] The biophysical extremists such as Vogt regarded their interest in materialism as allied to the larger, more

---

[39] *Ibid.,* p. 500.

[40] Eyck, *op. cit.* (note 21), pp. 237, 239; G. Rosen, "Romantic Medicine: A Problem in Periodization," *Bull. Hist. Med., 25* (1951), 157; Robert Kann, *A Study in Austrian Intellectual History* (London, 1960), pp. 264–267; and Hermann Misteli, *Carl Vogt, seine Entwicklung vom angehenden naturwissenschaftlichen Materialisten zum idealen Politiker der Paulskirche (1817–1849)* (Zürich, 1938), pp. 20–21.

[41] There was a striking absence of extremism in 1848, and the predominate moderate liberals disliked the scientific materialists. See Thomas, *op. cit.* (note 21), pp. 50, 120. The reform movement gained much of its support from Catholic groups and hence made no overt move toward atheism even if, as individuals, some of the reformers were inclined toward atheism; Eyck, *op. cit.* (note 21), pp. 82–83, and Priscilla Robertson, *Revolutions of 1848: A Social Study* (Princeton, 1952), pp. 156–157.

[42] E.J. Hobsbawn, *The Age of Revolution, 1789–1848* (New York, 1962), p. 344. Eyck, *op. cit.* (note 21), pp. 78, 93, 98, estimates that of the fifteen percent of the Frankfurt Parliament representatives who were academics, only a miniscule number were scientists. See also Anderson, *op. cit.* (note 5), pp. 384, 390, 392, 432.

[43] Richard B. Goldschmidt, *Portraits from Memory: Recollections of a Zoologist* (Seattle, 1956), pp. 6–7, 57, 75–76. Fritz Ringer has recently shown how closely academics clung to bureaucratic and governmental power in a book appropriately titled *The Decline of the German Mandarins*; see (note 27), Chapter 1.

[44] There was a gradual growth in student numbers throughout the century; the growth accelerated after 1860, especially in the expanding medical facilities; see J. Conrad, *op. cit.* (note 27), pp. 141–148. On expansion in the physical and applied sciences, see Frank Pfetsch, "Scientific Organization and Science Policy in Imperial Germany, 1871–1914," *Minerva, 8* (1970), 558–580. The number of professors also increased to fill the new posts and to accommodate the larger student body.

[45] Eyck, *op. cit.* (note 21), p. 85.

widespread interest in rationalism and nationalism.[46] Most political reformers, however, were, in addition to being nationalists, sufficiently
idealist and conventional to reject the support of materialism.[47] The
extremism of Vogt, Moleschott, and even of Ludwig Büchner was neither
the most popular nor the most effective basis for political action.[48]

The lack of feeling by the biophysical extremists for the intellectual
mainstream of Germany's national awakening can be seen in their politics,
careers, and science. Moleschott did not profit from government support
of science, spending his mature years on the periphery of German science
in virtual exile, first in Switzerland and later in Italy; he preached to a
nonexistent political movement. Büchner was.to quit university teaching
and to enter private practice. Ludwig lost his Marburg post and worked for
a time in Vienna before returning to Leipzig shorn of his youthful
radicalism. Vogt was able to continue teaching only by leaving Germany
for Switzerland. It seems to be a rule that the greater the political extremism of the biophysicists the greater their distance from Berlin.

The spokesmen Moleschott and Vogt, devoid of the hierarchical evaluation of man of Enlightenment natural law systems, appeared willing to
accept the view that strict determinism meant the loss of human freedom.[49] Yet in Vogt's speeches before parliament, he advocated the right
of man to be free as though he were still in the natural law tradition.[50]
Later in his treatise on anthropology, Vogt argued that man was not a
beast-machine; rather, man was the high point and end product of
evolution.[51] The anti-Enlightenment approaches to the problem of human
freedom can also be seen in an apparent exception to my case of anti-
natural law political extremists: Rudolf Virchow. Although not one of the

[46]Harold Höffding, A History of Modern Philosophy, trans. B.F. Meyer, 2 vols.
(1900; reprint New York, 1955), 2, 500: "The entire materialist movement in
Germany was supported by an idealistic interest in humanity and progress, and
Büchner was quite right when he protested against conjuring materialism as a method
and theory with materialism in the sense of a practical direction of life." Goldschmidt, op. cit. (note 43), p. 35, notes that the works of Moleschott and Büchner
were suppressed in the next generation.

[47]Eyck, op. cit. (note 21), pp. 237, 262ff.; Thomas, op. cit. (note 21), pp. 156–157.

[48]Ludwig Büchner, Force and Matter: Empirico-Philosophical Studies, Intelligently
Rendered, trans. J.F. Collingwood from the last (8th) German edition (London,
1870), pp. 35, 41. On pp. v and vii of the introduction, Büchner intimates that his
reception in Germany was poor.

[49]Moser, op. cit. (note 35), p. 41.

[50]Misteli, op. cit. (note 40), p. 230.

[51]Karl Vogt, Lectures on Man: His Place in Creation, and in the History of the
Earth, trans. and ed. James Hunt (London, 1864), p. 449.

biophysicists, Virchow is the best known scientist-politician in nineteenth century Germany. He vigorously fought to bring about medical reforms in 1848, while at the same time holding to natural law conceptions of nature and society.[52] He was a typical nineteenth century German in his preoccupation with cultural nationalism and in his hope for political unification on this basis. He was typical, too, in deriving from his understanding of human consciousness the cultural uniqueness of the German people as the basis for unifying political action. He believed that consciousness was a cumulative memory passed from generation to generation, surfacing as the culture of a nation.[53] For him natural law was not an obstacle to the political goals that he and his countrymen held for Germany. Political action was a response to an innate natural force; and natural authority was not violated in reform or revolution leading to national unity, since that authority belonged to the collective memory. Consequently, the freedom of the individual in harmony with his authoritarian cultural destiny was also preserved.

The biophysical spokesmen such as Moleschott and Vogt—and Virchow, too—shared certain distinguishing characteristics: First, they were committed to antigovernment or antitheological subplots, a commitment uncommon among the biophysicists.[54] The extremist position was similar to the earlier political idealism and scientific mechanism of Johann Gottlieb Fichte.[55] The second distinguishing characteristic of the spokesmen, setting them apart from the practitioner, was their preoccupation with what today might be called biochemistry.[56] Their sensitivity to biochemical arguments may be attributed in part to the wide influence of Justus von Liebig and Johannes Müller, both of whom placed physiological chemistry on the side of vitalism. The spokesmen Moleschott, Büchner, and Vogt were forced by their antivitalist goals to discuss the subject of nutrition and to investigate it by the techniques of organic chemistry;

---

[52] R. Virchow, "On the Mechanistic Interpretation of Life" (1858), in *Selected Essays by Rudolf Virchow. Disease, Life and Man*, trans. Lelland J. Rather (Stanford, 1958), pp. 116–117, 125, 129.

[53] Virchow, "Atoms and Individuals" (1859), *ibid*, pp. 154–155.

[54] Moser, *op. cit.* (note 35), pp. 9–10; Erwin Ackerknecht, *Rudolf Virchow* (Madison, 1953), pp. 185–186; for Vogt, see Jacques Droz, *Les revolutions allemandes de 1848* (Paris, 1957), p. 498.

[55] R. Haym, *op. cit.* (note 10), pp. 219–220; M.J. Schleiden, *Ueber den Materialismus. Zur Kritik der Schrift ueber den Materialismus der neueren deutschen Naturwissenschaft, sein Wesen und seine Geschichte* (Dorpat, 1864).

[56] Chemistry was the ideal science in many romantic works; see Haym, *op. cit.* (note 10), p. 590.

since the formation of flesh from bread was one of the major arguments for vitalism in Germany, nutritional research entered into their polemics.[57] The practicing biophysicists tended to shy away from chemical arguments, not because of any theoretical objections; they usually did not need such arguments, since their researches and methods depended on electrical and pressure-related physical apparatus. Although the practicing biophysicists would accept chemical arguments when they were to their advantage, they turned to physical chemistry, not to organic chemistry. The third distinguishing characteristic of the spokesmen was their concern with the source of human thought. They desired to give thought a wholly physical explanation. Moleschott equated thinking with the decomposition of phosphates and Vogt, following Cabanis, suggested that thought may be secreted by the brain just as bile is secreted by the liver; few people took either of these positions seriously. By contrast with the spokesmen, the practitioners did not try to explain thought; they preferred instead to analyze the process of sensation.

Keeping these distinctions in mind, I want now to discuss the work of the practitioners of biophysics. The historical view that biophysicists advocated the complete reduction of all phenomena to matter and motion needs correcting; rather they claimed that biophysics was able to explain all biological phenomena that were capable of definition by matter and motion. The biophysics movement was less original and countercultural than has generally been assumed. This reinterpretation is supported by three characteristics of the practitioners. First, in their actual scientific work the practitioners were seldom dogmatic. Second, their stated goals did not include that of unlimited or complete knowledge of life; this sense of limit occurs on practical, epistemological, and methodological levels. Third, DuBois-Reymond, who is usually cited as the programmatic spokesman for a biophysics that would encompass all of biology, assumed that role only in defensive, not in offensive, argument.

The major thrust of biophysics followed two lines of research: first, electrical experiments on muscle and nerve tissue, and second, pressure related problems such as diffusion, osmosis, absorption, and liquid flow properties. The connection between electricity and life is the older of these two themes and has important links to attitudes of the romantics and *Naturphilosophen* at the beginning of the nineteenth century. The pressure and

[57]Misteli, *op. cit.* (note 40), pp. 37–38; Büchner, *op. cit.* (note 48), pp. xlii, 135–136; Moleschott, *op. cit.* (note 38), p. vi.

diffusion laws were the creation of W. Henry, J. Dalton, H. Dutrochet, and T. Graham; Graham's work, appearing in the 1830's, was especially important for German scientists. Biophysics implies the existence of an applicable physics, and electricity and fluid dynamics provided biological scientists what rational mechanics could not; namely, a direct way to compare, measure, or produce dynamical models of contraction, blood flow, secretion, assimilation, cell formation by crystallization, and energy transfer. The use of such physical techniques and concepts did not require any drastic revision of prior experimental trends in the biomedical disciplines. Albrecht von Haller had focused attention on muscle and nerve tissue in the eighteenth century with his concepts of irritability and sensibility; and eighteenth and early nineteenth century medical systems commonly relied upon the circulatory system to explain inflammation, irritation, and general pathology. Thus the new physical principles and apparatus in the middle of the nineteenth century were easily adapted to questions that had long been of concern to biomedical scientists.

In their application of physical principles to biology, the biophysicists were seldom able to reconstruct what might be called a totally physical living system, let alone define all life functions physically. In 1837, for example, Magnus claimed that oxygen and carbon dioxide were absorbed and released from the blood stream according to Dalton's laws of gaseous absorption;[58] in other words, oxygen, the fundamental element in the steam engine analogy of the body, was transferred by wholly physical means. By 1845, however, Magnus had admitted the inadequacy of a wholly physical interpretation of blood gas exchange; chemical analyses had shown in the meantime that blood contains far more oxygen and carbon dioxide than could be explained by the absorption laws.[59] Nonetheless, he regarded himself as no less a biophysicist in 1845 than in 1837; his methodology was adequate for all of biological reality.

In the 1840's Valentin and Vierordt attempted to explain pulmonary gas exchange on the basis of Graham's law of diffusion, which predicted that if oxygen and carbon dioxide were placed on either side of a membrane, less carbon dioxide would cross over the membrane than would oxygen; the law had a precise mathematical formulation based on molecular

[58]G. Magnus, "Ueber die im Blute enthaltenen Gase," *Ann. d. Physik, 40* (1837), 589–590.

[59]G. Magnus, "Ueber das Absorptionsvermögen des Blutes für Sauerstoff," *Ann. d. Physik, 66* (1845), 195–196.

weights. Since animals give up a smaller volume of carbon dioxide than the volume of oxygen they breathe (respiratory quotient less than one), Valentin and Vierordt thought they had found an important, precise physical mechanism.[60] In 1852 Valentin admitted that the similarity between the results of diffusion law experiments and the respiratory quotient was merely mathematical, not physiological.[61] Vierordt, too, admitted that his own efforts had not confirmed the strict operation of physical laws in living systems, and although he believed that confirmation would come one day,[62] he coined the term "parenchymatic diffusion" to characterize the diffusion process in living animals and to distinguish it from the simpler form of diffusion known to physicists.[63] Retaining a strong faith in the future of his physical methodology, Vierordt recognized that there are no simple, direct analogies between the organic and the inorganic.

Valentin, Vierordt, and Ludwig were militant defenders of biophysics, yet their defense did not rely upon any expectation of attaining ultimate knowledge of life through physics or through a materialist philosophy. They believed that physical laws were the best *approximations* to knowledge of physiological processes that themselves could never be exactly known.[64] Ludwig was even responsible for discrediting the early mechanistic pronouncements of Valentin and Vierordt, carefully pointing out the differences between Graham's stucco plugs and the multilayered living tissue of the lung whose properties were not understood. Until *biological*

---

[60]T. Graham, "On the Laws of the Diffusion of Gases," *Trans. Roy. Soc. Edinb.*, *12* (1834), 255-257. Valentin first applied Graham's law in G. Valentin and C. Brunner, "Ueber das Verhältniss der bei dem Athmen des Menschen ausgeschiedenen Kohlensäure zu dem durch jenen Process aufgenommenen Sauerstoffe," *Arch. f. physiol. Heilkunde*, *2* (1843), 412, 414-415. Vierordt's statement appeared in R. Wagner's *Handwörterbuch* (note 19), *2*, 900.

[61]G. Valentin, *A Text Book of Physiology*, trans. from the 3rd German ed. by W. Brinton (London, 1853), pp. 249-250.

[62]Karl Vierordt, *Physiologie des Athmens mit besonderer Rücksicht auf die Ausscheidung der Kohlensäure* (Karlsruhe, 1845), p. 95; Wagner, *op. cit.* (note 19), *2*, 852, 875-877.

[63]Vierordt, *ibid.*, p. 222.

[64]Gabriel Valentin, *Lehrbuch der Physiologie des Menschen*, 2 vols. (Braunschweig, 1844), *1*, 1, 6, 173ff.; Vierordt, *ibid.*, pp. v, 184ff., and in Wagner, *op. cit.* (note 19), *2*, 828, 895; Carl Ludwig, *Lehrbuch der Physiologie des Menschen*, 2nd rev. ed., 2 vols. (Leipzig, 1861), *2*, 472. The Hegelian influence on the historian Leopold von Ranke led him to believe that the historian, like the scientist, would never exactly know his subject; see G.P. Gooch, *History and the Historians in the Nineteenth Century*, 4th ed. (London, 1928), p. 107.

tests were completed, Ludwig could not accept the diffusion hypothesis.[65] Yet to distinguish between the living and the nonliving is not the same as believing that the former requires vitalistic explanation; some twenty years later, after extensive animal testing, Ludwig did establish that physical diffusion and absorption, interacting with complex chemical processes, constituted an explanation of some phenomena involved in respiratory physiology.[66] He qualified his initial enthusiasm for mechanical mechanisms of secretion in the kidney and the submaxillary gland, and he did so without visible signs of resentment, despair, or sense of failure. Physical principles alone could not save the phenomena;[67] if biophysics were to be the new biology, the "bio" was as important as the "physics."

Other major biophysicists showed similar caution in their expectations for a physical understanding of life. Helmholtz, a master of both the physical and the biological sciences, expected no more of a derivative science such as biology than he expected of pure physics. For example, he stated that one can never know the Kantian thing-in-itself;[68] knowledge was limited by the fact that the senses could not grasp reality in a "real way." Sensate knowledge was only a symbol, an inexact copy, of the reality outside man; the symbol in fact need not even be similar to that outer reality. All that causality in scientific explanation required was that man perceive the same symbol in response to the same set of conditions; whatever laws man placed upon the world outside himself were symbolic of reality, not an absolute, ideal, transcendental, or universal abstraction drawn in Aristotelian or Platonic fashion from that outer reality. Helmholtzian laws would

---

[65] C. Ludwig, "Erwiderung auf Valentin's Kritik der Bemerkungen zu seinen Lehren vom Athmen und Blutkreislauf," *Z. f. rationelle Med., 3* (1845), 147–164; *ibid., 4* (1846), 183–190; and A. Schmidt (Ludwig's student), "Ueber Vierordt's Methode der Blutanalyse," *ibid.,* N.F., *2* (1852), 22–25.

[66] C. Ludwig, "Zusammenstellung der Untersuchungen über Blutgase," *Med. Jahrbücher Wien, 9* (1865), 145–166.

[67] For Ludwig's reevaluation of his own purely physical explanations in physiology, see Arthur Cushny, *The Secretion of Urine* (London, 1917), p. 43, and C. Ludwig, "Mittheilung eines Gesetzes welches die chemische Zusammensetzung des Unterkiefer-Speichels beim Hunde bestimmt," *Z. f. rationelle Med.,* N.F., *1* (1851), 278–284; "Neue Versuche über die Beihilfe der Nerven zur Speichelabsonderung," *ibid.,* pp. 254–277; and Ludwig, *op. cit.* (note 64), *1,* 141–165. For discussions over the physical nature of biological secretion, see W.H. Howell, "Secretion, Physiology of," in *A Reference Handbook of the Medical Sciences* (New York, 1888), *6,* 363–378; L. Wilson, "Starling's Discovery of Osmotic Equilibrium in the Capillaries," *Episteme, 2* (1968), 3–25; and the editorial "Carl Frederick Wilhelm Ludwig (1816–1895), Modern Physiologist," in *J.A.M.A., 200* (1967), 183–184.

[68] H. Helmholtz, "Founders Day Lecture, University of Berlin," in *Helmholtz on Perception,* ed. and trans. Roslyn and Richard Warren (New York, 1968), p. 212.

be universal in the sense of an empirically verifiable law, but not universal in any idealist sense; such laws are laws of relationship; i.e., phenomenological, not ontological, laws.[69] Belief in the inherent limitations of man's knowledge was common to historians and statesmen, romantics and idealists, philosophers and scientists.[70]

Clearly understanding that there could be no refutation of a vitalist argument, Helmholtz, like the earlier *Naturphilosophen*, was not concerned with mechanical versus vitalistic explanations, but with the scope of organic phenomena that could be explained by the principles of physics.[71] Just as the sense of the limits of knowledge was not purely Kantian, but generally cultural, the sense of a need to impose unity upon science and to discover causal relationships was a cultural imperative with roots in more than the work of a single philosopher. There was no emphasis upon mathematizing biological knowledge, as one would expect in an ideal Kantian science; indeed, antimathematical sentiments were expressed by Moleschott, DuBois-Reymond, and Ludwig as well as by the larger group of German humanists.[72] Instead of a bold Kantian demand to mentally impose causality and unity on nature from necessary empirical relationships, one finds constant doubt and caution among many biophysicists, some

[69] *Ibid.*, pp. 175, 179, 201.

[70] On humanists, see Iggers, *op. cit.* (note 6), pp. 51, 77, 80; Gueroult, *op. cit.* (note 7), p. 61; Schelling, *op. cit.* (note 7), pp. 52, 94; Schopenhauer, *op. cit.* (note 7), *2*, 96; Lotze, *op. cit.* (note 7), pp. 165, 381–382, 406–407, 535; Spencer, *op. cit.* (note 1), *1*, 491; J.B. Stallo, *The Concepts and Theories of Modern Physics* (1881; reprint Cambridge, Mass., 1960), p. 40. Below are additional references to statements by scientists on their sense of the limitations of knowledge. Lorenz Oken, *Lehrbuch der Naturphilosophie*, 3rd rev. ed. (Zürich, 1843), tempered his argument for the material basis of the origin of life (p. 111) by making a special case for higher species such as man (in his conclusion p. 515). Büchner, *op. cit.* (note 48), pp. 303–304, thought that the application of a materialist philosophy to biology should stop at the mental level. Ernst Haeckel also recognized limits in his *General Morphology;* see Erik Nordenskiöld, *The History of Biology* (New York, 1928), p. 515. This German attitude can also be seen in the Russian scientist Mendeleev; see A. Vucinich, "Mendeleev's Views on Science and Society," *Isis, 58* (1967), 343.

[71] Warren, *op. cit.* (note 68), pp. 227–228.

[72] For antimathematical sentiments, see Iggers, *op. cit.* (note 6), pp. 6–7; Lotze, *op. cit.* (note 7), p. 11; Moleschott, *op. cit.* (note 38), p. 265; DuBois-Reymond, "Ueber die Lebenskraft," in *Reden*, 2 vols. (Leipzig, 1912), *1*, 1–4; on Ludwig, see J. Burdon-Sanderson, "Carl Ludwig," reprinted in *The Golden Age of Science*, ed. Bessie Z. Jones (New York, 1965), p. 411, and E. Neil, "Carl Ludwig and his Pupils," *Circulation Research, 9* (1961), 973. On the cult of experience, see Merz, *op. cit.* (note 6), *3*, 205. The awareness of a need for antimetaphysical empiricism appeared early in the century; see W.v. Humboldt, "University Reform in Germany," reprinted and translated in *Minerva, 8* (1970), 247.

having learned caution the hard way. Idealism was in disrepute after the 1820's, and the biophysicist practitioners favored an empiricism that stressed experiment in place of mere observation.

German biophysical empiricism had, in addition to its native roots in romanticism and idealism, foreign roots as well. French science was emulated by at least some of the trained scientists in Germany; lines of intellectual communication between France and Germany have been noted often by historians.[73] It is well known that Carl Rudolphi brought back to Germany an empirical bent through his Parisian training and that he passed it on to Johannes Müller.[74] Such linkage of German to French educational circles dated from the Humboldt and Stein era of reform,[75] and it extended to the German medical school curricula in the first quarter of the nineteenth century.[76] Laplace's astronomy represented the high point of French scientific rigor for many German biophysicists such as Brücke, DuBois-Reymond, Moleschott, Ludwig, and Vogt and for influential philosophers such as Lotze and Schopenhauer who acted, in part, as spokesmen for the biophysical cause.[77] Laplace's appeal lay in his claim that the entire future and past of the world was within the grasp of a

[73] Shryock, op. cit. (note 13), pp. 293–294; Eyck, op. cit. (note 21), pp. 4, 19, 21; Temkin, op. cit. (note 36), pp. 322–327; and F. Schnabel, "Von den geschichtlichen Grundlagen der Wissenschaft," in Geist und Gestalt, op. cit. (note 13), p. 11.

[74] W. Riese, "The Impact of Romanticism on the Experimental Method," Stud. in Romanticism, 2 (1962), 12–22; M. Müller, "Ueber die philosophischen Anschauungen des Naturforschers Johannes Müller," Arch. f. Gesch. Med., 18 (1926), 138; and Gottfried Koller, Das Leben des Biologen Johannes Müller, 1801–1858 (Stuttgart, 1958), pp. 33ff.

[75] Thomas, op. cit. (note 21), p. 28.

[76] There were several German professors whose duty it was to report on foreign developments in medicine; see H. F. Kilian, Die Universitäten Deutschlands in medicinisch-naturwissenschaftlicher Hinsicht (Leipzig, 1828).

[77] On the parallel interests of romantics and biophysicists in science, see Wetzel, op. cit. (note 10), pp. i–v, 30, 32, 40; Haym, op. cit. (note 10), pp. 578–579; H. Pilz, "The Conceptions of Vital Energy by the Physician and Physiologist Johann Christian Reil (1759–1813)," Actes XI Congrès Hist. d. Sci., 1968, pp. 189–192; and Schelling, op. cit. (note 7), pp. 171, 218ff. On French crystallography, compare Wetzel, ibid., Chapter 3 with Oken's entire approach (note 70) and with Lotze's approach in "Lebenskraft," in Wagner, op. cit. (note 19), 1, xiii. On the importance of comparative anatomy to Weber, see Ludwig, op. cit. (note 33), pp. 6–7; and for Schelling's view on French comparative anatomy and its relation to German science, see Haym, op. cit. (note 10), p. 580. On the Laplacian image in general, see Estelle DuBois-Reymond, ed., Zwei grosse Naturforscher des 19. Jahrhunderts: Ein Briefwechsel zwischen Emil DuBois-Reymond und Karl Ludwig (Leipzig, 1927), pp. 172, 218; on Brücke, see Temkin, op. cit. (note 36), p. 326; on Moleschott, see Moleschott, op. cit. (note 38), pp. 133, 333; on Vogt, see Misteli, op. cit. (note 40), pp. 45, 192. For the views of the philosophers, see Schopenhauer, op. cit. (note 7), 3, 41, 72–73, and

superbrain that knew the positions and velocities of all material particles and all the forces acting on these particles. Inherent in this claim lay the method by which all natural phenomena could be reduced to matter and motion.[78] Yet Laplace's claim also pointed to the limits of scientific explanation that German biophysicists felt so strongly; there was no superbrain nor even means of knowing the initial conditions of a fraction of the cosmos.

The areas of physiology that most interested biophysicists—sensation, comparative anatomy and physiology, electrical phenomena (muscle and nerve tissue), and pressure phenomena (diffusion, osmosis, hemodynamics) —also had French as well as native roots. Magnus went to France to study physical chemistry, and Vogt improved his techniques under the supervision of French chemists. Weber, who was the pioneer of biophysics in the eyes of Ludwig and Helmholtz, took an interest in pressure related phenomena through the French physiolcgist Jean Poiseuille; Ludwig worked on circulatory problems as a student under Weber. Liebig, who became the vitalist enemy of his students Vogt and Moleschott, also worked in Parisian chemical laboratories. Electrical phenomena and sensory theory have well known roots in the work of German romantic scientists. Cuvier, a German transplant in France, raised comparative anatomy to a high level of precision, one that was admired for its ability to reveal unity in the animate world. Comparative anatomy was immensely popular in Germany where it served to draw together waning speculative tendencies and the new demands for empiricism.

Goethe and Schelling, in addition to Hegel, played an important role in bringing about a transition from Kantian and Fichtean idealism to an empirical approach in biology. In addition to establishing the general influence of *Naturphilosophie* on physiologists,[79] K. Rothschuh has traced

---

Lotze, *op. cit.* (note 19), *1*, xiv. In his "Ueber Neo-Vitalismus," DuBois-Reymond writes as if there were no physiologists between the Frenchman Magendie and the German J. Müller (*Reden* [note 72], *2*, 495).

[78]Moleschott, *op. cit.* (note 38), p. vi, never claimed that he knew how to account for or to circumvent consciousness; yet, he asserted that if he could not account for all higher animate functions with a materialist model of the brain, there could be no physiology.

[79]Rothschuh, *op. cit.* (note 31), p. 101; *op. cit.* (note 7), pp. 396–402; *Physiologie im Werden* (Stuttgart, 1969), pp. 45, 162ff.; *Physiologie. Der Wandel ihrer Konzepte, Probleme und Methoden vom 16. bis 19. Jahrhundert* (München, 1968), pp. 191–203; and "Joseph Görres und die romantische Physiologie," *Med. Monatsschr.*, *5* (1951), 128–131. For an overview of the themes in physiology between the romantic and the biophysical era, see Rothschuh, "Deutsche Biedermeiermedizin, Epoche zwischen Romantik und Naturalismus (1830–1850)," *Gesnerus*, *25* (1968), 167–187.

the use of argument by analogy in biology back to Schelling.[80] The description of the physical world by matter and motion was not the exclusive right of French Newtonians; historians have traced some proto-scientific ideas back to the romantic period, but they have overlooked the tendency of German romantics to describe the physical world in terms of matter and motion.[81] Such tendency furnishes further strong support to the argument for German cultural and romantic roots of biophysical ideas.

To understand the German biophysicists' sense of limits of knowledge, it is useful to examine their treatment of consciousness, a phenomenon which they saw as the final, ultimate problem of biology. No biophysicist defined consciousness by physical or chemical means. The popularizing spokesmen—Vogt, Büchner, and Moleschott—came closest to doing so, but fell short;[82] thought for them might well be physico-chemical, but the interpretation of consciousness (*Bewusstein*) as awareness of thought or free will remained for them unresolved.[83]

The biophysicists in fact tended to avoid treating the problem of consciousness; given the political ethos in Germany, it would be strange indeed for a German scientist to propose to explain it away. The most influential early statement of biophysics—Lotze's article on "Lebenskraft" in 1842 in R. Wagner's *Handwörterbuch der Physiologie*—claimed that a causal chain might be rigorously determined, but that the last element in the chain could be the divine creator.[84] Since the final link in the chain lay outside the jurisdiction of science, its mention might seem superfluous. But it was not superfluous for Lotze, who believed that man had free will.

[80]Rothschuh, *op. cit.* (note 7), pp. 398–400; and "Ursprünge und Wandlungen der physiologischen Denkweisen im 19. Jahrhundert," *Technikgeschichte, 33* (1966), 348.

[81]See John Unzer, *The Principles of Physiology,* trans. Thomas Laycock (London, 1851), pp. 4–5, 25; G. Prochaska, "A Dissertation on the Functions of the Nervous System," reprinted and trans. in Unzer, pp. viii, xiii–xiv; Schelling, *op. cit.* (note 7), pp. 13, 94; Haym, *op. cit.* (note 10), p. 588; Brandt, *op. cit.* (note 7), pp. 49, 83–87; Willy Moog, *Hegel und die Hegelische Schule* (München, 1930), p. 137; Gueroult, *op. cit.* (note 7), p. 159; Iggers, *op. cit.* (note 6), p. 51; Oken, *op. cit.* (note 69), p. 515; Lotze, *op. cit.* (note 7), p. 373, and "Lebenskraft," in Wagner, *op. cit.* (note 19), p. xxi; Schopenhauer, *op. cit.* (note 7), *3,* 43.

[82]See notes 50 and 51.

[83]For interpretations of consciousness, see the references in note 19 and Johannes Rehmke, *Das Bewusstsein* (Heidelberg, 1910).

[84]Lotze, "Lebenskraft," in Wagner, *op. cit.* (note 19), p. xii. Consciousness-based epistemologies similar to Lotze's were common at the time; see Hartmann, *op. cit.* (note 18), p. 1; Plessner, *op. cit.* (note 8), p. 128; and Iggers, *op. cit.* (note 6), p. 147.

In stripping nature of its final causes, vital principles, essences, and souls, the scientist must still endow the human organism with the freedom that man perceives in himself. For Lotze, who was influenced by Schelling's *Naturphilosophie,* preserving freedom of the will was as important as removing purpose from biological models.[85] Lotze regarded consciousness as something more than the summation of sensations.[86] For biophysicists, to cease defining the soul was not the same as eliminating the soul's "known" functions; they accepted the soul as part of man, even if they called it the mind or consciousness and did not recognize it as part of physiology.

Cranefield has suggested that DuBois-Reymond set consciousness apart from biophysics only after trying and failing to incorporate it.[87] But from the beginning DuBois-Reymond readily admitted the limitations of biophysics; he did not say that all phenomena, including consciousness, are subject to definition by matter and motion, but only that all phenomena

[85]Lotze, "Lebenskraft," in Wagner, *op. cit.* (note 19), p. xiii. The issues of consciousness and freedom were closely linked from the time of Leibniz, but they became more important during the romantic era. For example, Wordsworth referred to the mind as a lamp, not as a mirror; see M. Abrams, *The Mirror and the Lamp, Romantic Theory and the Critical Tradition* (New York, 1958). For similar views, see Paul Kluckhorn, *Die Idee des Menschen in der Goethezeit* (Stuttgart, 1946), especially pp. 33-38 on Fichte, F. Schlegel, Schelling, and C.G. Carus; and Wetzel, *op. cit.* (note 10), pp. 145-146. The Germanophile Thomas H. Huxley enjoyed pointing out the British contributions to *Bewusstsein* by Hume and Berkeley in his *Essays on Hume with Helps to the Study of Berkeley* (London, 1897), pp. 95-96, 103, 279, 318. Even Huxley believed methodological materialism was acceptable, but not philosophical materialism; see G. Geison, "The Protoplasmic Theory of Life and the Vitalist-Mechanist Debate," *Isis, 60* (1969), 273-292. For the views of Schiller, Fichte, Hegel, Schleiermacher, Schelling, Herbart, Beneke, and Schopenhauer in that order, see: A. Mette, "Die physiologischen Dissertationen Fr. Schillers im Blickfeld der heutigen Medizin," *N.T.M., 1* (1960), 35-49; F. Copleston, *A History of Philosophy,* 7 vols. (New York, 1965), 7, Pt. 1, pp. 60, 64, 69, 79; Egon Friedell, *A Cultural History of the Modern Age: The Crisis in the European Soul . . . (1931),* trans. C.F. Atkinson, 3 vols. (New York, 1953), 3, 109; Van der Meulen, *op. cit.* (note 7), pp. 251, 260; Brandt, *op. cit.* (note 10), p. 46; J. Lindsay, "The Philosophy of Schelling," *Phil. Rev., 19* (1910), 259; Merz, *op. cit.* (note 6), 3, 216; and Schopenhauer, *op. cit.* (note 7), 2, 389, and 3, 1, 12, 76-77, 411ff. Ernst Cassirer was still troubled by the interrelatedness of consciousness and freedom in the twentieth century; see D. Verene, "Kant, Hegel and Cassirer," *J.H.I., 30* (1969), 33-46.

[86]Lotze, "Lebenskraft," in Wagner, *op. cit.* (note 19), p. xxi. R. Effron has recently shown that without a consciousness-oriented view, the reflex arc could not have been defined and used as it originally was in the nineteenth century ("Biology without Consciousness," *Persp. in Biol. and Med., 2* [1967-1968], 9-36).

[87]Cranefield, *op. cit.* (note 27), p. 409.

up to (*bis zu*) consciousness are.[88] This sense of the limits of biological knowledge is in harmony with the methodological, epistemological, and cultural arguments of the time. With biophysics unable to provide an answer to the ultimate problem of consciousness, DuBois-Reymond—here acting as spokesman more than as practitioner—anticipated that physics, the science from which biophysics was derived, might eventually yield an answer. In his "Seven Riddles of the World," written in 1882, he spoke of the possibility that when the next subdivision of matter was achieved thought and the freedom of the will would be explained: "If matter thus exhibits different modes of action according to the degrees of its division, why may it not even think when under still a finer division?"[89] Only if this came about would the epistemological problem be resolved; for only then would consciousness be translated from the mind into measurable, empirical reality, only then would determinism become an acceptable philosophy.

German romantics, philosophers, and biophysicists held similar views on consciousness. The romantics and their successors came under the influence of French ideas, but they Germanized them so that the ideas had little contact any more with French epistemology or psychology. French ideas, however important to German science, did not alter the strong pietist, nationalist, and essentially romantic-idealist tradition in Germany. That tradition underlay the separation of consciousness from the subject matter of science. Schelling believed consciousness was the prerequisite for observation, not an observable itself; consciousness was action, not substance. He said that "I would be nothing if I were not I."[90] The ego (*das Ich*) existed only in so far as it was conscious of itself, a nineteenth century version of Descartes' *cogito ergo sum*. Consciousness was a hallowed cultural concept; it was a source of self-definition, awareness, freedom, and, for idealists like Kant, of law, causality, and unity in the physical world. Biophysicists, having accepted their cultural heritage, mirrored romantic ideology while disavowing its method, i.e., its formal metaphysics. The later romantics greatly abetted the movement away from formal metaphysics by their insistence upon empirical study and methods. Hence, it should not be surprising that Lotze, DuBois-Reymond, and Helmholtz dif-

[88]*Ibid.,* and DuBoid-Reymond, *op. cit.* (note 72), *1,* 9.

[89]DuBois-Reymond, "The Seven World Problems," trans. from the German in *Pop. Sci. Mon., 20* (1882), 400.

[90]Copleston, *op. cit.* (note 85), p. 127; W. Wieland, "Die Anfänge der Philosophie Schellings und die Frage nach der Natur," *Natur und Geschichte* (Stuttgart, 1967), pp. 420ff.

fered only slightly in their positions on consciousness, even though they differed greatly in their scientific methods. T. Ribot, who, like James, pioneered the study of consciousness, complained of the lack of published material on his topic: he attributed the lack to the self-imposed limits of German biophysicists and psychologists.[91] Biophysicists could have provided some kind of explanation of consciousness, but they did not choose to, and for good reasons. They, like romantics, drew a line beyond which they seldom if ever ventured, and consciousness was beyond that line.[92]

If biophysics was not absolutist, it was also not relativist, not at least if one respects Helmholtz' theoretical symbol as standing for correspondence with reality. The biophysicists believed that the fit between theory and data was possible, but that the fit lay in the realm of probable cause, not in that of strict, absolute causality. Ludwig, the most typical of the practitioners, stated that completely deterministic answers to biological questions were possible only when the positions and forces of atoms comprising an organism were known in their original condition of coming together.[93] He certainly never claimed to possess the Laplacean superbrain; the "never will be known" phrase of Ludwig and other biophysicists was not merely the result of their awareness of an incomplete state of knowledge that could be completely overcome at some future date, but of their awareness of what to expect from the pursuit of knowledge. Helmholtz' recognition that there can be no proof or disproof of a vitalist argument was but another reflection of that same awareness.

Viewing their science as a causally probable enterprise, biophysicists were, as we should expect, especially concerned with certain problems. One was the role of analogy; that role had to be constantly probed when one science, physics, was applied to another, biology. Another was the problem of sensation; since sensate knowledge was only a symbol of nature, studies of sensation took on a heightened significance, just as they had in the romantic era (see Appendix). A third was the problem of methodology; the preoccupation with sensation and analogy in biophysics was

[91] T. Ribot, German Psychology of Today, trans. from 2nd rev. ed. by J. Baldwin (New York, 1886), p. 13.

[92] Hartmann, op. cit. (note 18), pp. xxii–xxiii: "I was simply compelled to have recourse to older works, or to the writings of Burdach, because the more recent physiology carefully ignored everything that could not be forced into the materialistic mould." See also Lotze, op. cit. (note 7), pp. 422–443, 535; Merz, op. cit. (note 6), 3, 197, 261; and A. Bain, Mind and Body. The Theories of Their Relation (New York, 1897), p. 194.

[93] Ludwig, op. cit. (note 67), 1, 1-2.

naturally accompanied by a preoccupation with methodology.[94] The concern with analogy, method, and sensation is clear in Mach's treatise on sensation: "Animism, or anthropomorphism, is not an epistomological fallacy; if it were, every analogy would be such a fallacy. The fallacy lies merely in the application of this view to cases in which the premises for it are lacking or are not sufficient."[95] Mach added that "physics therefore still has much that is new to learn from a study of the organic before it is in a position to control the organic."[96] Biophysics, even according to physicists like Mach, was not synonymous with physics.[97] In raising his voice in the interest of the unity of knowledge, Mach was not responding to a sense of failure either on his own part or on that of his predecessors in biophysics; rather, like DuBois-Reymond, he thought that physics in its present state was inadequate to the task of developing a completely physical biology.

Mach and DuBois-Reymond hoped that the incompleteness of biophysics was only temporary, owing to the inadequacy of contemporary physics; the practitioner of biophysics, however, was apt to see the incompleteness through the eyes of biological experience. Helmholtz showed the same openminded and cautious questioning as Mach, but with the attitude of the biologist, even of the biophysicist, rather than the physicist: "The animal body . . . does not differ from the steam engine as regards the manner in which it obtains heat and force, but does differ from it in the manner in which the force gained is to be made use of."[98] Helmholtz was aware of the pitfalls of analogy; like Lotze, he knew that only by the careful choice of a methodology could one obtain good results from analogy.[99] Kant, Schelling, Hegel, and Schopenhauer had voiced similar concerns with method.[100] Ludwig's famous dictum, "die Methode ist alles," was not the

[94]Johannes Müller's inaugural lecture at Bonn University on 19 October 1824, "On the Requirements of Physiology according to a Philosophical Understanding of Nature"; see Wolfgang Jacob, *Medizinische Anthropologie im 19. Jahrhundert. Mensch, Natur, Gesellschaft* (Stuttgart, 1967), pp. 84ff.

[95]Mach, *op. cit.* (note 2), p. 97.

[96]*Ibid.,* p. 99.

[97]Mach's pronouncement is surprisingly similar to the well known one by Max Delbrück about why he, a twentieth century physicist, entered biology.

[98]Hermann von Helmholtz, *Popular Scientific Lectures,* trans. E. Atkinson (1893; reprint New York, 1962), p. 82.

[99]On Lotze, see "Lebenskraft," in Wagner, *op. cit.* (note 19), *1,* xiii, xvii; on Helmholtz, see Weischedel, *op. cit.* (note 17), *2,* 392ff.

[100]Hegel's thinking on process and method in dialectical terms is well known. On the romantics in general, see Wetzel, *op. cit.* (note 10), pp. 33–34, 195–198. Schelling, *op. cit.* (note 7), p. 95, wrote:

statement of a philosophically naive biologist; the method of research elucidated and defined "the manner in which the force gained is to be made use of." Biology and physiology were to be understood with the aid of physics, not reduced in all particulars to physical laws. The biophysicist practitioners were not so much intent upon a materialist philosophy or biology as on a mechanistic, physical biology that would build a unity of the sciences. If they left biology intact with physically irreducible, biological elements, there were cultural as well as methodological and scientific reasons for doing so. Reviewing the development of medicine in his lifetime, Helmholtz observed that: "Our generation has had to suffer under the tyranny of spiritualistic metaphysics; the newer generation will probably have to guard against that of the materialistic hypothesis."[101]

For the biophysicists, the unity of knowledge was the real issue and rationale for the reductionist program. Mach said that "I only seek to adopt in physics a point of view that need not be changed the moment our glance is carried over into the domain of another science; for ultimately, all must form one whole."[102] He believed that physics would change through its relation to physiology: "The result of this investigation will not be a dualism, but rather a science which, embracing both the organic and the inorganic, shall interpret the facts *that are common to the two departments*."[103] Mach did not imply a complete understanding in either physics or physiology.

---

For if they wish to comprehend all in one, they can admit only an absolute thesis, but they must forgo science.

Thus it is indeed clear that in true science each proposition has only a definite and, so to speak, local significance, and that, taken away from its definite locus and posited as an absolute (dogmatic) one, the proposition either loses sense and meaning or entangles us in contradictions. In so far then as method means the way of progression, it is evident that here method is inseparable from the essence, and aside from the method even the subject matter is lost. Whoever then believes that he may take the last [essence] for the first [method], and vice versa, or that he can recoin the proposition which should be valid only in a definite locus, into a universal or unlimited one, may indeed stir up sufficient confusion and contradictions for the ignorant in this way, but he has really not touched the matter itself, much less harmed it.

Schopenhauer stated his view on method more succinctly, *op. cit.* (note 7), *3*, 310: "Rule and application, method and achievement, must, like matter and form, be inseparable."

[101] Helmholtz, *On Thought in Medicine* (1877), trans. E. Atkinson (1893; reprint Baltimore, 1938), p. 23. For favorable comments on the beneficial effects of early nineteenth century romantic thought on science, see Temkin's reference to C. Nägeli in *Bull. Hist. Med.*, *41* (1967), 191; Warren, *op. cit.* (note 68), p. 227; and Lotze, "Seele," in Wagner, *op. cit.* (note 19), p. 142.

[102] Mach, *op. cit.* (note 2), p. 30.

[103] *Ibid.*, p. 101, italics added.

Cranefield has argued that the biophysics movement was a failure.[104] This is too harsh a judgment. The biophysicists were not as successful in their program for biology as they had hoped, but they did not completely fail. They worked towards a biology that would be as rigorous as the physical sciences which, as Lotze, Helmholtz, and DuBois-Reymond had shown, possessed limits of their own.[105] In their search for a unified *Wissenschaft,* they sought to banish from science the spiritual metaphysics of their predecessors and to eliminate teleological arguments from biology.[106] Their failure was certainly no greater than that of German biochemists, Darwinists, or socialists, just as their preoccupation with unity, limits of knowledge, sensation, individual freedom, matter and motion, methodological emphasis, and use of analogy were the concerns of the culture that shaped the politics, history, and science of Germany. The methods of biophysics emerging in this era cannot have avoided being touched by these concerns. Although the Berlin group of biophysicists has received the greatest historical attention, the Leipzig group—Weber, Ludwig, and Vierordt—is more typical of the successful practitioners than the Berlin group.

In evaluating the success or failure of biophysics, it must be kept in mind that not all of biology came under its influence. The biophysicists were a small minority of physiologists, whereas the majority of biological scientists were trained in traditional chemical techniques.[107] Organic chemistry in Germany reached its zenith during the lifetimes of the biophysicists and did not relinquish its leadership in chemistry until World War I. Cranefield has provided a convincing analysis of the social reasons for a lack of "take off" in biophysics.[108] Training and research in physiology were largely a medical school phenomenon, and few medical students had the necessary training in the physical sciences to work in an increasingly difficult field like biophysics. The expansion of physical institutes from the 1860's offered sufficient opportunity for physicists who might otherwise have be-

[104] Cranefield, *op. cit.* (note 23), pp. 420–423.

[105] See DuBois-Reymond on Helmholtz in "Ueber Neo-Vitalismus," *op. cit.* (note 72), *2,* 500. Lotze's view is predictably similar; see his "Lebenskraft," in Wagner, *op. cit.* (note 19), *1,* xiii, and in his *Metaphysic, op. cit.* (note 7), pp. 14–15, 165–166, 381–382, 406, 422.

[106] W. von Humboldt, *op. cit.* (note 72); Schelling, *op. cit.* (note 7), pp. 4–5, 44, 53–54; Peckham, *op. cit.* (note 7), pp. 33, 70; Treitschke, *op. cit.* (note 17), *2,* 326, and *4,* 571; Moleschott, *op. cit.* (note 38), p. 35.

[107] C. Culotta, "Respiration and the Lavoisier Tradition: Theory and Modification, 1777–1850," *Trans. Am. Phil. Soc., 62* (1972), 39–40.

[108] Cranefield, *op. cit.* (note 27), pp. 421–423.

come interested in biophysics. Evolution, the cell, bacteriology, and clinical work provided biological scientists with opportunity for achievement with far less preparation than that required for achievement within biophysics.

The application of physics to biology could not alter the fact that consciousness was inexplicable for cultural as well as methodological reasons.[109] Even on the basis of the use of analogy for achieving unity of knowledge, consciousness remained untouched by physics and biology. The early nineteenth century's explicit concern for consciousness was not continued by practicing biophysicists in their attempt to establish physiology as a rigorous science. Consciousness, however, lost none of its deep significance for the practitioners by their pretension that it did not apply to their science. The spokesmen for biophysics pointed to the overall cultural importance of consciousness by arguing for its inclusion in the biophysical outlook. If there is any marked failure of the biophysics movement, it must be attributed to the spokesmen and their extremist goals, not to the biophysical practitioners. The spokesmen could not escape the unwanted Cartesian dualism.

If the unity of the sciences, the unity of all knowledge, were imposed upon nature by the mind, as the biophysicists believed, then consciousness could not be eliminated from the scientists' concern, although it could be ignored in laboratory practice and in the language of science. The dominant issues of consciousness and unity of knowledge lead us once again to Kant and Hegel, whose philosophies supposedly ruled the century in Germany. The separation of consciousness from physiology, the use of consciousness as a mirror of knowledge, and the critical concern for method point to the fact that, deliberately or not, the biophysicists came down heavily on the side of Hegel;[110] method, process, and the significance of the observer in romantic biology slowly evolved into the dialectic of biophysics.

Given the cultural roots laid down by German romantics and idealists, any change in the sense of self, or the unity of knowledge, or the unity of the sciences, or consciousness-based epistemology would lead to changes in

[109] George Mead, *Movements of Thought in the Nineteenth Century* (Chicago, 1936), pp. 85, 109; Haym, *op. cit.* (note 10), pp. 641, 654–655; Iggers, *op. cit.* (note 6), p. 20; Copleston, *op. cit.* (note 85), p. 127; and Schopenhauer, *op. cit.* (note 7), *3*, 55. See also notes 62, 84, 85, and Johann G. Fichte, *Werke* (Leipzig, 1922), *3*, 430ff.

[110] Ernst Lass, *Idealistische und positivistische Erkenntnistheorie*, 2 vols. (Berlin, 1884), *2*, 522.

each of the other of these interrelated cultural parameters. By the turn of the century, consciousness, in its full context of meaning, had resurfaced in the frequently discussed topics of the new sciences, psychiatry and sociology. Under the pressure of industrialization, the individual felt a heightened sense of alienation; his freedom, uniqueness, and unity with the outer world, which consciousness had conveyed previously to man, were threatened. In an age of crisis, consciousness was a subject for the social and psychological pathologist.[111] In this context the scientism of the turn of the century should not be thought of as the end of the unity of knowledge and value, but as the last of a long series of attempts to assure that unity. In psychiatry Freud dissected consciousness, and in naming its components the id, ego, and superego he sought to preserve consciousness by giving it once more a secure ontological status; its century-long epistemological foothold in German culture was no longer assured. It was far more common, however, to transfer allegiance from the values of the individual to the values of society. Value, unity, dynamical change, limits, freedom, and free will were transferred to the group by the sociologist, the nation by the statesman, and the whole organism by the biologist. Organicism once again became widespread and acceptable among biologists. Although organicism had never entirely disappeared from biology, it became a fashionable subject at the turn of the century.[112]

By recognizing that the biophysicists were not the dogmatic reductionists they have been said to be, we see that they fit much better into their intellectual period. The transition from romantic to biophysicist, e.g., from Johannes Müller to his pupils, becomes less episodic and more understandable. Further, by this recognition we see that late nineteenth century organicism was not such a drastic change. As Alfred North Whitehead pointed out in *Process and Reality,* the separation of consciousness from sensation is fundamentally an organismic approach to animate phenomena.[113] With the advantage of hindsight, one can see that the midcentury biophysicists were mildly organismic because of their German cultural background, and their successors, therefore, had not so far to go to acquire their stronger, more explicit organismic outlook. Finally, by this recogni-

---

[111] H. Stuart Hughes, *Consciousness and Society: The Reconstruction of European Social Thought, 1890-1930* (New York, 1958), and Floyd W. Matson, *The Broken Image. Man, Science and Society* (New York, 1964).

[112] Arthur Lovejoy, *The Revolt Against Dualism* (LaSalle, Illinois, 1960); Ludwig von Bertalanffy, *Problems of Life* (1952; reprint New York, 1960); and Marjorie Grene, *Approaches to a Philosophical Biology* (New York, 1968).

[113] A.N. Whitehead, *Process and Reality* (New York, 1929).

tion we avoid the mistake of connecting biophysics and materialism, a mistake that the historian of medicine O. Temkin has pointed out.[114]

The spokesmen for biophysics succeeded in conveying the impression that science was radical, antitheological, and materialistic to certain people. So too the practitioners succeeded in establishing a securer place for the physical sciences in biology. Since few biologists, whatever their philosophical stance, ever completely denied the physical sciences a place in their own science, the accomplishment of the practitioners was not their program but their specific, exact, and successful explanation of certain limited biological phenomena with the aid of physical principles and methods. Insofar as the practitioners were also spokesmen, they shared the spokesmen's failure to reduce biology to physics and chemistry.

Nineteenth century science is beginning to come into historical perspective. I would like to see historians explore the cultural values of scientists, their motivations, and their expectations as well as the scientific problems internal to specific disciplines. In this paper I have studied only one area of biological research. I have made no attempt to distinguish those philosophers and scientists who saw consciousness as prior to sensation from those who saw it as the result of sensation; the significance of the widespread belief in innate ideas for conceptions of scientific method is still to be determined. I have not dealt with the other biological disciplines: i.e., embryology, biochemistry, bacteriology, histology, and general zoology. Nor have I dealt with the second generation of biophysicists; knowing to what extent their immediate cultural, intellectual, and social contexts resemble or differ from patterns I have discussed in this paper could greatly aid in understanding the motivations and expectations of scientists and hence the overall course of science.[115]

[114]Temkin, *op. cit.* (note 36), pp. 322–327.

[115] For an example of a similar pattern of cultural relationships of a scientific discipline, see Pierce C. Mullen, *The Preconditions and Reception of Darwinian Biology in Germany, 1800–1870,* unpublished University of California dissertation (Berkeley, 1964).

# APPENDIX

The purpose of this appendix is to further support my distinction between the practitioners and spokesmen of biophysics. I have used an independent source of statistics on the discoveries of the biophysicists I have discussed in this paper. Karl Rothschuh's *Entwicklungsgeschichte physiologischer Probleme in Tabellenform* (München, 1952) breaks down the subject matter of physiology according to anatomical parts and systems and lists major discoveries together with source and author references. I have constructed Table I from Rothschuh's index of the total number of discoveries listed for individual biophysicists. It should be noted that peripheral nerves and sensory organs were the subject of considerable biophysical research, but that the brain and spinal cord, representing the higher nervous and mental functions, were not. If biophysicists had conceived of thought as wholly materialist, they ought to have shown interest in the brain and spinal cord. That they preferred to study the organs of sensation reflects their attitudes on method, epistemology, and consciousness.

I have used data from Table I to construct Table II, which gives areas of research reflecting broad methodological approaches rather than Rothschuh's anatomical areas. Table II agrees by and large with the biophysical approaches and interests as defined in this paper.

The third column in Table II is a relative measure of the significance of biophysical discovery for biological research as a whole. The fourth column is a relative measure of the significance of any one specialty or method within the biophysical discoveries of the group as a whole. A comparison of the two columns indicates that subjects most frequently appearing in historical discussions of biophysics, namely, animal heat and metabolism, were not the major concerns of nineteenth century biophysicists. Undoubtedly the historical imbalance is the result of paying greater attention to the spokesmen of biophysics than to its practitioners. The dominant concerns of the practitioners were phenomena measurable by pressure related methodologies, sensory organs and sensation, and electrical and electrically testable phenomena.

Table III is a graphic representation of the schema in Table II, but here broken down into the contributions of each biophysicist according to the method or specialty.

Table III clearly indicates that the biophysical work of the militant spokesmen was limited in scope by comparison with that of the other bio-

## TABLE I

### Discoveries Made by the Biophysics Group According to Rothschuh's Categories

| | Helmholtz | Ludwig | Vogt | Weber | DuBois-Reymond | Brücke | Valentin | Vierordt | Moleschott | Büchner |
|---|---|---|---|---|---|---|---|---|---|---|
| Blood | | | | | | 1 | | 1 | | |
| Respiration | | 3 | | | | | 3 | 2 | | |
| Heart | 2 | 5 | | 1 | 4 | 1 | | | | |
| Circulation and Circulatory Regulation | | 9 | | 5 | | | 1 | 2 | | |
| Energy and Heat | 3 | | 5 | 1 | | | 1 | | | |
| Metabolism | | | 13 | 1 | | | | | 1 | 1 |
| Secretion | | 5 | 1 | | | 3 | 1 | | | |
| Kidney | | 2 | | | | 1 | | | | |
| Muscle | 6 | 2 | | 1 | 5 | 2 | | 1 | | |
| Peripheral Nerves | 2 | | | | 5 | | | | | |
| Spinal Nerves | 2 | | | | | | | | | |
| Brain | 1 | | | | | | | | | |
| Physiological Optics | 15 | | | 1 | 1 | 3 | | | | |
| Hearing | 9 | | | | | 1 | | | | |
| Other Senses | | | | 9 | | | 3 | 1 | | |
| Total No. of Discoveries | 40 | 26 | 19 | 19 | 15 | 12 | 8 | 7 | 1 | 1 |

TABLE II

Relative Significance of Research within the Biophysical Group

| Areas of Discovery Grouped by Method or Specialty | Number of Discoveries | | Percentage Representation of All Discoveries in Rothschuh's Categories % | Percentage of Total Discoveries in Biophysical Group % |
|---|---|---|---|---|
| Metabolism | 16 | | 8.0 | 10.8 |
| Energy and Heat | 8 | | 8.8 | 5.4 |
| Pressure | 52 | | 7.0 | 35.1 |
| Secretion | | 11 | | |
| Respiration | | 8 | | |
| Circulation | | 17 | | |
| Heart | | 13 | | |
| Kidney | | 3 | | |
| Electricity | 27 | | 6.0 | 18.2 |
| Muscle | | 16 | | |
| Peripheral Nerve | | 8 | | |
| Spinal Nerve | | 2 | | |
| Brain | | 1 | | |
| Sensation and Sensory Organs | 43 | | 11.7 | 29.1 |
| Physiological Optics | | 19 | | |
| Hearing | | 11 | | |
| Other | | 13 | | |
| Blood | 2 | | 1.5 | 1.4 |

physicists. The frequency with which any one method or specialty is represented in Table III is, of course, not a clear indication of the ingenuity or
success with which the method was applied or the specialty pursued; it is
only a measure of the degree of diversity of research of each biophysicist.

Table IV provides two additional ranking systems which can be used for
comparative analyses.

By correlating the data in the ranking scales in Tables III and IV certain
facts become clear. The militant spokesmen were attracted to metabolism
problems, and the practitioners were not. On all three scales, Büchner and
Moleschott were less typical, less successful, and less diverse in their inter-

Table III Rank of Biophysicists by Methodology and Specialty

(Each bar represents 100% of research according to Rothschuh)

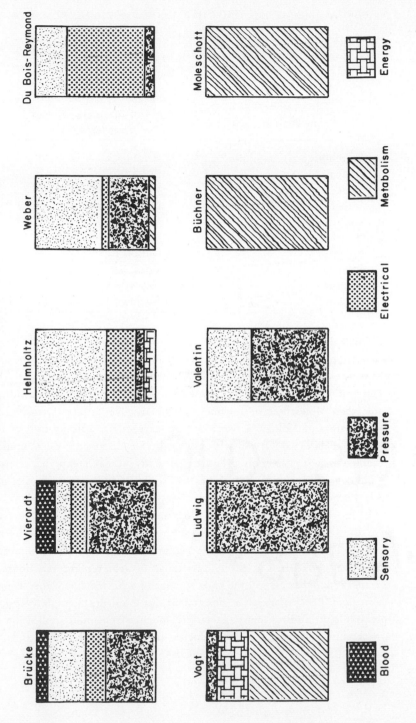

TABLE IV

Rank of Individual Biophysicists by Success in Discovery

| Rank by Number of Discoveries (from Table I) | | Rank by Number of Specialties Represented by Individual Discoveries (from Table I) | |
|---|---|---|---|
| Helmholtz | 40 | Helmholtz | 8 |
| Ludwig | 26 | Brücke | 7 |
| Vogt | 19 | Weber | 7 |
| Weber | 19 | Ludwig | 6 |
| DuBois-Reymond | 15 | Vierordt | 5 |
| Brücke | 12 | Valentin | 4 |
| Valentin | 8 | DuBois-Reymond | 4 |
| Vierordt | 7 | Vogt | 3 |
| Moleschott | 1 | Moleschott | 1 |
| Büchner | 1 | Büchner | 1 |

ests than the others. The second column of Table IV merits special attention. It measures the degree of success that each man had in applying biophysics to a variety of animal functions; in it, Vogt is ranked with the other militant materialists. As a scientist Vogt was more diverse and capable than Moleschott or Büchner, yet his discoveries were restricted to specific areas of biology, as were DuBois-Reymond's. Column two of Table IV correlates rather well with my qualitative discussion: the militancy of a biophysicist is inversely proportional to his success in applying physics to biology. A breakoff point of less than four to five specialty areas of notable discovery separates spokesmen from practitioners.

The breakoff point is marked by those men such as Ludwig and Vierordt who were willing to modify their youthful exuberance and mold physics to biological parameters. The second column of Table IV places intermediate level spokesmen in the middle range of achievement and nonprogrammatic biophysicists in the highest range of achievement. Weber, Helmholtz, and Brücke reveal a rich talent for biological and biophysical methodology; Ludwig achieved nearly as much by ingenious application of a more limited range of methodologies. In sum, the spokesmen and the successful practitioners can be distinguished by performance as well as by style and objective.

# Irving Langmuir and the "Octet" Theory of Valence

BY ROBERT E. KOHLER, JR.*

## 1. INTRODUCTION

In a brief paper published in March 1916 Gilbert N. Lewis (1875–1946) proposed that the chemical bond consisted of a pair of electrons shared by two atoms.[1,2] Within a decade the shared pair bond was widely recognized as the first principle of molecular structure; but for over three years it was almost completely ignored. Its recognition and acceptance were due chiefly to Irving Langmuir (1881–1957) of the General Electric Research Laboratory in Schenectady. Shortly after the end of the First World War Langmuir realized the full significance of Lewis's ideas, and through a series of dramatic lectures and long papers in 1919–1920 he brought the new "Lewis-Langmuir" theory rapid and widespread popularity. The early neglect of Lewis's theory is readily understandable in terms of the intellectual context of 1916. More difficult to understand is the tremendous popularity of Langmuir's version of Lewis's views only three years later. In this paper I argue that the contrasting popularity of Lewis's and Langmuir's versions is due mainly to the different personal styles of Lewis and Langmuir and to their different professional situations. Langmuir had a gift and a taste for popularization and a popular reputation that Lewis did not, especially among the sizeable group of industrial chemists. The new theory was well received in 1919 because it was Langmuir's theory.

Although Lewis was pleased at first at the belated recognition of his views, he soon came to resent the popular acclaim Langmuir alone enjoyed. A series of letters between them in 1919–1920 illuminates the complex intellectual, personal, and social issues involved in the brief dispute over priority. From these letters and other unpublished sources, the origin of Langmuir's rediscovery of Lewis's theory can be traced in some detail.

*Department of History and Sociology of Science, University of Pennsylvania, Philadelphia, Penna. 19104.

[1]G.N. Lewis, "The Atom and the Molecule," *J. Am. Chem. Soc.,* 38 (1916), 762–785.

[2]The probable sources of Lewis's theory are discussed in R.E. Kohler, "The Origin of G.N. Lewis's Theory of the Shared Pair Bond," *Hist. Stud. Phys. Sci.,* 3 (1971), 343–376.

The circumstances of Langmuir's rediscovery explain the real differences between Lewis's and Langmuir's versions of the "Lewis-Langmuir" theory as well as their very different attitudes toward the question of priority.

For both Lewis and Langmuir valence theory was a brief episode in their careers. In 1921 Langmuir abruptly abandoned work on the subject, as did Lewis after the publication of his book *Valence and the Structure of Atoms and Molecules* in 1923.[3] By that time the intense interest in Langmuir's "octet theory" had died down, and the shared pair bond as presented in Lewis's book was already being used by progressive chemists in England and America. Whereas Langmuir was responsible for popularizing the new valence theory, Lewis's version of it proved to be more influential in the long run. The general acceptance of the new ideas by the chemistry profession in 1921–1926 will be the subject of a subsequent paper.

## 2. THE NEGLECT OF LEWIS'S THEORY, 1916–1919

Why was Lewis's 1916 theory so completely neglected at first? The war undoubtedly hindered its recognition in Europe, but America was not involved until one year after Lewis's paper appeared. In all likelihood, the main reason for the neglect is simply that the problem Lewis's theory so elegantly solved was not recognized as a problem by most chemists. For nearly twenty years the prevailing belief had been that all chemical bonds were polar bonds, formed by the transfer of a single electron from an electropositive atom to an electronegative one. All bonds were believed to be the same as the polar bond of $Na^+Cl^-$, even the bonds of nonpolar organic molecules. By 1916 the electrochemical theory as set forth by Richard Abegg in 1904, J. J. Thomson in 1907, and others was a firmly entrenched orthodoxy.

Although both Abegg and Thomson (at first) explicitly denied the existence of a nonpolar bond, there was a small current of dissent from their opinion. In 1913 W. C. Bray and Lewis proposed that a nonpolar bond must exist, and more detailed theories of a nonpolar bond were proposed by J. J. Thomson himself in 1914, W. Arsem in 1914, Alfred Parson in 1915, and others.[4] But in 1916 the dissenting theories were isolated; moreover, they were highly individual, even eccentric, and led to strange and dubious consequences. To see how Lewis's theory looked in historical context, we must keep in mind that the shared pair bond, represented by dou-

---

[3]G.N. Lewis, *Valence and the Structure of Atoms and Molecules* (New York, 1923; reprinted, New York, 1967).

[4]See R.E. Kohler, "Origin," *op. cit.* (note 2).

ble dots, was part of a small avant garde of theoretical speculation, for which the vast majority of chemists had little interest or sympathy. For most chemists the simple, more familiar electrochemical bond was perfectly adequate.

The few references to Lewis's paper before 1919 reveal just how little Lewis's contemporaries, including Langmuir, understood it. The reviewer for *Chemical Abstracts* discussed only the familiar part of Lewis's theory, namely, how the cubic atom explained electron transfer bonds.[5] He mentioned without comment the tendency of atoms to hold even numbers of electrons and also Lewis's idea that "atoms were interpenetrable," i.e., that they could share electrons; one suspects he was passing along an intriguing bit of mystification without really understanding what it meant. In a lecture on valence to the American Association for the Advancement of Science in 1918 William Noyes (1857–1941) briefly referred to Lewis's theory.[6] He admitted that some exceptional organic compounds might have nonpolar bonds, but he saw the exceptions as a minor appendage to the polar orthodoxy. Noyes had been one of the earliest supporters of the polar theory, and for him the most important advance in valence theory was still the electron transfer bond and "the study of positive and negative atoms in inorganic compounds."[7]

In 1917 Lewis's theory was more sympathetically discussed in a long review of recent theories of atomic structure by Saul Dushmann (1883–1954), a colleague of Langmuir's at General Electric.[8] Dushmann too failed to understand Lewis's most novel points. He provided methane with electron transfer bonds, and used Abegg's old terminology of polar valences and contravalences to explain Lewis's cubic atom. He did not mention Lewis's view that electrons could be shared, or that they could form stable pairs.[9] His attempt to explain Lewis's formula for the ammonium ion with its shared electron pairs reveals how little he understood what Lewis was doing; he tried to force Lewis's elegant formula into the cramped framework of the familiar polar theory.[10] Yet Dushmann did find Lewis's ideas "extremely suggestive," and in view of later events at General Electric that fact has the greatest historical importance.

Langmuir too was familiar with Lewis's theory and had referred to its

[5] E.B. Milland's review in *Chem. Abst., 10* (1916), 112.
[6] W.A. Noyes, "Valence," *Science, 49* (1919), 175–182.
[7] *Ibid.*, pp. 180–181.
[8] S. Dushmann, "Structure of the Atom," *Gen. Elec. Rev., 20* (1917), 186–196, 397–410.
[9] *Ibid.*, pp. 403–406.
[10] *Ibid.*, p. 405.

importance as early as 1916. But Langmuir was primarily interested in Lewis's theory of the cubic atom; his understanding of the shared pair bond was no more profound than Dushmann's, and his interest apparently less. The limitations of Langmuir's viewpoint in 1916 are closely related to his activities at General Electric, to which we must now turn.

## 3. LANGMUIR AND GENERAL ELECTRIC, 1909-1916

Irving Langmuir had come to General Electric in 1909 from an unhappy teaching position at Stevens Institute of Technology in Hoboken.[11] His interest in chemistry had been an early enthusiasm acquired from his older brother Arthur, a successful industrial chemist. Irving had studied metallurgy at Columbia (because it required much physics and chemistry), and had made a brilliant record. After graduating in 1899 he studied physical chemistry with Walther Nernst at Göttingen, where with characteristic energy he also performed fifty-mile hikes and sent fifty-page letters to his family. His Ph.D. dissertation in 1906 was a study of the dissociation of gases by a hot filament. Langmuir was a studious, shy, and intense young man, fascinated by ideas. His ambition was to spend his life at the frontier of physical-chemical research. In 1906, however, few American universities had facilities or resources for research, and with Arthur's encouragement he accepted the teaching position at Stevens.

Langmuir certainly realized he would have little chance at first for research at Stevens, but was assured that within a few years he would have the opportunity.[12] He threw himself into teaching, trying to upgrade the low teaching standards and to build up the slender and neglected laboratory facilities. Langmuir's athletic intellectual ideals and his eagerness to provide rigorous laboratory training were not well received by his students, who grew recalcitrant and unruly at the new regimen, or by his colleagues, who resented his efforts to shake them up.[13] The burdens of single-handed reform and a heavy teaching load left no time for research. His letters from this period reveal him as an intensely energetic, ambitious young man, confident of his abilities, but unaware of the problems of communication and naive in his expectations that his superior abilities would be quickly acknowledged by others.[14] In 1909 Langmuir demanded a large raise and a

[11] A. Rosenfeld, *The Quintessence of Irving Langmuir* (Oxford, 1966). See pp. 98 ff.

[12] Letter from I. Langmuir to F.J. Pond, 2 July 1909. Langmuir Papers, Manuscript Division, Library of Congress.

[13] Letter from I. Langmuir to (?) Grant, 12 April 1909. Langmuir Papers.

[14] Letters in the Langmuir Papers. I am preparing a more detailed study of Langmuir's early career.

promotion; his colleagues were only too happy to call his bluff, and in the summer of 1909 he found himself jobless and with no prospect for a university post.[15]

Fortunately Langmuir had another prospect. In 1908 a former classmate, Colin Fink, had described to him the stimulating intellectual atmosphere at General Electric and the interesting research he was doing there. In January 1909 Langmuir had contacted Willis R. Whitney, director of the General Electric Laboratory, about a summer research job.[16] In March Langmuir gave an informal talk at Schenectady and returned "more eager than before" for summer research.[17] Whitney was apparently also impressed, for it seems that a more permanent post was discussed.[18] Langmuir was confident when he left for Schenectady in July that he would be offered a job. He wrote to his mother that he planned to accept, since a year of research at General Electric would be excellent experience and would give him time to look around for what he really wanted, a university post.[19] His year at General Electric proved such a success, however, that he never left. In industry Langmuir unexpectedly realized his ideal of complete freedom to pursue research wherever his interests led him.

The General Electric Laboratory was unique at the time. It had been founded in 1900 by E. W. Rice, Jr., General Electric's technical director, who was disturbed by the paucity of new developments in electrical technology. Rice believed that new technical applications would only come about through fundamental research in chemistry and physics.[20] It was a propitious time for such a faith, since physical chemistry was then in one of its most productive periods. The discovery of the electron in 1897 revolutionized electrochemistry and the study of the electrical properties of matter—subjects of obvious importance to the electrical industry. Rice persuaded Willis R. Whitney (1868–1958), then a young professor of chemistry at Massachusetts Institute of Technology, to become the first director, and his choice was a happy one.[21] Whitney was convinced that the way to get results for industry was not to force creative men such as Langmuir to

[15] Letter from I. Langmuir to F.J. Pond, 2 July 1909; letter from F.J. Pond to I. Langmuir, 14 July 1909. Langmuir Papers.

[16] Letter from I. Langmuir to W.R. Whitney, 30 January 1909. Langmuir Papers.

[17] Letter from I. Langmuir to W.R. Whitney, 15 March 1909. Langmuir Papers.

[18] Letter from I. Langmuir to Mrs. Charles Langmuir, 16 July 1909. Langmuir Papers.

[19] Ibid.

[20] A. Rosenfeld, op. cit. (note 11), pp. 109–112.

[21] G. Suits, "Willis R. Whitney," Biog. Mem. Nat. Acad. Sci., 34 (1960), 350–367. See also Laurence Hawkins, Adventures into the Unknown, the First Fifty Years of the General Electric Research Laboratory (New York, 1950).

pursue immediate applications, but to allow them to follow their own interests. Whitney protected his most able chemists from routine administration and red tape, and encouraged them to work freely on anything that interested them without regard to immediate payoff for General Electric.[22] According to legend it was Whitney's custom to visit his men regularly and to ask them if they were "having fun." Langmuir, who invariably was having fun, remarked one day that he did not know what good his having fun was doing for General Electric. "That is not your worry; it's mine," Whitney replied.[23]

Whitney's style created at General Electric a spirit of research that was in striking contrast to that at most industrial and many academic institutions. Open discussion of recent chemical and physical theory was encouraged; and in 1910–1915 there was much to discuss, especially in electron and atomic theory. Seminars and review sessions on the latest topics were organized by Saul Dushmann.[24] Publication and discussion of the results of work at General Electric were encouraged, and there was vigorous communication with the best academic scientists in America and Europe. In short, the General Electric Laboratory was one of the liveliest, most forward-looking and productive centers of chemical and physical research in America.

The atmosphere at General Electric was strikingly similar to the atmosphere of G. N. Lewis's department at Berkeley. Lewis too believed in a free and open spirit of research, and he encouraged independence and a broad interest in fundamental theories. Cooperation and discussion were fostered by free-wheeling weekly research conferences.[25] Lewis, like Langmuir, was addicted to theoretical speculation; it is perhaps no coincidence that the new theory of molecular structure emanated from Berkeley and Schenectady, where innovation was encouraged and new ideas were sure to be enthusiastically debated.

Langmuir's first project at General Electric made good use of his early research with Nernst. In 1909 William Coolidge (b. 1873) had just developed a ductile tungsten filament that could be heated to much higher temperatures than any before. Langmuir began to study the effect of very high temperatures on various gases, and within about five years this work had yielded a series of major results: the dissociation of molecular hydrogen,

[22]*Ibid.*, pp. 354ff.

[23]A. Rosenfeld, *op. cit.* (note 11), pp. 124–125.

[24]I. Langmuir, "Saul Dushmann, A Human Catalyst," in *Langmuir. The Man and the Scientist* (Oxford, 1962), pp. 409–410.

[25]R.E. Kohler, "Origin," *op. cit.* (note 2).

the invention of the atmospheric light bulb, and the construction of a new theory of the constitution of matter. An anomalous heat loss from very hot filaments led to the discovery that $H_2$ molecules dissociated to free hydrogen atoms,[26] and a series of important papers in 1912-1913 on the properties of atomic hydrogen brought Langmuir widespread recognition among physicists and chemists, including Nernst, Rutherford, Lewis, and Bohr.[27] Simultaneously, investigations of the evaporation of tungsten filaments (which caused the blackening of vacuum bulbs) led Langmuir to the idea of an improved light bulb filled with an inert gas. The nitrogen (later argon) bulb, developed in 1913 and patented in 1916, proved an enormous commercial success and gave Langmuir an unparalleled fame among industrial chemists. His success became the most often cited proof that basic research did pay off.

Langmuir's new theory of matter also grew out of his studies on filaments. He observed that oxygen formed a monomolecular film on tungsten so phenomenally stable that it reacted only with atomic hydrogen. He was deeply impressed; he began to suspect that surface adsorption, which was generally ascribed to weak "physical" forces, was in fact due to the formation of true chemical bonds. His opinion was strengthened about that time, 1915, by William Bragg's work on x-ray crystallography. Bragg showed that a crystal of NaCl was a regular lattice in which each sodium atom was bound to six chlorine atoms and vice versa, although both atoms were traditionally regarded as monovalent.[28] Langmuir concluded that the force between atoms in crystals, usually regarded as a "physical" force, was identical with the "chemical" force between atoms in a molecule, and that separate molecules existed as such only in the vapor state. For Langmuir a crystal was one vast molecule, and a change in state was a chemical change.[29] In his two long papers of 1916-1917 he applied his new theory to a vast array of chemical and physical phenomena, a feat he enthusiastically described as "merely an outline."

While Langmuir's dramatic and very ambitious new theory of matter was never widely accepted (it had a brief life), it did attract a good deal of attention. Indeed, everything he did was attracting attention. In 1915 he was awarded the Nichols Medal by the American Chemical Society, and in

[26] A. Rosenfeld, *op. cit.* (note 11). See Chapter 9 and references, pp. 340-352.

[27] Letters in the Langmuir Papers.

[28] I. Langmuir, "The Constitution and Fundamental Properties of Solids and Liquids," *J. Am. Chem. Soc., 38* (1916), 2221-2295. Part II, *ibid., 39* (1917), 1848-1906. See especially pp. 2221-2223.

[29] *Ibid.*, pp. 2222-2225.

1917 the Hughes Medal by the Royal Society. Already the author of over fifty papers and many patents, touted for his theoretical and practical discoveries and increasingly in demand as a lecturer, Langmuir was acknowledged to be one of the brightest stars in American physical chemistry.

In his 1916 paper on the constitution of matter, Langmuir tried to reconcile his new theory with the various existing theories of the chemical bond.[30] Although his taste in theorizing was eclectic, it is not clear that he took any of these theories entirely seriously, or even that he understood all of them. His treatment of Lewis's theory is a case in point. Langmuir singled out Lewis's theory as an "extremely important" one; yet he gave it the least attention of all those he discussed. He emphasized Lewis's distinction between polar and nonpolar types, but did not even mention Lewis's ideas of shared electrons and electron pairs. Yet in his discussion of Stark, Thomson, and Bohr he picked out precisely those features that were closest, at least in appearance, to Lewis's shared pair bond; e.g., Thomson's two electron bond. Langmuir clearly was intrigued by Lewis's shared pair bond but did not understand it, and that may be why he avoided closer discussion. A remark concerning Thomson's two electron bond reveals that Langmuir had completely missed the point: "This theory would seem to fit in badly with the facts of organic chemistry, for we find no evidence of organic compounds in which carbon acts as if it had a valency of eight or hydrogen a valency of two."[31] Langmuir had not escaped the traditional identification of one bond with the transfer of *one* electron.

The key to his confusion is simply that Langmuir was not concerned with the chemical bond or the structure of molecules, but with the forces between molecules in crystals and surface films. His conviction that chemical affinity was identical with physical cohesive forces would hardly have led him to appreciate Lewis's theory. The shared pair bond was designed to explain the rigid, stable geometry of organic molecules; Langmuir went so far in the opposite direction as to suggest that solid methane might be regarded as solid hydrogen held together by carbon atoms.[32] There was very little in Langmuir's own interests in 1916 that would have forced him to understand Lewis's theory of the chemical bond.

Langmuir's notebook for 1916 reveals what it was in Lewis's paper that he did find "extremely important."[33] Langmuir's chief concern was

[30]*Ibid.*, pp. 2225–2230.
[31]*Ibid.*, p. 2229.
[32]*Ibid.*, pp. 2232–2233.
[33]I. Langmuir, Notebook 803. Container 46, Langmuir Papers.

*atomic* structure, and in his first entry, dated 20 October 1916, he went directly to the crucial point: Bohr's orbital electrons and their violation of classical dynamics.[34] He thought that there were better theories than Bohr's, such as Alfred Parson's magneton theory which he had just been studying.[35] Parson had proposed that electrons, or "magnetons," consisted of circular bands of electricity rotating around fixed points at the corners of cubic octets. He had also adopted J. J. Thomson's positive sphere, and this Langmuir felt was "a greater violation of classical dynamics than . . . a failure of Coulomb's law at short distances (Lewis)." Langmuir was referring to Lewis's 1916 paper, which proposed that the atom consisted of concentric cubic shells of electrons (one electron at each corner) around the nucleus. Lewis was adamantly opposed to Bohr's dynamic orbital atom, which he felt ignored the facts of stereochemistry. He stated that Bohr's quantized planetary atom was designed simply to "save Coulomb's Law" at short distances. Lewis abandoned Coulomb's law and hinted that the stability of his static atom was due to a reversal of the attractive electrostatic force between electrons and nucleus at short distances. Langmuir went along with this view and said so in print.[36]

In a second entry of 26 October Langmuir went further to say that the electrons in atoms were situated in concentric, nonrotating rings.[37] Rings of two electrons were stable, and rings of eight were very stable "as in Parson's theory" (with no mention of Lewis). On these principles Langmuir constructed an *Aufbau* table of the elements with shells of 4, 6, 8, 12, and 16 electrons, these numbers apparently determined quite arbitrarily.

On 28 November Langmuir set down some ideas on crystal structure suggested by a reading of W. Kossel's 1916 theory of electron transfer bonds.[38] The polar theory, he noted, entailed that both $Na^+$ and $Cl^-$ atoms in NaCl have complete *cubic* groups of eight electrons; Langmuir had clearly accepted Lewis's cubic octet, though he did not mention Lewis's name. However, Langmuir's colleague Albert W. Hull (1880–1966), an x-ray crystallographer, had found that the lattice data of NaCl crystals fit poorly with outer cubic shells, but well with octahedral ones. Langmuir proceeded to devise an appropriate theory, once again based on an idea

[34]*Ibid.,* pp. 34–39.
[35]A. Parson, "A Magneton Theory of the Structure of the Atom," *Smithsonian Misc. Coll., 65* (1915), 1–80.
[36]In "Constitution . . . Part II," *op. cit.* (note 28), pp. 1850–1856.
[37]I. Langmuir, Notebook 803, *op. cit.* (note 33), pp. 82–84.
[38]*Ibid.,* pp. 107–116.

from Lewis's paper: "Lewis has found an *exceptionally* strong tendency for the total number of electrons in the shells in any molecule to be an *even number*. Let us assume that this is an *invariable rule*."[39] Langmuir argued that in NaCl crystals the strong repulsions of the cubic octets caused the electron shells to rearrange to Na (2,2,6) and Cl(2,10,6), retaining a stable, even number of electrons in each shell and an octahedral sextet in the outer shell.[40]

In his last entry of 1 January 1917 Langmuir set down a revised *Aufbau* table and a statement on atomic structure.in terms of stationary electrons, the stable pair and octet, and the reversal of Coulomb's law within the atom.[41] Although Lewis's name was mentioned only in regard to the first point, all three were essential points in Lewis's theory of atomic structure. But it is also clear how little Langmuir was concerned with Lewis's theory of molecular structure and the shared pair bond. Langmuir's primary interest was the physics of matter, not chemical structure. It was not Lewis's lengthy discussion of the sharing of electron pairs that interested Langmuir, but his brief hint of non-Coulombic forces. So too it was Parson's elaborate, but obsolete, physics that he noticed, not Parson's more suggestive ideas on the chemical bond. A list Langmuir compiled of sixteen points any atomic theory must explain included fifteen from physics, including gravitation and positive electrons, and only one from chemistry, namely, "the nature of chemical affinity."[42]

Langmuir did touch on one important problem of molecular structure: he proposed that the very stable $N_2$ molecule consisted of a single cubic octet surrounding *both* kernels with their inner shells.[43] But instead of arranging the six inner electrons in one shared pair and two free pairs, as he did after his rediscovery of Lewis's shared pair in 1919, Langmuir depicted them as two groups of three electrons. His paradigm was the *Aufbau* of stable electron groups, not the spatial arrangement of electron pair bonds.

To understand Langmuir's later attitude on his indebtedness to Lewis, it is essential to see how in 1916 he adopted isolated parts of Lewis's theory without seeing it as a whole on Lewis's own terms. The most striking example is his theory of crystal structure, in which he used Lewis's observation that most molecules contained even numbers of electrons. For Lewis

[39]*Ibid.*, p. 109.
[40]*Ibid.*, pp. 113–116. Entry dated 29 November.
[41]*Ibid.*, pp. 151–157.
[42]*Ibid.*
[43]*Ibid.*, p. 115.

this fact was evidence of a more general theory; but as usual Langmuir was totally occupied with his own thoughts and saw in this fact only what was relevant to his current enthusiasm. For Langmuir to see more would require a special occasion.

## 4. LEWIS'S WORK ON VALENCE THEORY, 1916-1919

Lewis made curiously little effort to publicize his theory. He even failed to discuss the shared pair when opportunity presented itself. In September 1916 he published a short paper on the color of triphenylmethyl compounds, which he ascribed to the presence of an "odd" or unpaired electron.[44] Such "odd molecules" had been one of Lewis's key pieces of evidence for the electron pair, yet he only referred in passing to his "recent paper" and did not even mention the electron pair bond. He did draw an elegant picture of the dissociation of several compounds to free radicals, using his double dot bonds;[45] but without any explanation it must simply have baffled his readers in 1916.

Lewis was more eager to defend his cubic atom against Bohr's orbital one. In December 1916 he revealed his plan for a counter-revolution at the joint meeting of the American Chemical and Physical Societies in New York.[46] He had been slated to speak on the relation between atomic structure and valence bonds—a fine opportunity to give the shared pair bond some publicity. But in view of the "wide acceptance" of Bohr's model among physicists, he chose instead to defend the position that electrons in atoms were at rest. He even tried to meet the physicists on their own ground with a crude mathematical theory, developed some years previously on the basis of "electron theory alone" (i.e., without quanta). Lewis proposed that the force between electrons at short range was some damped periodic function alternating between attraction and repulsion. The dips determined the equilibrium positions of electrons and explained the regular series of atomic spectra, obviating the need for orbital or quantum hypotheses. It seems unlikely that Lewis's sketchy, ad hoc physics made much of an impression on the physicists. At the end of his lecture Lewis mentioned his idea that atoms could share electron pairs, but immediately linked it to his idea of non-Coulombic forces. Few chemists

[44] G.N. Lewis, "Steric Hindrance and the Existence of Odd Molecules," *Proc. Nat. Acad. Sci., 2* (1916), 586-592.
[45] *Ibid.*, p. 591.
[46] G.N. Lewis, "The Static Atom," *Science, 46* (1917), 297-302.

would have been stimulated to look up Lewis's earlier paper on the subject.

Langmuir, however, was very interested in Lewis's theory. He was in New York for the meeting, giving a paper on "The Structure of Solids and Liquids and the Nature of Interatomic Forces." He and Lewis had lunch together on 28 Decmeber, "but there was so much left over to talk about that they arranged to meet again the following day to continue the discussion."[47] Presumably the discussion centered on the static atom theory, not the chemical bond.

In April 1917 the entry of the United States into the war put an end to atomic discussion, as laboratories mobilized for war research. In November 1917 Lewis was commissioned in the chemical warfare service, and in January 1918 he went to France where he was soon in charge of anti-gas defense training.[48] He returned to Washington in September 1918 and to Berkeley some months later. During his first months at Berkeley Lewis suffered from a brief case of postwar letdown, and was occupied with a severe administrative crisis in the university. In June 1919 he wrote Millikan:

> When I reached Berkeley I found I had the greatest aversion to chemistry and the chemical laboratory. For several weeks I hardly entered the building; but this feeling has entirely disappeared and I have never enjoyed my work more than I have for the last few months. . . . As you perhaps know, outside of the department the conditions in the university are extremely unsettled, and have been at times extremely discouraging. But we are hoping that our worst predictions will not come true.[49]

Soon Lewis was again hard at work on his compilation of thermodynamic data, a project of fourteen years standing. He apparently had no inclination to pursue his neglected ideas on the cubic atom and the shared pair, and had no inkling that they would soon be a nine days wonder.

## 5. THE ORIGIN OF LANGMUIR'S "OCTET" THEORY, 1919

Even before April 1917 Langmuir had begun war research, and throughout 1917 and 1918 he was largely occupied with submarine detection devices and other projects.[50] He had the opportunity, however, when Ruther-

[47] A. Rosenfeld, *op. cit.* (note 11), p. 168.

[48] J.H. Hildebrand, "Gilbert N. Lewis," *Nat. Acad. Sci. Biog. Mem.*, *31* (1958), 209–235.

[49] Letter from G.N. Lewis to R. Millikan, 7 June 1919. G.N. Lewis Archive, College of Chemistry, University of California, Berkeley.

[50] A. Rosenfeld, *op. cit.* (note 11), pp. 156–163.

ford visited Schenectady in June 1918 to air his speculations on atomic structure. According to Rosenfeld, Rutherford was impressed and urged Langmuir to publish.[51] But it was not until early 1919 that Langmuir's interest was aroused by the question of molecular structure and the shared pair bond.

In his enthusiastic letter to Lewis of 22 April 1919 Langmuir revealed the general course of his rediscovery of Lewis's theory (Letter 1, Appendix). The occasion for his renewed interest in Lewis's paper was a colloquium organized by Dushmann in January 1919, at which Langmuir presented Lewis's theory and his own extensions of it. The entry in Langmuir's notebook[52] for 12 January 1919 begins: "Yesterday I gave a colloquium at the lab on 'Relation between Atom Structure and Properties of Elements' based mostly on Lewis' paper on the Atom and Molecule. I gave the ideas that I have developed during the last 2 or 3 years."[53] Langmuir's notebook reveals that his postulates had undergone slight but significant modification since 1916. The three postulates, all concerning the stability of groups of electrons in the atom, now read: the most stable group was that of two electrons with one or two nuclei; the next most stable was the group of eight electrons, some of which could be common to two groups; the third most stable was any even number of electrons.[54] These postulates show a new concern with the bonds between atoms; the first two clearly refer to the shared electron pair bond, and the third was apparently meant to cover atoms with two or three electron pair bonds. Nevertheless, Langmuir's first interest was clearly still the structure of the static atom. He noted that he had often discussed the static atom with Albert Hull, and had even suggested to Hull that they write a joint paper in which Hull would provide the experimental evidence for stationary electrons (presumably from x-ray crystallography) and Langmuir the chemical evidence.[55]

Langmuir was also still concerned with the problem of reconciling the static atom with the Bohr model. He made some attempts to derive spectra from a static atom and discussed at length the failings of Bohr's mechanism for quantum transitions. He returned to his 1916 idea that transitions involved changes in the structure of the electron itself,[56] which he now conceived might be a continuous band of electricity around the nucleus.

[51]Ibid., p. 173.
[52]I. Langmuir, Notebook 966. Container 46, Langmuir Papers.
[53]Ibid., pp. 99–107.
[54]Ibid., p. 99.
[55]Ibid., p. 100.
[56]Ibid., pp. 101–107.

His excitement grew: an entry of 22 January 1919 on "Structure of Electron" records speculations, stimulated by discussions with Whitney and Hull, that the band electron might be wound up, the number of turns corresponding to Bohr's quantum number $\tau$.[57]

In his next entry of 24 January 1919 Langmuir returned to the *Aufbau* of the higher elements.[58] He also added to his postulates—which covered the first three rows of 2, 8, and 8 elements—another covering the next two rows of 18 elements each,[59] and an entry for 25 January elaborates the *Aufbau* of these groups.[60] His atom model became more elaborate: to explain why there were two rows of 8 and 18 electrons, he postulated a planar symmetry in the atom, every electron above the plane paired with one below.[61] In the following pages of his notebook Langmuir's theory of the atom emerges, differing in only some refinements from the form in which it was published.

Thus far Langmuir was occupied wholly with his new ideas of atomic structure. His insight into Lewis's theory of molecular structure first appears in an entry of 6 February 1919. Langmuir referred to this crucial insight in his long letter to Lewis of 3 April 1920 (Letter 6, Appendix, pp. 76–87). Although he had accepted Lewis's idea that a single bond consisted of an electron pair (postulate one) and presumably held the common belief that a molecule was most stable when each atom had a full octet (postulate two), he had not seen that the electron pairs in bonds and the free unshared pairs together comprised a full octet. The four edges (electron pairs) of Lewis's cubic atom, whether free or shared with other cubic atoms, still constituted a complete cube. Langmuir had also failed to see that the number of shared pair bonds of any atom was strictly limited to four. With the exception of his model of $N_2$, he had never been concerned with the number and disposition of electrons present in a molecule. Until the end of January 1919 Langmuir still assumed that the number of shared pair bonds in a molecule was no less arbitrary than the number of simple line bonds in ordinary structural formulas—hence his third postulate (Letter 6, Appendix, pp. 76–87). Langmuir's new insight was that the number of shared pair bonds $p$ was strictly determined by the total number of valence electrons $e$ and the number of octets $n$. This insight he called the "octet theory" and expressed it by the equation: $e = 8n - 2p$.

---

[57]*Ibid.*, pp. 118–119.
[58]*Ibid.*, pp. 126–133.
[59]*Ibid.*, p. 130.
[60]*Ibid.*, pp. 134–142.
[61]*Ibid.*, p. 134.

Langmuir's notebook provides some hints as to how he rediscovered this crucial point of Lewis's theory. In an entry of 24 January 1919 he returned to the structure of $N_2$ he had suggested in 1916, in which one octet enclosed both nuclei. He now brought it more in line with his new postulates, and proposed that the inner group of six electrons consisted of one free pair associated with each nucleus and one pair lying between the two nuclei[62] (presumably Langmuir had a single bond in mind). A similar structure was also proposed for NO, the inner group of which consisted of one pair for each nucleus and one electron lying between the nuclei.[63] He tried to devise a similar formula for $NO_2$, but this line of reasoning failed him:

I cannot think of any very satisfactory structure for $NO_2$. It is probable that the two O atoms have their full quota of electrons [i.e., eight] and that the N nucleus with one electron is between the two oxygen atoms.

Such a molecule is very unstable and readily polymerizes to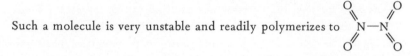

in which N behaves normally [as in $N_2$?] two electrons being held in common between the two N kernels. Because of this fact that there is a *pair* of electrons around the kernels (the two not forming any part of a group of 8)[64]

Langmuir broke off at a crucial point, precisely where he explicitly states that the electron pair between the nitrogen atoms does not form part of any octet. In his letter to Lewis (Letter 7, Appendix) Langmuir particularly recalled his difficulties in deriving structures for the nitrogen oxides from his three *Aufbau* postulates, and I strongly suspect that this specific problem with $NO_2$ was the germ of his "octet theory." For it is obvious in the next entry of 29 January 1919, five days later, that Langmuir had understood the role of octets.[65] He gives a table of compounds of chlorine and oxygen ($ClO_2$, etc.), with each atom represented as a square, the four edges of Lewis's cubic octet, and joined at the corners by shared pair bonds. Langmuir had realized that these free and shared pairs constituted an octet, for he wrote: "In each of these Cl compounds the chlorine atom has gotten its surrounding cube of electrons. Thus an oxy-

[62]*Ibid.*, p. 127.
[63]*Ibid.*, p. 132.
[64]*Ibid.*, pp. 133–134.
[65]*Ibid.*, pp. 142–145.

gen atom O> [with three electron pairs] can add itself to the edge of any *completed* cube of eight."[66]

In the next entry, dated 6 February 1919 and entitled "Theory of Valence,"[67] the "octet" equation appears for the first time.[68] The following pages are filled with specific structures derived by the octet rule for compounds of nitrogen, sulfur, phosphorus, and carbon. For atoms of normal electrovalence ($Cl^I$, $O^{II}$, $N^{III}$, $C^{IV}$) the new structures matched the traditional ones, but for compounds traditionally represented with pentavalent nitrogen or hexavalent sulfur Langmuir derived new structures with only four shared pair bonds per atom. For Langmuir all this must have been an intensely exciting revelation, and rather marvelous too, for he was not sure why his theory worked so well: "Why is it that the valence bonds in organic compounds check with the pairs of electrons held in common but not so in nitrogen etc. compounds?"[69] It is abundantly clear that Langmuir's rediscovery of Lewis's theory was wholly independent of Lewis: it began with his idea of the structure of $N_2$ in 1916, leading in January 1919 to his puzzlement over $NO_2$, to his cubic structures of $ClO_2$, etc., and finally, in February 1919, to his general octet equation. The form of Langmuir's rediscovery was distinctively his own; it was intimately related to the unique events of his own intellectual history.

## 6. THE ANNOUNCEMENT OF THE "OCTET" THEORY, 1919-1920

Throughout February Langmuir expanded and refined his new theory of valence for publication. As usual he lost no time in sharing his enthusiasm with the rest of the scientific world, and it proved contagious. His diary of 1 March 1919 records an interested response from a group of physicists—an acid test:

Have been working all month on "Arrangements of Electrons in Atoms and Molecules." Most interesting paper to write I have attempted. New York: Amer Phys Soc Meeting. I read 10 min paper on Atomic Structure. Am asked at end of meeting to show slides etc. Talk for $1/2$ hour.[70]

The real clamor over the "new theory" began with Langmuir's address

[66] *Ibid.*, p. 145.
[67] *Ibid.*, pp. 146–155.
[68] *Ibid.*, p. 147.
[69] *Ibid.*, p. 154.
[70] A. Rosenfeld, *op. cit.* (note 11), p. 173.

on 9 April 1919 to the annual meeting of the American Chemical Society at Buffalo. This meeting was normally held in December, but the war had led to its postponement—as if to serve as Langmuir's springboard. As he noted in his diary, the response was so enthusiastic that he was asked to repeat it for those who had missed it the first time:

> April 9: I read paper $1^1/_4$ hrs (section Inorg & Phys Chem) on Electrons in Atoms & Molecules. It arouses very great interest (more than among physicists).

> April 10: I am asked to repeat the reading of my paper. E. C. Franklin asks me to take Phys Dept at Stanford Univ. but I am not interested. GE Lab too good.[71]

In 1920, when Langmuir again received the Nichols Medal for his work on valence, it was noted that his repeat performance at Buffalo had set a precedent.[72]

The response to his theory led him to consider its application to organic chemistry, and it led to more requests for lectures:

> April 11: After night on train, back to Schen. L. W. Jones, Clewes & Others called my attention to agreement of my theory with organic comps. I will examine them more fully.

> April 12: Sat: Tel call from Washington to give my paper there. Spend morning in library & afternoon at home studying organic, N, S, & O compounds. Find wonderful agreement with octet theory.[73]

The invitation from Washington was to address the American Association at its annual meeting. On April 29 Langmuir also addressed a large and eager assembly at the National Academy of Sciences, which included "four hundred chemists from the National Bureau of Standards."[74] Throughout the rest of 1919 Langmuir gave lectures at a number of universities, including a series of seven to W. A. Noyes' department at the University of Illinois.

Langmuir was an extremely effective lecturer; he loved the part, and his enthusiasm swept his audiences before him. He was almost compulsively pedagogic; as a boy he had lectured his little brother into a corner until

[71] *Ibid.*, pp. 173-174.
[72] Editorial, "Wm. H. Nichols Award," *J. Ind. Eng. Chem., 12* (1920), 386.
[73] A. Rosenfeld, *op. cit.* (note 11), pp. 173-174.
[74] Editorial, "The Structure of the Atom," *Scientific Monthly, 8* (1919), 572-573.

poor Dean had yelled for help.[75] His son-in-law has described Langmuir's passion for educating the neighborhood children:

> He was like a great big magnet. . . . There was a charged atmosphere around him. Anything he wanted to tell you seemed exciting because he was excited about it. It couldn't seem dull if he thought it was important. If he wanted to tell you about it, you wanted to hear. . . . He always described things in simple, down-to-earth terms, and always thought up graphic demonstrations. And he made it all fun.[76]

Langmuir clearly had the same effect on his adult audiences.

The dramatic success of Langmuir's Buffalo speech was soon noticed by the popular scientific press.[77] The editor of *Scientific Monthly* hailed the "new conception" of chemical combination: "it explains the ordinary theory of valence and indicates when this must be modified." It also corrected Bohr's atomic theory—"while Bohr's results were correct, the theory was wrong."[78] Such statements are a measure both of Langmuir's enthusiasm for his theory and of chemists' enthusiasm for Langmuir. In like vein the editor of the industrial journal *Chemical and Metallurgical Engineering* hailed the "new philosophy of chemistry and matter,"[79] and this editorial was followed by a full-length exposition[80] of Langmuir's paper. The tone of this popular presentation is a curious mixture of diffidence and enthusiasm:

> The main difficulty is that we must take a new point of view, and anything new is likely to be bothersome. . . . The theory opens up vast possibilities. We can imagine periods of perplexity and dizziness after we have tried with sticks and balls of wax to build up atoms and molecules, . . . and we almost dread the task.[81]

To aid the "dread" task, the editors later published a description of plaster models illustrating Langmuir's postulates and offered a kit for making them, designed by Leffert Lefferts, a consulting chemist in New York.[82]

[75] A. Rosenfeld, *op. cit.* (note 11), p. 49.

[76] *Ibid.*, p. 180.

[77] Editorial, "Scientific Meetings," *Prog. of Sci.* (1919), p. 569.

[78] Editorial, *op. cit.* (note 74).

[79] Editorial, "A New Philosophy of Chemistry and Matter," *Chem. Met. Eng., 21* (1919), 57–58.

[80] E. Hendrick, "The Langmuir Postulates," *ibid.*, pp. 73–81.

[81] *Ibid.*, p. 77.

[82] O.R. Foster, "Some Remarkable Models of Atomic and Molecular Structure," *Chem. Met. Eng., 23* (1920), 690–692.

Such exhortations to the reader betray a profound ambivalence among industrial chemists to the more prestigous world of academic theoretical chemistry. Industrial chemists were not noted for an interest in new ideas, and one senses here the companion feelings of diffidence and distrust, as well as enthusiasm. The attraction of the new theory was certainly due to Langmuir, who belonged to both the academic and the industrial world. Probably only Langmuir could have aroused such interest in a group that did not ordinarily bother much about new philosophies. Since the group of industrial chemists made up a large fraction of the chemical profession, Langmuir's high reputation in this group was no small element in the success of the new theory.

Equally important for Langmuir's success was his almost compulsive desire to publish and proselytize. Here he differed strikingly from Lewis, who was content to quietly offer a single brief and polished statement of his ideas with a few key illustrations. Langmuir covered every detail and spoke from every pulpit. Langmuir's theory was published in brief form in the National Academy's *Proceedings*[83] and in the *Journal of the Franklin Institute*[84] in June 1919. In the same month a long exposition of it appeared in the *Journal of the American Chemical Society*,[85] followed by two papers on special applications, written in May and June and published around the turn of the year.[86,87] The second of these also included a resume of Langmuir's most important ideas. Thus by the end of 1919 Langmuir's ideas were available in detail and in summary to the American chemical community, and were being widely acknowledged as a sensational breakthrough in chemical theory.

Langmuir's version of the new valence theory differed from Lewis's in a number of important respects. In sheer bulk and detail it was far more impressive. Langmuir's theory consisted of no less than eleven "postulates," the first seven of which concerned the structure of atoms and the *Aufbau* of the elements. Lewis had applied his theory only to the first three rows of the periodic table, to which the cubic atom applied best. Langmuir, on

[83] I. Langmuir, "The Structure of Atoms and the Octet Theory of Valence," *Proc. Nat. Acad. Sci., 5* (1919), 252–259.

[84] I. Langmuir, "The Arrangement of Electrons in Atoms and Molecules," *J. Franklin Inst., 187* (1919), 359–364.

[85] I. Langmuir, "The Arrangement of Electrons in Atoms and Molecules," *J. Am. Chem. Soc., 41* (1919), 868–934. Received 3 March 1919.

[86] Langmuir, "Isomorphism, Isosterism, and Covalence," *ibid.*, pp. 1543–1559.

[87] I. Langmuir, "The Octet Theory of Valence and Its Applications with Special Reference to Organic Compounds," *ibid., 42* (1920), 274–292.

the other hand, applied his more complex atom, with its shells and planes of symmetry and "cells" of electron pairs, to the higher elements, including the rare earths and transition metals. He took up each element systematically, discussing its chemical and physical properties.

Langmuir's last four postulates concerned the chemical bond and molecular structure. They were essentially the principal points of Lewis's paper; namely, the pairing and sharing of electrons and the stable octet.[88] For Langmuir, however, these postulates were only the starting points for his new theory; as he put it, "they lead directly to a new theory of valence which we may call the Octet Theory."[89] From the octet equation Langmuir calculated the number of shared pair bonds in a molecule, characterizing all other bonds as mobile ionic bonds. To make this distinction clear he proposed the name of "covalent bond,"[90] a choice that, like the term "octet theory," immediately caught the public fancy. Using the octet equation Langmuir systematically discussed compounds of each element in turn.

In method as well as terminology Langmuir's treatment differed from Lewis's. For one thing Langmuir paid much more attention than Lewis to the physical properties of compounds. This attention reflects Langmuir's practical concern at General Electric with physical properties of materials as well as his deep theoretical interest in adsorption and surface chemistry and his taste for theoretical models of physics, notably the *Aufbau* model. Langmuir's basic idea was that groups of two and eight electrons had weak "external fields" and conferred nonreactive, nonpolar chemical properties on compounds, whereas Lewis had relied more on the empirical distinction between polar and nonpolar compounds. Langmuir's approach to molecular structure was also based on the mathematical deductive method of physics, as shown by his octet equation and his vision of a "deductive chemistry."[91] Although Lewis too spoke of postulates and fancied himself an amateur physicist, his approach to molecular structure was essentially a structural one, like that of an organic chemist.

In the matter of style, Lewis was far more informal and intuitive than Langmuir. Their stylistic difference is well illustrated by their treatment of the structure of $NH_4Cl$, Lewis's key illustration of his theory. Langmuir

88 I. Langmuir, "Arrangement of Electrons," *op. cit.* (note 85), pp. 887–889.
89 I. Langmuir, "Structure of Atoms," *op. cit.* (note 83), p. 254.
90 I. Langmuir, "Arrangement of Electrons," *op. cit.* (note 85), p. 926.
91 I. Langmuir, "Future Developments of Theoretical Chemistry," *Chem. Met. Eng.,* 24 (1921), 553–557.

calculated from $e = 8n - 2p$ $(e = 16, n = 2)$ that $p = 0$; i.e., that there is no covalent bond between the nitrogen and chlorine atoms, but only an ionic bond. His long and complex discussion involved physical considerations such as polarization and residual fields.[92] Lewis, by contrast, simply drew the formula for $:NH_3$ in terms of double dot bonds, with its free pair available for binding a proton. He pointed to the striking analogy between $NH_4^+$ and $CH_4$, both with complete octets, remarking that "it will be sufficient to write an equation in terms of the new symbols in order to make the explanation obvious."[93] Indeed, Lewis never did spell out that part of his theory, but merely left it implicit in his examples. In the short run the significance of Lewis's elegant pictorial formulas was not obvious, and Langmuir's more abstract but more familiar deductive treatment, with its seemingly inexorable logic, was more understandable and convincing. But once the basic ideas were familiar, Langmuir's roundabout "deductions" became superfluous, and Lewis's intuitive chemical approach prevailed.[94]

One of Langmuir's most original points was his recognition that two compounds with the same values of $e$ and $n$ should have similar structures and physical properties; he termed such compounds *isosteres*. Thus a table of a dozen properties of $N_2O$ and $CO_2$ $(e = 16, n = 3)$ revealed a striking quantitative similarity that had gone unnoticed.[95] Langmuir made the most of this dramatic discovery, and it made a great impression at the time. It was widely reported that it was now possible to predict the properties of compounds even before they were synthesized, and even Lewis showed signs of envy. Langmuir later devoted a whole paper to isosterism.

These differences between Lewis's and Langmuir's theories and the great difference in their reception by the chemical world inevitably led to a clash over priority.

## 7. LEWIS AND LANGMUIR: THE DISPUTE OVER PRIORITY

On 22 April 1919 Langmuir sent Lewis a manuscript copy of his first paper and mentioned some of his latest ideas (Letter 1, Appendix). Some-

[92] I. Langmuir, "Octet Theory," *op. cit.* (note 87), p. 276.
[93] G.N. Lewis, "The Atom and the Molecule," *op. cit.* (note 1), p. 778.
[94] An example of the limits imposed by Langmuir's lack of structural intuition is his treatment of the water molecule in "Arrangement of Electrons," *op. cit.* (note 85), p. 893.
[95] I. Langmuir, "Structure of Atoms," *op. cit.* (note 83), p. 257.

what naively, he also gave Lewis a brief history of the origins of his theory, beginning with Lewis's own work. Lewis was at first not displeased; Langmuir's work was, after all, a belated recognition of his own ideas. In a letter to Langmuir of 15 June 1919 Lewis approved Langmuir's treatment of the higher elements and their physical properties, subjects that Lewis had scarcely touched on (Letter 2, Appendix). Lewis was less impressed with Langmuir's atom model and his treatment of the nitrogen oxides, subjects he had had something to say about. Langmuir replied eagerly on 28 June 1919, looking forward to a stimulating competition with Lewis in applying their new theory (Letter 3, Appendix). Lewis, however, undoubtedly did not share Langmuir's enthusiasm for a public footrace, since Langmuir was the marathon hiker and had a headstart as well. Lewis delighted in debate, but also had a strong sense of intellectual property rights. By that time the extent of Langmuir's success was beginning to be clear to him; in June Millikan had written from Chicago that "Langmuir seems to have created quite an impression by adopting your ideas and re-presenting them to the public. I have not gone into them very carefully as yet, but in so far as I have studied them I see little which he has added to what you had already presented."[96]

Lewis's uneasiness over Langmuir's popularity is explicit in his letter to Langmuir of 9 July 1919 (Letter 4, Appendix). It was clear to him by then that much of Langmuir's work concerned the first two rows of elements, which his own cubic atom covered. Many of Langmuir's statements must have struck Lewis as rephrased versions of his own insights, for which Langmuir was getting all the credit. In particular Lewis objected to Langmuir's catch phrase "octet theory" and to Langmuir's avoidance of Lewis's term "odd molecule." He might also have complained that Langmuir had religiously avoided Lewis's double dot symbol for the covalent bond, certainly an intentional omission. Lewis's concern with nomenclature is understandable; although he could do nothing about the public enthusiasm for Langmuir, nomenclature was a professional concern and, in theory, subject to professional agreement. Nomenclature also had an obvious bearing on priority; if Langmuir's terms were accepted, the theory would be linked forever with Langmuir's name. The emotional overtones involved are clear in Lewis's slightly acid reflection that "sometimes parents show singular infelicity in naming their children, but on the whole they seem to enjoy having the privilege." Lewis made it politely but per-

[96] Letter from R. A. Millikan to G.N. Lewis, 19 June 1919. Lewis Archive.

fectly clear that he thought Langmuir had added little but a new name to Lewis's own ideas.

By the end of 1919 Lewis no longer felt so diplomatic; two events in particular finally led him to seek arbitration. In late 1919 W. A. Noyes submitted a paper to the *Journal of the American Chemical Society,* based on a lecture he gave at Chicago that spring, which took issue with some points of Langmuir's work.[97] Noyes had long been interested in valence theory and had already corresponded with Langmuir at some length about it in May.[98] They arranged that Langmuir would draw up a rebuttal to be published with Noyes' paper. Through William Bray, a member of the editorial board and a close colleague of Lewis's at Berkeley, Lewis learned of these plans and was furious. It seems that Noyes had discussed the same questions with Lewis and that Lewis had told him of relevant experimental work going on at Berkeley (Letter 5, Appendix). Lewis also felt that he should have been the one to defend his theory, not Langmuir. On 13 January 1920 Lewis wrote the editor of the *Journal,* Arthur B. Lamb (1880–1952), complaining of his neglect by Noyes and Langmuir and objecting to their use of Langmuir's term "octet theory" and of the popular term "Lewis-Langmuir theory." He also objected to Langmuir's paper, "The Octet Theory of Valence," which appeared that month and which included several key illustrations of the "octet theory" (e.g., the formation of the ammonium ion and the stereochemistry of carbon and nitrogen) that Lewis had explicitly covered in his paper.[99]

Lamb sent copies of Lewis's letter to several leading chemists, who agreed that Lewis's position was reasonable.[100] On 24 March Lamb informed Langmuir that the editors "with much heart-burning" had decided not to publish Noyes' paper: "the greater part of his paper, while a graceful and fitting response to the presentation of the medal was not just the type of paper which we feel should be printed in the Journal." Langmuir's rebuttal was also refused.[101] Lamb enclosed a portion of Lewis's letter, presumably to suggest the difficulties involved in his decision. He hoped that the dispute would be resolved: "I feel that we shall all suffer irreparably if there is anything but friendliness and harmony between the two men whom I consider promise most for the future of our

[97] Letter from I. Langmuir to G.A. Abbott, 16 March 1920. Langmuir Papers.
[98] Letters in the Langmuir Papers.
[99] I. Langmuir, "Octet Theory," *op. cit.* (note 87), pp. 278–280, 286–288.
[100] Letter from A.B. Lamb to G.N. Lewis, 2 April 1920. Lewis Archive.
[101] Letter from A.B. Lamb to I. Langmuir, 24 March 1920. Langmuir Papers.

science in America."[102] To Lewis, Lamb counseled patience and understanding: "It would appear to me that if proper recognition is now given
to you for your work in this field, opportunities for discord in the future
will be less than at present. Langmuir is so intensely interested in this
problem, and has a mind of such activity and power, that he is sure to
evolve modifications of this theory sufficiently distinctive so that there
will be no confusion."[103]

Prompted by Lamb, Langmuir finally replied to Lewis's letter of July
1919; as he confessed in his long letter of 3 April 1920, the question of
priority was extremely distasteful to him (Letter 6, Appendix). His letter,
however, was hardly calculated to smooth Lewis's ruffled feelings. Langmuir's forthright remarks on the question of priority must in fact have
seemed calculated to displease; he said that he could not "perpetually be
giving credit," and then proceeded to give credit to Kossel, Parson, and
Bohr—to practically everyone except Lewis. Knowing as we do Langmuir's
intense interest in 1916 in the physical basis of atomic structure, we can
see how for him the physics of Kossel, Parson, and Bohr was more impressive than Lewis's hints of a non-Coulombic force. There is no doubt
that Langmuir was perfectly open and honest; he was simply defending
himself with the same vigor—indeed, relish—with which he would defend
an abstract idea. His insensitivity to the human context of ideas was well
known; Rosenfeld observed:

> Langmuir was always "pointing out errors" in other men's work. And
> occasionally the erring soul would get angry, and Langmuir would be
> surprised and puzzled. He liked other people to correct his own errors—
> which were not rare, since he did not mind sticking his neck out with
> positive assertions. . . . He assumed, therefore, that others would not
> mind—in fact, would welcome—his criticism of their ideas. Were not
> scientists after all in pursuit of truth? "Having Langmuir 'point out an
> error'," one of his old colleagues recalls, "was like having a boulder land
> on you."[104]

In a reply to Lamb, Langmuir hoped his letter would "help to reconcile
our differences of opinion, although for the sake of frankness I have had
to criticize his 1916 paper in a way that he may not like."[105] He was

[102] Ibid.
[103] Letter from A.B. Lamb to G.N. Lewis, 2 April 1920. Lewis Archive.
[104] A. Rosenfeld, op. cit. (note 11), pp. 190–191.
[105] Letter from I. Langmuir to A.B. Lamb, 4 April 1920. Langmuir Papers.

naively unaware of the social value of tact and restraint, but his failings were honest ones, as his final touching confession suggests: "I am rather at a loss to know what I can do or what I should do" (Letter 6, Appendix).

Lewis was not assuaged. In December 1920 he declined to collaborate with Langmuir in a report on theories of atomic structure for the National Research Council—for geographical reasons. But he added that "in general it might be best to ask me to defend such theories as I have originated, and to ask Dr. Langmuir to sponsor the theories which are his."[106] He steadfastly refused to adopt the terms "octet," "covalence," and the "Lewis-Langmuir theory."[107] In a letter to Noyes in 1926 he complained of Noyes' reference to a structural formula (of $HClO_4$) as the "Lewis-Langmuir" formula:

> This formula . . . should be called the formula of Lewis, Langmuir and W. A. Noyes, and so on, adding the name of every author who quotes it hereafter. Or perhaps it would be simpler to call it the formula of Lewis, and not mention the names of all the others who have quoted it.
>
> Perhaps I am inclined to be too caustic in this matter, but I really do feel that while people were justified in being carried away a bit by Langmuir's personal charm and enthusiasm some years ago, to persist, especially as they do in England, in speaking of the Langmuir theory of valence is inexcusable. If anyone feels the contrary I would like to ask him to mention any one original principle of Langmuir's regarding valence which has proved tenable. I do not, however, wish this ancient grudge to make me unduly critical of your present paper.[108]

By then both Lewis's and Langmuir's interests had long since turned elsewhere, and a friendly exchange of letters in 1930 suggests that at least between them the "ancient grudge" was ancient history.[109]

In retrospect, what can be said about the question of priority? Langmuir religiously gave Lewis credit at the beginning of every paper, noting that his work was "an extension of Lewis's theory." But having thus discharged his obligation, he rarely referred again to Lewis's work. He also spoke of his "octet theory" as if it were a novel deduction from Lewis's principles, when in fact it is clearly implicit, if not spelled out, in Lewis's paper. The crux of the priority matter was Langmuir's rediscovery of the octet theory;

---

106 Letter from G.N. Lewis to F.A. Saunders, 24 December 1920. Lewis Archive.
107 G.N. Lewis, *Valence, op. cit.* (note 3), pp. 87, 105.
108 Letter from G.N. Lewis to W.A. Noyes, 13 July 1926. Lewis Archive.
109 Letters in the Lewis Archive.

the sense of revelation was so strong that his new insight felt as if it were his own discovery. Psychologically it was, and it would have taken a less fervent man than Langmuir to see that it was in fact a rediscovery.

## 8. LANGMUIR, 1921–1923

Despite his intense activity in the subject in 1919 and early 1920, Langmuir's interest in valence theory per se was really only an interlude in his career. Previously his main theoretical interest had been atomic structure, and in 1920 he returned to it. That fall he attempted to derive, by classical mechanics, a rigorous theory of the helium atom and the $H_2$ molecule.[110] The basic idea behind this ambitious effort had been suggested by A. Landé, who had proposed in 1919 that only the angular momentum of the electrons in atoms circulated around the nucleus, while the electrons themselves remained in limited regions or "octants" analogous to Langmuir's "cells." Langmuir proposed an "oscillating" model of the static atom in which two electrons described oscillating semicircular paths. This model seemed an ideal compromise between the chemists' static atom and Bohr's dynamic one. By modifying the quantum postulate he was also able to calculate the ionization potential of helium.

But quantum theory was not familiar ground to Langmuir; in a letter to Bohr in October 1920 he confessed he might not have used the quantum theory correctly and asked for Bohr's criticism.[111] He also told Bohr that he felt Landé and Bohr himself had underestimated the importance of coupling between electron orbits in the stable groups of two and eight electrons. Bohr's reply in December 1920 was enthusiastic: he too had been deeply impressed by Landé's ideas, and also had come to realize the need for coupling electron orbits.[112] Bohr was already at work developing these ideas into what was to be his highly successful *Aufbau* theory of atomic structure. But Bohr confessed he was dubious about Langmuir's models: the motion of electrons, he felt, was too complex to be described by a mechanical model. Despite Bohr's skepticism, however, Langmuir published his complete, mechanical calculations in November 1921.[113]

[110] I. Langmuir, "The Structure of the Helium Atom," *Science, 51* (1920), 605–607.

[111] Letter from I. Langmuir to N. Bohr, 25 October 1920. American Institute of Physics Archives.

[112] Letter from N. Bohr to I. Langmuir, 3 December 1920. American Institute of Physics Archives.

[113] I. Langmuir, "The Structure of the Helium Atom," *Phys. Rev., 17* (1921), 339–353.

In February 1921 Langmuir had another inspiration, the result of his efforts to write a report on recent theories of atomic structure for the National Research Council. He explained to his mother:

I started to write it [the report] up about two weeks ago and soon found that I began to get new ideas on the subject. These have developed into the most important scientific discoveries that I have yet made. Especially since last Sunday I have been working night and day. . . . I am able to prove now with certainty that the electrons of which matter is made are not moving in orbits, but remain relatively stationary and I can now calculate exactly the forces that act on each electron.[114]

Langmuir rejected orbital motion and replaced the centrifugal force in Bohr's model with a new "quantum force" that kept the electrons in equilibrium positions. From Bohr's equation for the hydrogen atom he calculated the new force law and from that derived all the results of Bohr's theory, admitting, a little naively, that "of course the law of force was chosen to give just this result."[115] He had already begun to tackle the helium atom, but his expectations were premature; the promised extensions of his theory never appeared.

Langmuir published one more paper on valence theory, a logically condensed form of his octet theory.[116] He reduced his eleven postulates to three: one concerned the *Aufbau* of atoms; one concerned the shared pair bond; and the third stated that the sum of electrovalences and covalences (the "residual atomic charge") for any atom in a molecule tended to a minimum. The latter statement was a highly abstracted form of the equation $e = 8n - 2p$, and from it Langmuir "deduced" all the empirical valence rules. He was convinced that the "residual atomic charge" had important physical significance, apparently having in mind his mysterious quantum force: "It is felt by the writer that this postulate is a crude expression of a very important and fundamental law. When we understand the repulsive forces between charged particles better we shall be able to state the law in a more nearly quantitative form."[117] Since he wrote nothing further on this subject, Langmuir must have realized after Bohr published his new theory later in 1921 that both the "residual atomic charge"

---

[114]Letter from I. Langmuir to Mrs. Charles Langmuir, 9 March 1921. Langmuir Papers.
[115]I. Langmuir, "The Structure of the Static Atom," *Science, 53* (1921), 290–293.
[116]I. Langmuir, "Types of Valence," *Science, 54* (1921), 59–67.
[117]*Ibid.,* p. 62.

and the "quantum force" were totally obsolete. The long development of Langmuir's thoughts on atomic physics thus ended in a cul-de-sac.

Among chemists the direct influence of Langmuir's "octet theory" was short-lived. Its mathematical or axiomatic expression was soon dated as chemists became more facile with the double dot bond. Langmuir's failure to adopt Lewis's convention was a serious tactical error; so was his frequent use of the cubic atom in depicting molecular structures. By 1923 the cubic atom was an embarrassing relic (even Lewis did not depict it in *Valence*, though he still favored a modified tetrahedral atom model), and Langmuir's papers were accordingly obsolete. As Lewis pointed out, Langmuir also insisted too rigidly on the necessity of a full octet,[118] a consequence no doubt of his dramatic rediscovery of the "octet theory"; Lewis foresaw that molecules with incomplete octets defined a type of generalized acid (later termed "Lewis-acid").[119] Lewis's structural approach thus proved to be more flexible and useful. *Valence* was probably the decisive influence; although it bears the mark of Lewis's peculiar outlook and the historical context of its birth in the controversial years 1921–1922,[120] its numerous illustrations of the use of the double dot bond provided chemists with a firm basis for further applications. Langmuir too had planned to prepare a monograph on valence theory, but he never wrote it,[121] and in the long run Lewis's outlook was the more influential.

I want to return, finally, to the central problem: the contrast between the total neglect of Lewis's theory in 1916 and its immediate recognition only three years later. The initial failure of the theory was due to the unreceptive intellectual context; the theory fulfilled no obviously pressing need, and Lewis made no effort to persuade others of its advantages. Organic, physical, and inorganic chemists were generally content with their traditional points of view. Between 1916 and 1919 there was a slight change in the intellectual context as more chemists—even Noyes—recognized the need for a dualistic system and a nonpolar bond; and their concern over atomic models and atomic theories perhaps became more open and acute. But on the whole the context had not greatly changed. What made the difference was, of course, Langmuir himself, and his

[118]G.N. Lewis, *Valence, op. cit.* (note 3), p. 97.
[119]*Ibid.,* pp. 97–101, 142.
[120]It was the result of a seminar presided over by Lewis in these years.
[121]Letter from I. Langmuir to N. Bohr, 3 November 1921. American Institute of Physics Archives.

personal reputation. The new theory was well received because it was Langmuir's theory and not because of its intrinsic intellectual worth. Once received, of course, its worth became evident. What I wish to stress is that the advantages of the new theory were not immediately obvious, and that had it not been "Langmuir's theory" the rediscovery and adoption of Lewis's theory might well have awaited a real crisis in the theory of chemical bonding.

# APPENDIX: CORRESPONDENCE OF LEWIS AND LANGMUIR [122]

[1]  I. Langmuir to G. N. Lewis, 22 April 1919.

My dear Lewis:

Until a couple of weeks ago I was under the impression that you were still in France, and therefore have not written you in regard to the theory that I have been working on recently.

I am sending you under separate cover the manuscript of a paper which I have sent to the Jr. of the American Chemical Society, and which is to be published in the June number.

You will probably be interested in the history of the development of these ideas. When I read your paper on the "Atom and Molecule" in 1916, I was immediately struck by the very fundamental nature of the ideas you presented, and of their splendid agreement with the general facts of chemistry, so I very soon began to look upon all chemical phenomena from the viewpoint that you presented. It seemed to me that it accounted particularly well with so-called physical characteristics, such as boiling-points, freezing-points, etc. In talking to several other people about the theory, and explaining to them how it would apply to properties of the elements in the two short periods, I gradually began to ~~understand~~ extend the theory somewhat, especially in the direction of coming to a realization that the tendency to form groups of 8 or 2 was nearly without exception, the cause of the formation of compounds, at least in the case of the first 20 elements. While on war work at Nahant[123] I met Sir Ernest Rutherford, and later, Sir Richard Paget, and I told both of them in detail the importance of your theory, in showing them how it could be applied to the prediction and understanding of the properties of substances.

Early in January of this year Dr. Dushman, of this laboratory, asked me to give a talk at our Colloquium on the subject of "Adsorption." I told him that I thought a very much more interesting subject would be Lewis' theory of the Atom and Molecule, and, accordingly, I read your paper

---

[122] Lewis Archive. Except for Letter 5, the letters are also in the Langmuir Papers. The letters of G.N. Lewis are printed here by the kind permission of Dr. Richard N. Lewis, Dr. Edward S. Lewis, and Mrs. Mary Lewis.

[123] Langmuir worked at the naval research station at Nahant, Massachusetts.

again carefully, and began to study how I could present the matter in a way that it would arouse the most interest. In doing so I was impressed more than ever by the general applicability of the theory, and was surprised that chemists in general seem to have paid so little attention to your ideas.

My interest was then so thoroughly aroused that I spent nearly all of my time in the development of these ideas for about five or six weeks in January and February. I was especially interested in extending the theory to cover all the elements, and to broaden out the theory of valence so as to cover all types of compounds. I think you will be interested to see how I was able to accomplish this. It seems to me there is no field of chemistry where these ideas are not going to bring about radical changes in present conceptions.

Since writing the enclosed paper I have thought over the application of the theory in the field of organic chemistry, and have found, as is really to be expected, that the theory explains, as far as I can see, all of the facts of structural chemistry in a thoroughly satisfactory manner. The stereo-isomers of carbon, nitrogen, sulphur and phosphorus, all fit in much better with the new theory than with any theory previously proposed; also the oxonium compounds are fully in accordance with the theory. After having spent weeks in going over the literature I have only found one set of compounds that really puzzles me, and that is, the various hydrides of boron, in which the boron seems to act as though it were quadrivalent. I refer particularly to the compounds $B_2H_6$, $B_6H_{12}$, and $B_4H_{10}$. The only reasonable explanation that I can think of is that two boron atoms form an inner compound with two hydrogen atoms, leaving a pseudo atom with a single octet, (like that which I have found for the gases of $N_2$ and $CO_2$). This would account for the absence of such compounds as $BH_4$, $B_3H_8$, etc. On the other hand, I do not see on this basis how to explain the compound $KBH_3O$, even if we double this molecule in order to get an even number of electrons. It seems to me that experimental work on the physical and chemical properties of these compounds is needed to give us a basis for the proper theory. Of course, according to the octet theory, it is obvious that no gaseous hydrides of boron should exist.

It seems to me that the theory of the atom and molecule which we have developed should be capable of throwing a great deal of light on quantitative chemical relationships in such fields as molecular volumes, heat, and free energy, of reactions, dissociation-constants, etc. You will notice that in the case of compounds like $N_2$ and $CO$, and again in $N_2O$ and $CO_2$, quantitative relations are actually predicted by this theory. In the second paper that I am publishing I will show that hydronitric acid and cyanic acid have ions which have similar structures to the molecules of $CO_2$ and $N_2O$. As far as I have been able to find the physical properties (solubilities, etc.) of azides and cyanates are the same.

The next time you come East I hope very much that you will stop at the laboratory, for I think we could very profitably spend a day or so talking over the further extension of this work.

Yours very truly

[2]  G. N. Lewis to I. Langmuir, 15 June 1919.

My dear Langmuir:

I am sure you will pardon my long delay in acknowledging the manuscript copy of your article on "The Structure of the Atom and Molecule." The fact is I have been hoping to find opportunity to discuss with you at length the many interesting points which you have brought out; but conditions have been so unusual, and it has been so difficult to get the department back to its status quo ante that the opportunity has not come, and even now I am not able to discuss the matter at length as I should like. But as I am just leaving for a short vacation I wanted to let you know how much I appreciated your thoughtfulness in sending me an advance copy, and how much I have been pleased by finding that, after the searching investigation you have made, you find yourself in agreement with all of the main conclusions which I have reached in my papers.

Although I have speculated a good deal concerning the structure of the elements of the long periods, I have not yet developed any ideas which seem to possess a sufficient degree of certainty to warrant their publication. I have therefore been extremely interested in your hypothesis regarding these elements, and it strikes me as capable of explaining a considerable number of facts. The relations which you establish between atomic structure and magnetism must certainly have some real basis. I also feel sympathetic toward your tautomerism of nickel, and think that this is the direction in which the ultimate solution will be found. I cannot, however, accept as yet the details of your atomic structure, but perhaps I shall after I have thought of it further.

Your treatment of the elements of the two short periods seems to me extremely satisfactory, and it had not occurred to me to make the extensive use of arguments from physical properties which you do so success-fully. With respect to the structural formulae of nitrogen compounds, etc., there will always be some difference of opinion, and we must bear in mind the almost universal phenomenon of tautomerism in inorganic compounds. But it is great fun to play with these formulae, and I have worked out a great many which, in the main, agree with your own, and which I should have published long before this if it had not been for the war.

Your ideas concerning the drawing together of the atoms in the com-pounds of some of the elements of the first period with each other and with hydrogen corresponds entirely with a view which we have developed here, and which Bray and Branch have interested themselves in. The independent development of an idea of this sort seems to me to point pretty strongly to its validity.

The question of the co-ordination number is one which deserves a great deal of thought. E. Q. Adams[124] had a number of important ideas on this subject which he put into a paper that he showed me before he left Cali-fornia. I criticized it on the ground of too great brevity, and although he has promised several times to bring it out, it has not yet been published. I am afraid from the standpoint of publicity on this subject all of us here have been rather remiss. I wish that I could have a chance to talk all of these interesting things over with you, and perhaps before long I shall be able to get East. In the meantime I shall be very glad to hear if you have any new ideas on the subject. Will you be good enough to send me one or two reprints of your paper? I am not sure that mine have been sent out. I am sending them to you, therefore, under separate cover.

With best regards, I am,

Yours very sincerely,


[3] I. Langmuir to G. N. Lewis, 28 June 1919.


My dear Lewis

I am sending you reprints of all the papers I have published during the last four years, and a couple of extra reprints of the paper in the June Journal. Elwood Hendrick with my help has written up a popular account of this for Met. & Chem. Eng. and I have two papers I am sending to the

---

[124] E.Q. Adams was a graduate student at Berkeley (Ph.D. 1914), and had also worked summers with Langmuir at General Electric in 1909–1913. The paper re-ferred to was never published, and Adams informs me that the manuscript is lost.

Journal of the Amer. Chem. Soc. One is on the application of the valence theory to organic compounds particularly nitrogen compounds also oxonium, sulphonium, etc compounds. It also discusses the differences between salts and subtances whose molecules are held together by pairs of electrons in comolecules, and such subjects as: 1. why are there "weak acids" and "weak bases" but no "weak salts." 2. Why are there no isomers of HNCO, $HNO_2$ etc. or their inorganic salts while the organic derivatives exist in two isomeric forms?

The second paper deals with "Isomorphism, isosterism and covalence." By isosterism I mean to describe the relationship between two substances (or comolecules[125]) having equal numbers of electrons and in similar arrangements. Examples are $N_2$ and CO; $N_2O$ and $CO_2$; $HN_3$ and HNCO and all inorganic trinitrides and cyanates; $KClO_3$ – $SrSO_4$; $CaCO_3$ – $NaNO_3$; $SrHPO_4$ and $KHSO_4$; NaF and MgO; $Na_2O$ and $MgF_2$ etc. These pairs of substances have nearly identical crystalline forms or are isomorphous as is to be expected by the octet theory (at least as far as can be determined from available data). This affords direct proof by Mitscherlich's rule that the valence (better call it covalence) of N in $NaNO_3$ is 4, and the valence of the central atoms of $SO_4^{--}$, $PO_4^{---}$, $ClO_4^-$ etc. is four. Note further that corresponding salts of $CO_3^{--}$, $SO_3^{--}$ are not isomorphous since in the latter the covalence is three. By the ordinary theory however both should show valency of four in their compounds, and should be (and were) expected to be isomorphous.

I will be much interested in knowing your objections to the "details of the atomic structure."

It is too bad that E. Q. Adams cannot bring things to definite conclusions. I hope you can influence him to publish his work. I have had no plan of publishing anything more for the present on compounds of the types usually considered by Werner altho I realize that there is a great deal that needs clearing up—especially from the view-point of most chemists.

I am sorry that you had not published your results on the structures of inorganic compounds, and I hope you will be very active in extending the theory into new fields. Don't you think that competition of this kind between us will be stimulating to us both and assure more rapid progress? We should however keep each other posted as to the particular fields we are actually working on to avoid duplication.

I plan to be in California in August and early September, and hope I can

---

[125] "Comolecule" is a term coined by Langmuir to signify groups of covalently bonded atoms.

spend a day with you. I will let you know more definitely as to my plans as soon as I know them and will let you know where to write me.

Yours Sincerely

[4]  G. N. Lewis to I. Langmuir, 9 July 1919.

My dear Langmuir:

I am very glad indeed to have the complete set of your papers which you were good enough to send to me. You may be interested to know that in one of our recent seminars a considerable part of the time was devoted to a discussion of your paper on Surfaces.

I shall be very much interested in seeing your two new papers on Structure, and I shall not publish anything further in this line until I have seen them. Apparently you have found, as I did, that for the present the easiest progress can be made in the study of elements which I chose for consideration, being not only simpler in structure, but on account of the large number of compounds and the extensive study to which they have been subjected, giving also a much larger body of experimental. [Sic.]

It has been extremely gratifying to find that after the extended study to which you have given the matter you have found no one of the numerous and rather revolutionary conclusions of my paper which you have wished to amend. You have been remarkably successfull [sic] in applying this theory to a large number of concrete cases, and I do not know anyone who could have done it so well; but to be perfectly candid I think there is a chance that the casual reader may make a mistake which I am sure you would be the last to encourage. He might think that you were proposing a theory which in some essential respects differed from my own, or one which was based upon some vague suggestions of mine which had not been carefully thought out. While I realize what a short distance we have gone towards explaining chemical phenomena, it seems to me that the views which I presented were about as definite and concrete as was possible considering the condensed form of publication. I think if any confusion should arise it would be due perhaps to points of nomenclature. For example, while I speak of a group of eight, you speak of an octet. I think, as a matter of fact, your expression is preferable, and I shall be glad to adopt it, but I should be sorry to see the whole theory known as the octet theory, partly because it raises questions of the sort I have just mentioned, but especially because the octet is no more fundamental to the theory than the electron pair which constitutes the chemical bond. Many years ago, when I first began working on this subject, and before electrons were much known, it was the change of valence by steps of two which seemed to me about the most striking phenomenon which had to be explained by a theory of valence. It was for this reason that I laid particular stress upon the fact that so few compounds are known possessing odd molecules or odd atoms. These are terms which I believe you have not adopted. Did you think of anything better? It is of course important in a new development of this kind that the nomenclature should be as expressive and as simple as possible. Sometimes parents show singular infelicity in naming their own children, but on the whole they seem to enjoy having the privilege.

I trust that you will not misunderstand what I have said, or think for a moment that I am not delighted to see you working in this extremely interesting field. I shall look forward with great pleasure to seeing you in Berkeley, and hope that you will be able to spend more than the one day with us. Do let me know just when you can come and give us as much of your time as possible. We have a number of interesting things to show you, and I should like very much to have our students hear from you.

With best regards, I am,

Yours very sincerely,

[5]  G. N. Lewis to A. B. Lamb, 13 January 1920.

My dear Lamb:

Bray has asked me to write you a word regarding a series of statements by W. A. Noyes and by Langmuir which he has shown me. Bray tells me that you take the attitude that it is the duty of the editor, as far as he is able, to prevent misunderstandings which may arise through unfortunate statements in papers submitted for publication.

I feel that there is some danger of misunderstanding in connection with the new views of valence or molecular structure. When Langmuir aroused the interest and enthusiasm of Eastern chemists by his paper on the arrangement of electrons, atoms and molecules he performed a valuable service. His interesting and convincing personality, his admirable methods of presentation, and his opportunity of expounding the new views to many audiences gave the subject an impetus among chemists of all ranks which otherwise it might not have obtained in many years. I also appreciate highly the intrinsic value of Langmuir's work. He not only introduced new ideas which may prove to be very valuable, but he showed an unusual degree of acumen in elaborating the ideas which had preceded his. There is no one in this department, where we had discussed the whole subject very fully, who, in my opinion, could have given so thorough and so lucid a presentation of the matter.

In spite of all this I have felt during recent developments a growing sense of embarrassment. I have always avoided, and should like to avoid, anything in the nature of a polemic. Scientific discoveries are of greater importance than scientific credit, but there are certain established rules of priority which ought to be observed.

Langmuir's original article might be divided into two parts. One concerns the elements whose consideration I did not include in my paper. This one, which is new, is not the one which has been referred to in his and other recent publications. The second part is an amplification and an application to numerous concrete cases of the theory contained in my paper. Some of these developments had not occurred to me; others had been already fully worked out in this laboratory and would have been published except for the intervention of the war. But for all of these Langmuir, who first published them, is entitled by the established rule of priority to complete and sole credit.

However, in recent discussions by Langmuir and others that which is termed the octet theory, or the Langmuir octet theory is simply the theory of which I gave a complete though concise exposition in my paper, and does not ordinarily refer to the extensions or amplifications made by Langmuir. He has in no case suggested any subtractions from the theory which I advanced, and his additions, in which he pushes the theory rather farther than I am inclined to, are not ones which are involved in the application of the theory to most chemical problems. Looking at the matter, then, as impartially as possible I feel that it is not just to speak of the Lewis-Langmuir valence theory, nor do I like the term octet theory, for while the octet (which was called by Parson and myself the group of eight) is an important part of the theory it is by no means the whole or even the essential part.

To return to the communications from Noyes and Langmuir, I think it was unfortunate that Noyes' paper was sent first to Langmuir for a reply, and I am surprised too, by one or two of the statements in the paper by Noyes. For example, I had spent several hours last summer discussing with him the derivatives of the amine oxides,[126] showed him the explanation of this phenomenon from the standpoint of my theory of structure, and told him of an experimental investigation, which we have since got under way, which he admitted would show conclusively which of the two types of structure is correct.

With best wishes for the New Year, I am,

Yours very sincerely,

[6]  I. Langmuir to G. N. Lewis, 3 April 1920.

My dear Lewis:

Three separate times I have started to write you in reply to your letter of July 9, 1919 but in each case I have been interrupted and have so little liked what I had written that I put off writing. The fact is, that the points that you raise are ones which are most unpleasant to write about and could be much better straightened out if we could talk things over. I am therefore particularly sorry that I was not able to see you when I was in California last summer. With my brother, Mrs. Langmuir and I were taking an automobile trip thru California and had been to the Yosemite Valley and were staying for a few days at Lake Tahoe. I had fully planned to stop a day at Berkeley but a couple of days before we expected to leave Tahoe Mrs. Langmuir seriously injured her hand by a large falling stone while we were mountain climbing, and we had to make a hurried trip to Los Angeles (my brother's home) for medical attendance.

This morning I received a letter from Lamb in regard to a paper I had sent him some time ago, and he enclosed a copy of a portion of a letter which you had written him, and suggested that it would be unfortunate "if anything but friendliness and harmony" should exist between us. With this I fully agree and I therefore plan to write you in detail and with the utmost frankness in regard to the matter brought up in your two letters.

I have already written you at length about the part that your publications played in connection with my work on atomic structure and valence. Ever since your paper appeared in 1916 I have thought of chemical phe-

[126]According to Lewis, nitrogen in amine oxides had a valence of four ($R_3N^+ - O^-$), whereas Noyes believed it to have a valence of five ($R_3N = O$). See W.A. Noyes, "Ionization of Trimethylammonium Hydroxide," *J. Am. Chem. Soc.*, 47 (1925), 3025–3030.

nomena in terms of your theory. In January and February 1919 I did work, and developed ideas which at that time seemed to me (and still do) to constitute an important developement [sic] and extension of your theory. I therefore have felt that what I have published is not merely an exposition of *your* theory but is distinctly a joint theory, and that I have contributed at least as much as you have to the final result. I know from your letter to Lamb that you differ with me in this opinion. I hate to discuss matters of this kind and especially wish to avoid all public expressions in such matters, but I feel that the best way to straighten out the present difficulty is to discuss these things frankly. Let me then give my reasons for my opinion.

In the first place we must all realize that no one can or should have a proprietary right in a theory for all time. We must always hope that the theory will grow and that many chemists will contribute to it. It therefore soon becomes impossible to attribute the whole theory to the one who took the first steps. For this reason I think that it is highly desirable that theories should not be known by the name of those who propose them. For example, I think it is much better to speak of the Relativity Theory than of Einstein's theory; of the Quantum Theory rather than Planck's theory; of the Principle of Equipartition rather than that of Waterson. For the same reason it seems to me better to speak of the Octet Theory than of Lewis' theory of valence. (In my mind Parson is the originator of the Octet theory). (Or possibly it may be J. J. Thomson). The point is, the quantum theory grows much bigger than Planck.

Furthermore every new theory is based upon and is an extension of work that has gone before. We cannot perpetually be giving credit to all those upon which our work is based. A great many of the features of the theory which you proposed in 1916 had been previously published elsewhere. Stark[127] had identified a pair of electrons held in common between adjacent atoms with the valence bond. Bohr had had a pair of electrons not only between two atoms in the hydrogen molecule, but he proposed a structure for methane which is essentially identical with that which both of us now assume. This is shown by the following quotation from Bohr's paper of 1913 (Phil. Mag. Nov. 1913, p. 874):

"In systems such as the molecule $CH_4$ we cannot, however, assume the existence of an axis of symmetry, and consequently we must in such cases omit the assumption of exactly circular orbits. The configuration sug-

---

[127] J. Stark, *Prinzipien der Atomdynamik III. Die Elektrizität im chemischen Atom* (Leipzig, 1915).

gested by the theory for a molecule of $CH_4$ is of the ordinary tetrahedron type; the carbon nucleus surrounded by a very small ring of two electrons being situated in the centre, and a hydrogen nucleus in every corner. The chemical bonds are represented by four rings of two electrons each rotating around the lines connecting the centre and the corners."

This in my opinion is a much clearer and more nearly correct picture of the methane molecule than any given in your paper. I do not mean that Bohr gave a complete valence theory but it is clear that in the eyes of the world, Bohr must be given priority over you in identifying the pair of electrons held in common between atoms with the valence bond. You may claim that Bohr did not suggest that all bonds in organic compounds are of the same nature, but on the other hand Bohr himself might say that it is only an obvious extension of his theory to apply it to other substances. Similarly I feel that I am justified to a large degree in claiming that in your 1916 paper you did not show that your theory was of general application to inorganic compounds but merely gave a few illustrations and that it was by no means obvious that the theory laid the foundation for a comprehensive theory of valence of the kind that I believe I have developed.

Kossel's paper[128] appeared a couple of months (much to my regret) before yours and therefore "by the established rules of priority" should be given credit for a number of points which form an essential part of your theory. Thus the first, second and fifth postulates (page 768 of your 1916 paper) of your theory are fully developed in Kossel's theory. Furthermore one important feature of your theory, viz: that the properties of the elements adjacent to the inert gases are determined by their ability to take up or give up electrons, is brought out in great detail in Kossel's theory. As a matter of fact Kossel's whole theory is practically the same as yours in so far as the application to polar compounds is concerned. Your theory of course is far ahead of Kossel's in that it also takes into account the pairs of electrons held in common between atoms, but as we have just seen this is not exclusively a feature of your theory. Kossel emphasizes the stability of the pair of electrons in helium and in the kernels of other atoms, and also the octets in the heavier elements. The only important point that he misses is that these stable groups can share pairs of electrons with each other.

The ideas of the octet or stable group of eight is [sic] clearly advanced by Parson (perhaps by J. J. Thomson in some of his early work). Would it

---

[128]W. Kossel, "Über Molekülbildung als Frage des Atombaus," *Ann. d. Physik, 49* (1916), 229–362.

not be perhaps as logical to speak of the Octet theory as the Parson octet theory as the Lewis or the Lewis-Langmuir octet theory? It seems to me we must all frankly admit that the present theory is the outgrowth of the work of many.

So much for the question of priority.

In all that I have said so far and in what follows I am discussing only that part of my publications which covers a similar ground to that of your paper. I understand that your criticisms are not directed towards those parts of my papers which deal with the eighth group and rare earth elements etc.

In one of [the] paragraphs of your letter to Lamb you say that the second part of my June paper is an application of your theory to numerous concrete cases and that some of these would probably have been published by you if it had not been for the war. I assure you that I had no intention of stealing a march on you in this connection and that if I had thought that you were planning to publish further papers on this subject in the near future, I would have written you beforehand. As a matter of fact, since many papers had appeared from your laboratory during the interval of nearly three years, and since your paper before the American Chemical Society in Sept. 1916[129] dealing with the structure of atoms did not touch upon this theory of valence except in a very indirect way, it was natural that I should believe that you were not working very actively on this subject. Furthermore I had been told in Jan. 1919 that you had not yet returned from France, and it did not seem right to hold back any contribution that I might make.

In all of my publications on this subject I have endeavoured in every reasonable way to be what I have considered scrupulously fair. In every paper I have placed in as conspicuous a place as possible a statement to the effect that my work has consisted in a development and an extension of your theory. In many cases I have repeatedly referred to your paper in the course of one of mine. In all the personal letters I have written in connection with this work I have gone out of my way to be fair in giving you credit. As one illustration I enclose that first page of a letter which I wrote recently to Sommerfeld, and I assure you that this is typical of all of my letters of this kind. I am really at a loss to know what more I can do. For the reasons I have already give[n] and will give, I cannot honestly say that the theory that I am using is Lewis' theory of valence. In order to explain without needless repetition I must refer frequently to my own papers rather than to yours, but in doing so I do not mean to claim priority.

[129]The meeting was in December; see Lewis, "Static Atom," *op. cit.* (note 46).

In fact I have given little attention to priority except in so far as it seemed necessary for the sake of fairness. It seems to me that it is for other chemists to decide to what extent each of us has contributed to the present theory. We are necessarily prejudiced and can only with great difficulty form impartial judgements in such a matter. All we should do is to refer reasonably frequently to the work of the other and not make any claim as to priority. As far as I can remember I have not specifically made any claim at all in regard to the matter but have frequently disclaimed priority as far as I fairly could. I am willing to go as far in this direction as you think I should.

For example I have noticed in the last number of Nature a note referring to the theory as "Langmuir's Theory of the Atom."[130] This note then goes on to discuss some points which are clearly contained in your paper. I have just received a letter from H. S. Allen saying that he is also writing a letter to Nature and suggests that I write a reply. This I intend to do and in so doing I will point out that all the features in the discussion are contained in your paper and that the theory should never be referred to as Langmuir's theory of the atom. But except in those cases where the subject has been covered in your paper it does not seem reasonable that I should protest against the term Lewis-Langmuir, altho I would greatly prefer to have the theory referred to as the octet theory and have it forgotten (as will soon be the case) who first proposed the term octet.

The last paragraph of your letter which was quoted by Lamb contains many statements with which I cannot agree. Let us consider the statement "that which is termed the octet theory—is simply the theory of which I gave a complete though concise exposition in my paper." I have the highest admiration for the theory which you proposed in 1916 and admit frankly that you had a remarkably clear view of the nature of chemical valence. To me it was the most stimulating paper that I had ever read and (as I have repeatedly stated publicly in most of my lectures) was the direct cause of the work that I subsequently did in this field. But in my opinion we have progressed essentially beyond this point now, and I doubt if you will find any impartial student of the subject who will agree with you that you gave a *complete* exposition of the theory as given in my recent papers.

I will discuss your paper from my point of view and I think you will understand the basis of my opinion. I hate very much to be forced to criticize a paper as admirable as yours, but I honestly consider that it is very

---

[130]Langmuir was probably referring to S.C. Bradford, "On Langmuir's Theory of Atoms," *Nature, 105* (11 March 1920), 41.

unfair not to recognize some originality in the work I have done on the theory of valence. I believe in this matter you are doing me an injustice greater than that which you believe I am doing you.

In the first place let me ask you whether you have carefully tried to exclude from your mind *all* the developements [sic] which you have thought of since the spring of 1916? This is a particularly difficult thing to do. In reading over your paper now I am able to see a great many things in it which I did not get from it at all in Jan. 1919. Furthermore I see many statements which seem to me to be inconsistent with my present viewpoint, and I find a vagueness in many points which explains why no-one as far as I know recognized in your work a general and important new theory of valence. You will understand my point better from my own experience in working with your theory.

Prior to Jan. 1919 I had read over your paper at least twice and had been most struck by the ease with which the ordinary valence relations (valence and contravalence) were explained from *very few* fundamental assumptions. Also by the ease with which I was able (but this was not done in your paper) to derive the physical properties. But it did not occur to me that the theory was a perfectly general theory which covered all classes of compounds much *better* (not only with fewer assumptions) than any other theory of valence.

In Jan. 1919 (or perhaps it was Dec. 1918) in preparing to give a colloquium on this subject, I spent a couple of weeks in rather intensive study of the subject. I gave the colloquium without any thought of having contributed anything new to the subject. Several of those present who had read your paper urged me to publish an article on the subject for they insisted that they failed to get any such view of chemical phenomena from reading your paper, and claimed that many of the ideas which I had presented were not in your paper at all. For two weeks or so after I had no thought of writing a paper on the subject as it seemed to me that I had too little new matter to present.

In connection with this colloquium, and the discussion which followed, many questions arose as to the structure of particular compounds. I remember especially having a discussion in regard to oxides of nitrogen and nitric acid. I did not see that the theory gave any definite picture for the structure of compounds such as $N_2O$, $HNO_2$, $HNO_3$, $HClO_2$, etc. And I had no idea as to how to apply the theory to most of the acids of sulfur and phosphorus.

A couple of weeks later, after I had developed the ideas in regard to the arrangement of the electrons in what I call the third and fourth shells, I became impressed with the importance of the group of eight in the second shell *rather than the group of 2,4,6 or 8.* Up to this time I had kept in mind the view that ~~the only requirement was that~~ the total number of electrons was to be an even number. I had in mind particularly such statements as the following from your 1916 paper:

> top p. 770 "chlorine has 8 electrons in the outer shell in chlorides, 6 in hypochlorites, 4 in chlorites, 2 in chlorates and none in perchlorates."
>
> Middle p. 770 "In every substance in which each element has either its highest or its lowest *polar number,* E will appear in multiples of 8."[131]— "In compounds in which the elements have polar numbers intermediate between the highest and the lowest the number of electrons is not as a rule a multiple of 8, but is in almost all cases *an even number.*"

The impression one gets from these statements is that the polar numbers are to be *assumed,* just as the valences of $-1, +1, +3, +5,$ and $+7$ are assumed in the ordinary theory. There is no thought expressed in your paper of counting up all the electrons and *deducing* how many pairs of electrons must be held in common. The choice of polar number and number of electrons in the shell seems to be quite arbitrary. In this respect it was not at all obvious from your theory that your theory was any more definite than the ordinary theory. In fact it seemed much less definite, and in our discussions we were discouraged by the great number of compounds that seemed to be possible according to your theory.

I started to say that I had developed what seemed to me to be new ideas as to the stability of 8 (instead of 2, 4 or 6) electrons in the second shell and then for the first time began to see the necessity of having *all the electrons* take part in the *formation of octets.* I do not see that this idea is stated anywhere in your paper. I consider it an essential part of what I call the octet theory, *and without it I do not see how the equation $2p = 8n - e$ can be derived.*

It has seemed to me that the derivation of this equation or the viewpoint which underlies it is a vital step in making the theory a general theory of valence. I know that in my own case by the aid of this equation I was immediately enabled to derive definite structures for many substances, whereas without it I felt I had been groping in the dark. It seems to me that it is just this definitness [sic] which I have given to the theory that

---

[131]"Polar number" refers to the number of electrons transferred to or from an atom; $E$ refers to the total number of valence electrons in a molecule.

has more than any other fact led to its general recognition, whereas I have found no cases in the literature where your work had been considered at all as a general theory of valence. By making it possible to calculate $p$ the number of pairs of electrons shared between atoms I have very greatly decreased the number of possible structures which may be assumed to exist, and the fact that even with this limitation there is agreement with the chemical data is in my mind the strongest evidence in favor of the theory.

There are a few other points in your 1916 paper which I would like to call attention to. You seem to take a very indefinite stand in regard to the structure of such substances as sodium chloride. In several places you emphacise [sic] the "continuous transition between the most polar and the most nonpolar of substances." According to the octet theory as I understand it there is nothing corresponding to a pair of electrons which could possibly hold a chlorine and a sodium atom together. The structure of sodium chloride and an organic molecule are different in kind, not in degree, altho in a series of compounds I can see how it is possible to get transitions.

The statements in postulates 2 and 3 are quite at variance with what I have called the octet theory. These statements are:

"the number of electrons in the shell may vary during chemical change between 0 and 8." "The atom tends to hold an even number of electrons in the shell."

In the theory as I have presented it, there is a tendency to have 8 electrons in the shell (or 18 or 32 for the heavier elements) but little or no tendency to hold 2, 4 or 6. The fact that there is nearly always an even number of electrons follows from the fact that only *pairs* of electrons are shared between atoms. This you fail to emphacize [sic] (postulate 4 does not mention it). On p. 772 (top) where you discuss the interpenetrability of the shells you do not mention the importance of pairs. I think this lack of emphacis [sic] on this important point would have made it very difficult for the average chemist to extend your theory to any large number of cases. In fact I have met many chemists who were familiar with your paper who tried to put atoms together so that only electron [sic] [132] would be held in common between adjacent atoms.

I would also criticize the following statements:
p. 777. "Ammonium ion may be regarded as a loose complex due to the electrical attraction of the two polar molecules."

[132] Langmuir undoubtedly meant "only *one* electron."

p. 778. "The union of sulfur trioxide to oxide ion to form sulfate ion is similar to the addition of ammonia and hydrogen ion to form ammonium ion."

These of course are minor points.

These are *all* the statements in your paper with which I seriously disagree. I think it is a remarkably small number and it means of course that I have not felt any necessity of modifying any part of your theory. But I do think that I have really *extended* and *developed* the theory in an essential way and have not merely been expounding the Lewis theory.

In regard to the work that I have done I think you must also agree that in my postulates 9, 10 and 11, I have given a definiteness to the theory which was largely lacking in your presentation. You may not agree with all my ideas but if you do not then you must still more admit a trace of originality in the work I have done. Consider for example the mathematical proof in my paper of Feb. 1920 that the octet theory is identical with the ordinary [theory] of organic chemistry whenever we take valences equal to 8 – E. This seems to me to furnish the strongest proof we have yet had of the soundness of the theory. Yet I have not been able to see how this derivation could possibly be derived from your paper.

In the last sentence which Lamb quotes from your letter you say: "I feel that it is not just to speak of the Lewis-Langmuir valence theory, nor do I like the term octet theory, for while the octet is an important part of the theory it is by no means the whole or even an essential part."

Strictly speaking if the originators of the theory must be mentioned in connection with it I think the theory should be called the Thomson-Stark-Rutherford-Bohr-Parson-Kossel-Lewis-Langmuir theory. I really think you would have a hard time finding which one of these names has most reason to be attached to this theory. But joking aside don't you think I have done enough work and contributed sufficiently to even be mentioned in connection with the theory if names are to be mentioned? The question arises; is it physically possible to prevent my name from being mentioned in connection with it even if that were desirable? I am afraid that no protests on my part would be of much effect. I assure you that to whatever extent my name has been associated with the theory recently has resulted solely from the fact that I have published a series of papers on it and have brought the theory to the attention of a large number of people. In every case I have spoken of your work and have said that I have merely extended and developed it. But you know that people are inclined to associate (to too great a

degree) such ideas with those who *develop* them instead of those who originate them. It seems to me that the only effective way to counteract such
a tendency is for you to publish more work in this field. If you do not
continue to be active along these lines you surely cannot expect to be so
intimately associated with the work as are those who publish in this connection. In my last letter to you I expressed the hope that you would continue to develop this theory.

(I am getting very sleepy and I notice that I have been rambling rather
aimlessly but I will continue until I finish so as to get the letter sent off
this time. I am doing my own typewriting as you have surely guessed from
the mistakes.)

In regard to the term "Octet Theory." When I got your letter of last
July I tried hard to think of some way of meeting your objections to this
term. But I have never succeeded in doing this. I did not then any more
than I do now think it at all right or feasible to call it the Lewis theory.
Suppose I should at any time make an addition to the theory that would
be fundamental, should I then stop calling the theory by your name or
would I always have to name each part of the theory separately in order to
prevent someone else from making a mistake in regard to priority? If then
we are to have a name for the theory not to be associated with the originator, it seems to me that the term Octet Theory is more satisfactory than
[any] other. You will notice from what I have said that according to my
view the octets play a much more important part than in the theory which
you presented. Thus when you consider that *all the electrons* in the shells
of the atoms form octets (with the single exception of $H_2$) whereas only
certain ones as a rule form stable pairs, it seems to me that the term octet
theory is justified. I would like to get a name which would also express the
importance of the group of two, but I have not been able to think of anything satisfactory. For this reason I have continued to use the term in spite
of your objections. I hope you will let me know your present opinions in
the matter for I think we should come to an agreement if possible. I would
be perfectly willing to change the nomenclature if you can suggest anything better.

If other people insist in connecting our names with the theory have we
any right to object? It seems to me the case is quite similar to that of the
Stefan-Boltzmann Law, or the Bohr-Sommerfeld theory. In both cases the
second name is that of the one who made the theory more definite by extending it or developing it. In neither case was it necessary to modify the
original theory.

Well, I have now fully unburdened my mind on this subject. I think it is probably a good thing to have discussed all the points that I can think of which may have led to our differences of opinion. It is hardly reasonable to expect you to go to such length in explaining your views, but I do hope you will find time to tell me frankly and in some detail just what unfair statements I have made and in what way I can counteract their effect. Do you think we could publish a joint note or paper in which we could straighten out any misconceptions? I am rather at a loss to know what I can or what I should do. But I believe that no real good ever comes from friction of the kind that might develop between us if we let matters drift along. I have always had the highest regard for you and will continue to value your friendship, and would hate to see any misunderstandings undermine that friendship.

A couple of times while I have been writing this letter I have thought that certain parts of it (pages 5, 6, and 7)[133] perhaps ought to be sent to Lamb. It might be better to do this however, along with your letter to me. In any case I think we should let Lamb know what we finally agree upon as the fair thing. We might even ask Lamb to arbitrate in connection with any points that we cannot agree upon. I would be perfectly willing to adopt any policy in my publications etc. which he would advise. I doubt however whether such action will be necessary.

You will be interested in a general theory of chemical reactivity which Dushman (in our laboratory) has recently developed. An abstract will appear shortly in the Jour. of the Franklin Inst. and Dushman will read a paper at St. Louis. It is simply this:

The velocity of any monomolecular reaction is given by the expression

$$\nu e^{-\dfrac{Q}{RT}}$$

where $\nu$ is related to $Q$ by the quantum relation $Q = Nh\nu$. Thus there is only one empirical constant needed to express the reaction velocity at all temperatures. From this it is easy to derive the condition for equilibrium. The relation holds with remarkable accuracy for all known cases of dissociations into atoms, decomposition of $PH_3$ etc. I have also found that it [is] applicable to the rates of evaporation and the vapor pressures of all substances even the extreme cases such as He, $H_2$, W, Mo, Pt, Hg, $UF_6$ etc. It also applies to dissociations such as $CaCO_3$ etc. In the cases of so called associated substances there are the usual deviations. It is a beautifully simple

133 See pp. 52–55.

relation, but what does it mean? It seems to apply even where the mechanisms seem very different. Dushman is now applying it successfully to solubilities and to reactions in solution.

Well, it is now 2:30 A.M. and I am getting hopelessly sleepy. I will mail this just as it is and will trust that you will forgive me for not reading it over before I send it. It is probably full of mistakes but can nevertheless be read.

Yours sincerely,

# The Rise and Fall of Laplacian Physics

BY ROBERT FOX*

*By means of these assumptions, the phenomena of expansion, heat,
and vibrational motion in gases are explained in terms of attractive and
repulsive forces which act only over insensible distances (distances
imperceptibles). In my theory of capillary action I related the effects
of capillarity to such forces. All terrestrial phenomena depend on
forces of this kind, just as celestial phenomena depend on universal
gravitation. It seems to me that the study of these forces should now
be the chief goal of mathematical philosophy. I even believe that it
would be useful to introduce such a study in proofs in mechanics,
laying aside abstract considerations of flexible or inflexible lines
without mass and of perfectly hard bodies. A number of trials have
shown me that by coming closer to nature in this way one could make
these proofs no less simple and far more lucid than by the methods
used hitherto.[1]*

## 1. INTRODUCTION

The period from Napoleon Bonaparte's assumption of power as First
Consul in 1799 until his final overthrow in 1815 is generally recognized to
have been one of the most glorious in the whole history of French science.
It was a period when France led her European rivals in the quantity and
in the quality of her scientific contributions, especially in the physical
sciences. Great names, such as those of Laplace, Berthollet, Biot, Poisson,

*Department of History, University of Lancaster, Bailrigg, Lancaster, England.

Abbreviated versions of this paper have been read at meetings of the Northern
Seminar in the History of Science in Manchester on 7 May 1969 and of the British
Society for the History of Science in London on 23 November 1970, and parts of it
have since been discussed at seminars in Oxford and Cambridge. It is a pleasure to
express my thanks for the generous help and criticisms I have received from J.R.
Ravetz during the preparation of the paper for publication. I am also grateful to
E. Frankel, P.M. Heimann, and an anonymous referee for some valuable comments.

[1]P.S. Laplace, *Traité de mécanique céleste*, 5 vols. (Paris, 1799–1825), *5*, 99. Although the title page of the fifth volume bears the date 1825, the six books that
made up the volume were published and dated separately. Book XII, in which this
passage appears, is dated April 1823. For an earlier and slightly different statement
see *Connaissance des tems . . . pour l'an 1824* (Paris, 1822), p. 323; also *Journal de
physique, 94* (1822), 90. The translations throughout the paper are my own.

Gay-Lussac, Thenard, and Malus, abounded, and there were some remarkable successes, of which the most celebrated is perhaps the discovery and study of the polarization of light. It is not surprising, therefore, that both the "declinists" of Britain in 1830, such as Charles Babbage and David Brewster,[2] and those who complained no less bitterly about the state of French science in the 1860's and 1870's, notably Louis Pasteur and Adolphe Wurtz,[3] looked back to the years of Napoleon's rule as a truly golden age for science.

It is not difficult to identify at least some of the conditions that allowed French science under Napoleon to become a byword for excellence. As Maurice Crosland has shown, the supply of able graduates from the École Polytechnique, public recognition and encouragement given even by Napoleon himself, the attractive career possibilities that were available to young men trained in science, and the select research school centered on Berthollet's country house at Arcueil, just outside Paris, all played their part.[4] And equally, thanks above all to the work of L. Pearce Williams and Roger Hahn, we know something of the weaknesses of French science in the Consulate and First Empire. For example, although weaknesses were rarely acknowledged at the time, at least in public, Williams has identified grave deficiencies in education, especially at the elementary level,[5] and Hahn has pointed to the harm that was being done as the First Class of the Institute (the revolutionary successor of the Academy of Sciences) became increasingly a manifestation of Napoleon's *Kulturpolitik*.[6]

It is the purpose of this paper to take further the investigation of both the strengths and the weaknesses of Napoleonic science, with special

[2] In Britain admiration for Napoleonic science was naturally greatest some years after 1815 and was particularly strong about 1830. Babbage wrote glowingly of French achievements in his *Reflections on the Decline of Science in England* (London, 1830), especially pp. 25–27 and 30–36, maintaining that under Napoleon "the triumphs of France were as eminent in Science as they were splendid in arms" (*ibid.,* p. 26). An equally favorable view was given by David Brewster in his unsigned "Decline of Science in England," *Quarterly Review, 43* (1830), 313–317, although Brewster stressed that the enlightened policy toward science, which had been so characteristic of the First Empire, had continued under Louis XVIII and Charles X.

[3] See, for example, Pasteur's contribution of 1871 to the Lyons newspaper *Salut public,* quoted in R. Vallery-Radot, *La vie de Pasteur* (Paris, 1900), pp. 278–279, and C.A. Wurtz, *Les hautes études pratiques dans les universités allemandes* (Paris, 1870), pp. 5–6.

[4] M.P. Crosland, *The Society of Arcueil. A View of French Science at the time of Napoleon I* (London, 1967).

[5] L.P. Williams, "Science, Education and Napoleon I," *Isis, 47* (1956), 369–382.

[6] R. Hahn, *The Anatomy of a Scientific Institution. The Paris Academy of Sciences, 1666–1803* (Berkeley, Los Angeles, and London, 1971), pp. 310–312.

reference to physical science. In Section 2, I shall argue that the course and content of much of French physics and physical chemistry under Napoleon was determined by the zeal of the mathematician and physicist Pierre Simon Laplace and the chemist Claude Louis Berthollet for a program of research which they jointly sought to pursue. The program was seen, at least by them, as a natural culmination of eighteenth-century work in the Newtonian tradition, so that although it is described here as Laplacian, it was in reality not entirely the creation of Laplace himself, or indeed of Berthollet; it was Laplacian only to the extent that Laplace gave it a number of its characteristic features, stated it explicitly, and was its most brilliant exponent from the time he began to formulate it, probably in the 1790's, until his death in 1827.

In the years of its greatest success, from 1805 to 1815, the program both raised problems and laid down the general principles for solutions; and, by doing so, it gave French physical science a most uncommon unity of style and purpose. It also stimulated much good work; yet, as I hope to show, it owed its dominant position not merely to its merits, considerable though these appeared to be at the time, but equally to the effectiveness with which Laplace and Berthollet were able to control the scientific establishment of France in teaching as well as research. Once this control was lost (a process that I discuss in Section 3), the program became vulnerable, and, beset by the challenges of new discoveries and theories in heat, optics, electricity, magnetism, and chemistry and by a new generation of younger scientists who felt no allegiance to Laplace and Berthollet, it was abandoned, quite suddenly, between 1815 and 1825. By examining the downfall of the Laplacian program and its attendant doctrines, I hope to demonstrate the precariousness of what I see as the leading research tradition in physical science in Napoleonic France and to suggest that the successes of the period owed far more than has previously been recognized to Laplace's personal commitment to his program and to his ability to engage other men of exceptional ability in the same enterprise.

## 2. LAPLACIAN PHYSICS

Laplacian physics was a style of physics that depended on and was embraced by what J. T. Merz, with an acknowledgment to Maxwell, first called the astronomical view of nature.[7] It was a physics that sought to

[7] J.T. Merz, *A History of European Thought in the Nineteenth Century*, 4 vols. (Edinburgh and London, 1896–1914), *1*, 347–348.

account for all phenomena, on the terrestrial and, more particularly, the molecular scale as well as on the celestial scale, in terms of central forces between particles which, although treated by analogy with Newtonian forces of gravitation, could be either attractive or repulsive. Since attempts to "explain" gravitation had been generally abandoned long before, forces of this character could readily be accepted as "mechanical" and hence in need of no further explanation.[8] The forces were conceived as being exerted by and upon imponderable as well as ordinary ponderable matter; indeed, an essential and highly characteristic element in Laplacian physics was the system of imponderable fluids of heat, light, electricity, and magnetism. In accordance with beliefs that had come to be widely accepted by the end of the eighteenth century, each fluid was thought to consist of particles which were mutually repulsive but which in all cases were attracted by ponderable matter.[9] In the hands of the Laplacians, models of such fluids, founded on the assumption that the forces between imponderable and ponderable matter were effective only over "insensibly small" distances, were capable of being translated into systems of differential equations whose approximate solutions could "save" the phenomena already known and even predict new ones. And it was in the attempt to refine and quantify a theory of the imponderables which had hitherto been vague and qualitative that Laplacian physics found its main problems and had its most notable achievements.

The imponderable fluids, like the rest of Laplacian physics, did not originate with Laplace himself. As far as the basic model for their structure is concerned, they have their roots in Newton's speculations on the subtle electrical spirit in the General Scholium of 1713,[10] in his speculations on the ether which appeared in the second and subsequent editions

[8] However, the charge against the imponderables that they merely allowed the explanation of action at distance to be postponed, since their own properties presupposed the existence of such action, was raised in the late eighteenth and early nineteenth centuries, notably by Lavoisier and Davy; see R. Fox, *The Caloric Theory of Gases from Lavoisier to Regnault* (Oxford, 1971), pp. 17 and 118.

[9] Those who adopted the two-fluid theories of electricity and magnetism (see below, p. 93) made the additional assumption that there was attraction between the vitreous and resinous electrical fluids and between the austral and boreal magnetic fluids.

[10] Newton, *Philosophiae Naturalis Principia Mathematica,* 2nd ed. (Cambridge, 1713), p. 484. On the interpolation of the words "electric and elastic" to describe the spirit in Andrew Motte's translation of 1729, see A. Koyré and I.B. Cohen, "Newton's 'Electric & Elastic Spirit'," *Isis, 57* (1960), 337.

of the *Opticks*,[11] and even more clearly perhaps in what was generally recognized through the eighteenth century as the Newtonian view of gas structure—the view that the particles of gases were stationary and that repulsive forces between these particles accounted for gas pressure and the other characteristic gaseous properties.[12] This Newtonian model had been applied with increasing frequency in discussions of the properties of imponderable fluids since the 1740's, when Franklin used it in his widely read speculations on the nature of the electric fluid.[13] In fact, by about 1780 Franklin's belief that electrostatic phenomena could be explained in terms of the supposed repulsion between the particles of the electric fluid and the supposed attraction between the fluid and the particles of ordinary ponderable matter had become standard doctrine; and, as a result of the work of such men as Aepinus, Priestley, and Lavoisier, the same was true of the other "Newtonian" imponderables which had emerged by then, the fluids of magnetism, heat (or fire), and light.[14] There were divergences of opinion, of course, notably between the supporters of the "one-fluid" theories of electricity and magnetism, associated principally with the names of Franklin and Aepinus, and those like Coulomb who favored the "two-fluid" theories, in which a vitreous and a resinous electrical fluid and an austral and a boreal magnetic fluid were postulated.[15] But such differences did nothing to make the fundamental concept of the imponderable elastic fluid any less acceptable. By 1780 the

[11]Newton, *Opticks,* 2nd ed. (London, 1718), pp. 322–328 (Queries 17–24). In the *Principia* the subtle spirit was simply described as "electric and elastic" and no further details of its supposed structure were given. In Query 21 of the *Opticks,* however, it was suggested that the postulated ether might consist of mutually repulsive particles. Although the structure of Newton's ether was similar to that of the later imponderables, its function, primarily as the basis for an explanation of gravitation and optical phenomena, was quite different; see J.E. McGuire, "Force, Active Principles, and Newton's Invisible Realm," *Ambix, 15* (1968), 154–208.

[12]First stated (as no more than a mathematical hypothesis) in the first edition of the *Principia* (London, 1687), pp. 301–303 (Book II, Proposition xxiii).

[13]Most easily consulted in I.B. Cohen, ed., *Benjamin Franklin's Experiments* (Cambridge, Mass., 1941), especially pp. 213–215.

[14]For accounts of the rise of the imponderables between the 1740's and the 1780's see I.B. Cohen, *Franklin and Newton* (Philadelphia, 1956), pp. 365–554; R.E. Schofield, *Mechanism and Materialism* (Princeton, 1970), pp. 157–190; Fox, *op. cit.* (note 8), pp. 6–20; and J.E. McGuire and P.M. Heimann, "Newtonian Forces and Lockean Powers: Concepts of Matter in Eighteenth-Century Thought," *Historical Studies in the Physical Sciences, 3* (1971), 233–306.

[15]Also the Newtonians such as Gowin Knight, P.D. Leslie, Cadwallader Colden, Bryan Higgins, James Hutton, and Adam Walker, who worked in the predominantly British tradition discussed by Heimann and McGuire (see their paper cited in note

theory of the imponderables was recognized to be imperfect to the extent that it was still almost entirely qualitative, yet it was coherent, simple, and, above all, it had the merit of possessing what appeared to be a thoroughly Newtonian pedigree.

So for a Frenchman such as Laplace, whose interest in the experimental aspects of physical science, especially the study of heat, grew rapidly about 1780,[16] it was to be expected that the imponderable fluids would provide an entirely acceptable explanation of the phenomena of physics. This was a time when in a strongly Newtonian France few qualms were felt about accepting the possibility of forces acting at a distance and when in any case the physics of the eighteenth-century Newtonian tradition was seen as having had so many notable successes. Moreover, it was just at this time that the writings of Laplace's friend Lavoisier were beginning to attract favorable attention to the fluid or caloric theory of heat[17] and to give it the form it was to have for the next seventy years; and it was only shortly afterwards that Coulomb produced some of his most important work in electricity and magnetism,[18] work which did much to win

---

14), held views on subtle fluids that differed appreciably from those of Franklin, Aepinus, Lavoisier, and Coulomb.

[16]The stimulus for this new interest came from Lavoisier, according to Laplace's letter to Lagrange, 21 August 1783, in *Oeuvres de Lagrange,* 14 vols. (Paris, 1867–1892), *14,* 124. In a letter to Lagrange of 11 February 1784 (*ibid., 14,* 130), however, he made no show of reluctance, writing, with reference to Haüy's recently published *Essai d'une théorie sur la structure des cristaux,* which he and Daubenton had read on behalf of the Academy of Sciences: "It contains an interesting application of mathematics to nature, and the hope that we may be able to extend the realm of geometry cannot be put too strongly. It is with this in view that I have devoted a little of my time to physics, and I am not without hope that I shall be able to grasp some other physical problems sufficiently well to be able to apply the methods of analysis to them."

[17]Notably in his papers in the *Mémoires . . . de l'Académie Royale des Sciences* for 1777 (pp. 420–432 and 592–600), and the joint "Mémoire sur la chaleur," written with Laplace, which appeared on pp. 355–408 of the *Mémoires* for 1780 (although it was not read until June 1783 and was published only in 1784). It is important to note that Lavoisier was always cautious on the question of the nature of heat, and in the joint paper with Laplace the view that heat consists in the motion of the particles of ordinary ponderable matter was stated to be no less plausible than the fluid theory. However, especially in his *Traité élémentaire de chimie,* 2 vols. (Paris, 1789), *1,* 4–27, he was easily taken for a convinced calorist.

[18]The seven papers describing this work, which all date from the period 1785–1789, are most easily consulted in *Collection de mémoires relatifs à la physique, publiés par la Société Française de Physique. Tome 1. Mémoires de Coulomb* (Paris, 1884), pp. 107–318. For a study of Coulomb's work in electricity and magnetism see C.S. Gillmor, *Coulomb and the Evolution of Physics and Engineering in Eighteenth-Century France* (Princeton, 1971), pp. 175–221.

support for the two-fluid theories that Coulomb himself favored.[19] But Laplace, of course, did more than merely accept the legacy of Newtonian physics as this was normally understood towards the end of the eighteenth century. It was Laplace's great achievement to build on the Newtonian tradition, to restate many of its principles in a mathematical form, to take up its outstanding problems, especially with regard to the short-range forces that were thought to operate on the molecular scale, and thereby to create a physics which, although Newtonian in origin, was unmistakably and characteristically Laplacian.

Signs of what was later to emerge as the true Laplacian program can be detected as early as 1796. In the first edition of the *Exposition du système du monde,* published in that year, Laplace stated that not only optical refraction and capillary action but also the cohesion of solids, their crystalline properties, and even chemical reactions were the result of an attractive force exerted by the ultimate particles (*molécules*) of matter, and he looked forward to the day when the law governing the force would be understood[20] and when, as he put it, "we shall be able to raise the physics of terrestrial bodies to the state of perfection to which celestial physics has been brought by the discovery of universal gravitation."[21] In Laplace's view there was good reason to believe that the molecular forces might themselves be gravitational in nature, even though they did not obey the simple inverse-square law, a complication that resulted from the effect, on the molecular scale, of the shape of the individual molecules.

But in all this he was saying no more than what so many eighteenth-century Newtonians, with an eye on the Queries, had already accepted as standard doctrine. Throughout the eighteenth century, molecular forces, usually assumed to be negligible except over a very short range, had been invoked as a standard element of Newtonian physics in treatments of optical refraction, capillary action, surface tension, and crystal structure,[22]

---

[19]*Collection de mémoires . . . Coulomb* (note 18), pp. 250–252.

[20]P.S. Laplace, *Exposition du système du monde,* 2 vols. (Paris, an VII [1796]), *2,* 196–198.

[21]*Ibid., 2,* 198.

[22]The most important source for this acceptance was, of course, Query 31 of the *Opticks;* see Newton, *Opticks,* 4th ed. (London, 1730), pp. 350–382. For references to the work of Clairaut and Buffon, the leading exponents of the "molecular forces" tradition in eighteenth-century France, see notes 24, 25, and 26. Views on crystal structure are discussed in H. Metzger, *La genèse de la science des cristaux* (Paris, 1918), pp. 165–170, and J.G. Burke, *Origins of the Science of Crystals* (Berkeley and Los Angeles, 1966), pp. 34–35 and 78. Although Laplace did not discuss the matter in 1796, he almost certainly shared the belief of many eighteenth-century Newtonians that the molecular forces were operative only over a very short range. For

and they had been invoked also in a continuing tradition of work on chemical affinities.[23] Although molecular forces had been equally acceptable to British and to French Newtonians, it was probably the French, in particular Alexis Claude Clairaut and Georges Louis Leclerc de Buffon, who (next to Newton himself) exerted the greatest influence on Laplace, and it is by examining their work that we can see most clearly the continuity between Laplace and his Newtonian precursors in the eighteenth century. Clairaut, for example, had ascribed "the roundness of drops of fluid, the elevation and depression of liquids in capillary tubes, the bending of rays of light, etc." to gravitational forces that became large at very small (molecular) distances,[24] and Buffon had discussed similar forces, though in his case with special reference to the forces of chemical affinity.[25] Although both men were proud to call themselves Newtonians and stated explicitly that the molecular forces they postulated were of the same nature as those operating between celestial bodies, they disagreed fundamentally over the relationship between force and distance on the molecular scale. The debate in which this disagreement became apparent arose because of a discrepancy between the predicted and observed periods of the apogee of the moon.[26] To remove the discrepancy, Clairaut suggested, in 1747, that the force law should contain a term inversely proportional to the fourth power of the distance, $1/r^4$, in addition to the usual term proportional to $1/r^2$.[27] This additional term, he argued, would

---

earlier expressions of this belief see, for example, John Keill, "Epistola ad Cl. virum Gulielmum Cockburn, Medicinae Doctorem. In qua leges attractionis aliaque physices principia traduntur," *Philosophical Transactions, 26* (1708–1709), 97–110, especially p. 100; F. Hauksbee, *Physico-Mechanical Experiments on Various Subjects* (London, 1709), pp. 157–160; and, for a contemporary French statement, by Coulomb, *Collection de mémoires relatifs à la physique . . . Mémoires de Coulomb* (note 18), pp. 125–126. For Newton's earliest comment on the matter, see his *Optice* (London, 1706), pp. 322–348 (Query 23), especially p. 335.

[23] For references to this tradition see note 32.

[24] A.C. Clairaut, "Du système du monde dans les principes de la gravitation universelle," *Mémoires . . . de l'Académie Royale des Sciences* for 1745 (published 1749), p. 338. The paper was read on 15 November 1747. Cf. his later comment on p. 547 of the same volume.

[25] G.L.L. de Buffon, "De la nature. Seconde vue" (1765), in his *Histoire naturelle, générale et particulière,* 44 vols. (Paris, 1749–1804), *13,* xii-xv.

[26] The debate is best followed in the papers by the two men that were published in the *Mémoires . . . de l'Académie Royale des Sciences* for 1745, pp. 329–364, 493–501, 529–548, 551–552, and 577–587. For accounts of the debate see P. Brunet, *La vie et l'oeuvre de Clairaut (1713–1765)* (Paris, 1952), pp. 82–88, and A.W. Thackray, *Atoms and Powers. An Essay on Newtonian Matter-Theory and the Development of Chemistry* (Cambridge, Mass., and London, 1970), pp. 157–160.

[27] Clairaut, *op. cit.* (note 24), pp. 337–339.

at once remove the anomaly in question and be consistent with the existence of molecular forces that were very large at insensible distances. Concerned at what he saw as a loss of elegance and simplicity and hence as a threat to the Newtonian system, Buffon upheld the familiar $1/r^2$ law, though some years later he admitted that such a law would be modified at short range by the shape of the particles of matter.[28] The details of the debate do not concern us here, and it is sufficient to note that it ended abruptly in 1749 when Clairaut found that, after all, he could reconcile the motion of the apogee with a simple inverse-square law.[29] However, he was careful not to concede victory to Buffon with regard to the short-range forces, and the form of the law obeyed by such forces remained undiscovered at the end of the century, having attracted little further attention.

Laplace's comment on the effect of the shape of individual particles on the force law suggests that he was especially indebted to Buffon, but even though he was reticent about his precursors, there can be little doubt that he owed quite as much to Clairaut, who had treated refraction and capillary action in a mathematical way of which he would surely have approved.[30] There is, then, evidence of continuity between Laplace and at least one kind of eighteenth-century Newtonianism which had a strong following in France, and the degree of continuity is so great that it could be argued that Laplace merely brought together a group of ideas which previously had been rather disparate. However, his statement of the range of phenomena that could be treated in terms of molecular forces, even as given in 1796, was certainly more comprehensive than any made previously, and it did direct renewed attention to the unification of terrestrial and celestial physics which, in his view, would result from further research. Above all, it looked forward to future work, in the manner of a research program.

It was not until the publication of the fourth volume of the *Traité de mécanique céleste* in 1805 that Laplace's brief and rather formal state-

[28] Buffon, *loc. cit.* (note 25).

[29] "Avertissement de M. Clairaut . . . sur le système du monde, dans les principes de l'attraction," *Mémoires . . . de l'Académie Royale des Sciences* for 1745, pp. 577–578. This is dated 17 May 1749.

[30] See Clairaut, "Sur les explications cartésienne et newtonienne de la réfraction de la lumière," *Mémoires . . . de l'Académie Royale des Sciences* for 1739 (published 1739), pp. 259–275, and (on capillary action) his *Théorie de la figure de la terre, tirée des principes de l'hydrostatique* (Paris, 1743), pp. 105–128. In both of these discussions he used short-range molecular forces. For a reference to one of Laplace's very few comments on his precursors, in this case to Clairaut, see note 40.

ment of 1796 was transformed into the basis for a truly Laplacian style of science. It seems crucial to our understanding of this transformation that by 1805 Laplace had gained a close and highly influential ally in Berthollet, his intimate friend since the early 1780's, his next-door neighbor at the village of Arcueil from 1806, and a man who saw chemistry in precisely those Newtonian terms that Laplace sought to apply more particularly in physics. In the *Recherches sur les lois de l'affinité* of 1801 and more fully in the *Essai de statique chimique* of 1803, Berthollet had expounded his view that chemical affinity was the result of attractive forces between the particles of matter. Indeed, he had gone so far as to begin the *Statique chimique* by declaring:

> The forces that bring about chemical phenomena all derive from the mutual attraction between the molecules of bodies. The name affinity has been given to this attraction so as to distinguish it from astronomical attraction.
>
> It is probable that both are one and the same property.[31]

Of course, in putting forward this idea, Berthollet was making no claim to originality. The idea was taken straight from the Newtonian tradition in the chemistry of affinites as this had come down through the English Newtonians such as the Keills and Hauksbee, and in France through Buffon and the French chemists Macquer, Guyton de Morveau, and Lavoisier, among others.[32] But in his lengthy writings on affinity Berthollet, like Laplace, did far more than reiterate a conventional view. Perhaps he did not succeed in answering many (or any) of the outstanding problems of the eighteenth century, for neither he nor his disciples carried through the systematic determination of chemical affinities that good Newtonian chemists saw as their goal. And his recognition of the difficulty of the tasks ahead may well have spread more despondency than encouragement. But by his rigorous, critical restatement of the Newtonian

---

[31] C.L. Berthollet, *Essai de statique chimique*, 2 vols. (Paris, an XI [1803]), *1*, 1.

[32] For accounts of this tradition, which was virtually unaffected by the innovations of Lavoisier, see M.P. Crosland, "The Development of Chemistry in the Eighteenth Century," *Studies on Voltaire and the Eighteenth Century*, 24 (1963), 369–441, especially pp. 382–390; A.W. Thackray, "Quantified Chemistry—the Newtonian Dream," in D.S.L. Cardwell, ed., *John Dalton & the Progress of Science* (Manchester, 1968), pp. 92–108; and Thackray, *op. cit.* (note 26), pp. 199–233. The basic belief of eighteenth-century Newtonian chemistry was that chemical phenomena could be explained in terms of short-range forces which it was the goal of the chemist to quantify and systematize; hence the keen eighteenth-century interest in tables of affinity.

principles he succeeded in creating a coherent system and, what is even more important for our purpose, in laying down a program for future work, where before there had been a jumble of rather vague beliefs.

So when, between 1805 and 1807, Laplace published his theoretical studies of the refraction of light and capillary action in the fourth volume of the *Mécanique céleste*[33] and when he based these studies on the assumption that there were short-range attractive forces both between the particles of ponderable matter and between the particles of ponderable matter and those of light, he was using an approach which, in his own eyes and in those of his contemporaries, had the sanction not only of a strong and much admired eighteenth-century Newtonian tradition but also of the most eminent French chemist of the day. Berthollet's may indeed have been one of the last of all attempts to realize the "Newtonian dream" of a quantified chemistry based on the measurement of the forces between the particles of matter; it was also one of the most distinguished of all such attempts, and the fact that it was soon to be made obsolete by the new approach to chemistry initiated by the Daltonian atomic theory in no way diminishes its importance in helping to set the course and objectives of French chemistry in the Napoleonic period. Nor should its imminent rejection lead us to underestimate the influence that it must have exerted on Laplace in bringing him to publish his first detailed study of the molecular forces operating in physics just two years after the analogous forces of chemistry had been treated in the *Statique chimique*. Nor, indeed, should its influence on others be discounted, for it was no coincidence that the Abbé René Just Haüy developed his model for acid-alkali reactions in terms of short-range intermolecular forces in the three years following the publication of the *Statique chimique*.[34] We may be certain, of course, that by the period 1803–1806 Haüy was being influenced quite as much by Laplace as by Berthollet. But the precise circumstances of Haüy's work need not concern us; we need only note it as an important early product of the revival of interest in molecular forces that Berthollet and Laplace jointly fostered.

[33] Laplace, *Mécanique céleste* (note 1), *4* (1805), 231–281 (on refraction). The two supplements (separately paginated) contained his theory of capillary action. On the date of their publication see J.B. Biot, *Journal de physique, 65* (1807), 88; also *Académie des Sciences. Procès-verbaux des séances de l'Académie tenues depuis la fondation de l'Institut jusqu'au mois d'août 1835,* 10 vols. (Hendaye, 1910–1922), *3,* 344 (28 April 1806) and 553 (6 July 1807).

[34] See S.H. Mauskopf, "Haüy's Model of Chemical Equivalence: Daltonian Doubts Exhumed," *Ambix, 17* (1970), 182–191.

There can be little doubt that by 1805 Laplace already had a clear conception of his program for physics and for physical science as a whole. Certainly he had not yet set down his program formally, as he was to do rather sketchily some three years later[35] and again in 1823 in the definitive form of the passage quoted at the beginning of this paper; but the 1805 volume of the *Mécanique céleste* and its two supplements, published in 1806 and 1807, indicate clearly enough that Laplace had formulated the basic idea of the reduction of all physical phenomena to a system of densely distributed particles exerting attractive and repulsive forces on one another at a distance (albeit at a very short distance). In this earliest work on his program Laplace gave lengthy mathematical treatments of optical refraction and capillary action, basing both treatments on the supposed existence of short-range attractive forces of the type that had been first postulated by Newton and discussed so often through the eighteenth century.[36] In the case of capillary action these forces were assumed to exist between the particles of ordinary ponderable matter; in the case of refraction the attraction was between the particles of ordinary matter and those of the imponderable light.

Laplace's choice of optical refraction and capillary action as the subjects for his first *sorties* into the realm of molecular physics reveals clearly his caution at this stage in his work. For these were both manifestations of action at a distance on the molecular scale which had been of special

---

[35] This statement of his program appears in a note added to his "Mémoire sur les mouvemens de la lumière dans les milieux diaphanes," *Mémoires de la Classe des Sciences Mathématiques et Physiques de l'Institut de France, 10* (1809), 300–342. It dates presumably from between January 1808, when the main paper was read, and August 1810, when the volume was published. In the note (p. 329) he wrote, with reference to short-range molecular forces:

In general, all the attractive and repulsive forces in nature can be reduced, ultimately, to forces of this kind exerted by one molecule on another. Thus, in my *Theory of Capillary Action,* I have shown that the attractions and repulsions between small objects floating on a liquid, and generally all capillary phenomena, depend on intermolecular attractions which are negligible except at insensible distances. Similarly an attempt has been made to reduce the phenomena of electricity and magnetism to intermolecular action. The behavior of elastic bodies also may be treated in the same way.

Later (p. 338), after discussing the relevance of short-range forces to the study of heat flow, he stated the purposes of his note as follows: "I have sought to establish that the phenomena of nature can be reduced ultimately to action *ad distans* between molecules and that the theory of these phenomena must be based on a study of such action."

[36] For references to this earlier work see notes 22, 24–26, 29, 30, and 32.

interest to eighteenth-century Newtonians, as well as to Newton himself.[37] Moreover, both phenomena had raised problems that remained unsolved even in 1805. The detailed mathematical treatment of refraction in particular had proved difficult, and the study of the molecular forces that caused refraction, although of such obvious interest to Newtonians, had scarcely begun.[38] Likewise, even Clairaut's treatment of the theory of capillary action,[39] which for Laplace was the only discussion worthy of serious consideration,[40] was brief and incomplete. By contrast, Laplace's treatments of both refraction and capillarity were lengthy and, to all appearances, comprehensive. Not surprisingly, the problem of discovering the law relating molecular force and distance, which remained in much the same state it was in after the inconclusive confrontation between Clairaut and Buffon nearly sixty years earlier, was one that the *Mécanique céleste* and its supplements did not solve, but Laplace's demonstration that the form of the law was unimportant at least made the situation appear less scandalous, and to that extent it was a minor triumph.

However, in Laplace's mind there was obviously far more to be achieved by a study of short-range forces than the mere tying up of loose ends, and between 1805 and 1807 he appears to have immersed himself totally in the problems of molecular physics. In this period he brought his writings on capillary action to the notice of the Institute on no fewer than four occasions[41] and engaged others in experiments designed to confirm and enlarge on his theoretical work. For example, Haüy, the Parisian engineer Jean Louis Trémery, and Joseph Louis Gay-Lussac, then a young *protégé* of Berthollet, were all asked to undertake experiments on capillary action,[42] while Jean Baptiste Biot, perhaps Laplace's closest disciple at this

---

[37] Newton, *Opticks* (note 22), 4th ed., pp. 324–327, 345–349, and 367–371 (Queries 19–21, 29, and 31).

[38] Although the existence of the molecular force that caused refraction was not in doubt for Newtonians, they could say little more than that it diminished rapidly with distance. This was true even of a quite detailed mathematical treatment like Clairaut's (cited in note 30).

[39] See note 30 for reference.

[40] See pp. 2–3 of the first supplement on capillary action in Laplace, *op. cit.* (note 33). Hauksbee was the only other authority mentioned.

[41] *Procès-verbaux*, *3*, 293 (2 nivôse an 14; 23 December 1805); *3*, 344 (28 April 1806); *3*, 431 (29 September 1806); *3*, 553 (6 July 1807).

[42] Laplace, "Extrait d'un mémoire sur la théorie des tubes capillaires," *Journal de physique*, *62* (1806), 120–128, and the first of the two supplements on capillary action that were added to the tenth book of the *Mécanique céleste* (vol. 4), especially pp. 52–55.

time,[43] was chosen to undertake the experimental investigation of refraction in gases which was proposed to the Institute by Laplace. The paper that resulted from this last investigation, read in March 1806,[44] is an important one in the history of the Laplacian program, since Biot and his young collaborator François Arago were convinced that their observations on the bending of light rays had yielded an accurate measure, indeed the first accurate measure, of forces on the molecular scale which had hitherto almost defied quantification. If, as I believe, Laplace had already conceived his program by this time, the work of Biot and Arago must have marked an advance of outstanding significance in his eyes; and its significance was certainly not lost on Biot and Arago themselves. Adopting what appears to have been standard Laplacian doctrine—that the short-range forces which caused the refraction of light were also the forces of chemical affinity—they maintained that their work, quite apart from its more obvious consequences in the field of optics, might also help to solve the great problems of chemistry, by which, of course, they meant Berthollet's chemistry of affinities and molecular forces. And it was in fact with some justification that they proposed the study of optical refraction as a more promising tool for the investigation of the forces that governed the course of chemical reactions than the direct observation of the reactions themselves, in which the complexities were quite daunting.[45] A table of affinities for light, they believed reasonably enough, would be easier to establish than a table of affinities for, say, oxygen, such as Berthollet had proposed.[46]

Laplace's great strength in the Napoleonic period was, of course, the

---

[43]However, later there emerged certain issues on which Biot and Laplace were apparently not in full agreement. For example, in two contributions to the *Mercure de France* in 1809 Biot took the opportunity of pointing to the dangers of accepting the physical reality of the various imponderable fluids. Such fluids, he wrote, were no more than "a convenient hypothesis to which [true natural philosophers (*physiciens*)] are careful not to attach any idea of reality"; see Biot, *Mélanges scientifiques et littéraires,* 3 vols. (Paris, 1858), 2, 97–116, especially pp. 102–103 and 113–116, and (for the quotation) p. 114. There is further evidence of at least a temporary weakening of the bond between the two men in Laplace's decision to vote for Fourier rather than Biot in the election for the post of permanent secretary of the Academy of Sciences in 1822; see note 143.

[44]Biot and Arago, "Mémoire sur les affinités des corps pour la lumière, et particulièrement sur les forces réfringentes des différens gaz," *Mémoires de la Classe des Sciences Mathématiques et Physiques de l'Institut National de France,* 7 (1806), 301–387. Read 24 March 1806.

[45]*Ibid.,* pp. 327–330.

[46]Berthollet, *op. cit.* (note 31), 2, 3–6.

influence that he was able to wield in the scientific community, an influence that was matched in France only by that of Berthollet, whose zeal for Newtonian science was in any case no less than his own. Laplace naturally did not hesitate to use his position to promote his beliefs, and direct patronage which he and Berthollet dispensed to promising young graduates of the École Polytechnique—Biot, Arago, Gay-Lussac, and Siméon Denis Poisson among them—was only one of his methods.[47] Laplace also wielded to extraordinarily good effect the system of prize competitions organized by the First Class of the Institute. Hence it is not surprising to find him serving on, and presumably dominating, the five-man committee which in December 1807 proposed a mathematical study of double refraction as the subject for the prize for mathematics to be awarded some two years later.[48]

Clearly the intention in setting the subject was that Laplace's treatment of refraction, given in the fourth book of the *Mécanique céleste,* should be extended to embrace double refraction as well. The prospect of success in the enterprise was all the more attractive from the Laplacian point of view because the explanation of double refraction had presented such notorious problems since the discovery of the phenomenon in crystals of Iceland spar in 1669.[49] Even Huygens himself had admitted that his wave theory was inadequate to explain all the observations associated with double refraction;[50] in particular, the behavior of the ordinary and extraordinary rays when passed through a second crystal defied explanation by anyone who, like Huygens, postulated a longitudinal wave motion, and it was only when Fresnel introduced the concept of transverse waves in 1821 and so made an understanding of polarization possible that this grave weakness in the wave theory was removed. Although Huygens' failure was seized upon in the *Opticks,*[51] Newton's own explanation, in terms of the "sides" of rays of light, was vague and difficult to reconcile with a corpuscular theory, and even by the end of the eighteenth century it had

[47]For an excellent study of the patronage system of Arcueil see Crosland, *op. cit.* (note 4).

[48]*Procès-verbaux, 3,* 632-633 (21 December 1807). The other members of the committee were Lagrange, Legendre, Lacroix, and Lazare Carnot.

[49]For accounts of earlier theories of double refraction see A.I. Sabra, *Theories of Light from Descartes to Newton* (London, 1967), pp. 221-229, and V. Ronchi, *The Nature of Light. An Historical Survey,* trans. V. Barocas (London, 1970), pp. 153, 188-190, and 205-206.

[50]C. Huygens, *Traité de la lumière* (Leiden, 1690), pp. 88-91.

[51]Newton, *Opticks* (note 22), 4th ed., pp. 332-336 and 336-339 (Queries 25, 26, and 28).

been little improved. So to Laplace the theory of double refraction presented the enticing challenge of a long-notorious anomaly; it was, moreover, an anomaly that was likely to become increasingly troublesome, since, for some years in France, Haüy had been using double refraction as a valuable exploratory tool for the investigation of crystal structure, and his work was still proceeding.[52]

Predictably, it was a confirmed supporter of the corpuscular theory of light and one of the most brilliant of Laplace's disciples at Arcueil, Étienne Malus, who was awarded the prize of 3000 francs on 1 January 1810. Indeed, it is probable that the subject for the competition was conceived by Laplace not simply in the hope of a glorious victory for the corpuscular theory but with Malus specifically in mind. For by 1807, despite some ten years of hard military service in the obscurity of Egypt and provincial France, Malus had already become closely associated with the style of physics that prevailed at Arcueil and appears even to have made contact with Laplace himself. In his earliest paper on light, which he read in 1807, he did not hesitate to assume the existence of short-range attractive forces,[53] and Laplace, in his own preliminary study of the theory of double refraction, which he read to the First Class of the Institute in January 1808, referred favorably to Malus' experimental work on the subject.[54] Presumably with the competition in view, Laplace, in this paper of 1808, also took the opportunity of pointedly laying down certain principles that he took to be established beyond doubt. Huygens' wave theory, he maintained, was inadequate for the explanation of double refraction,[55] so that the task ahead was clear: it was simply to devise a new explanation in terms of those short-range attractive and repulsive molecular forces that Newton had invoked in explaining ordinary refraction.[56] Since Laplace himself had already made inroads into the prob-

[52] See, for example, R.J. Haüy, *Traité de minéralogie,* 5 vols. (Paris, 1801), *1,* 229–235, and *2,* 38–51 and 196–229. For a brief account and further references see Burke, *op. cit.* (note 22), pp. 139–140. Haüy gave cautious support to Newton's theory of double refraction.

[53] See his "Traité d'optique," *Mémoires présentés à l'Institut National des Sciences, Lettres et Arts par divers savans et lus dans ses assemblées. Sciences mathématiques et physiques, 2* (1811), especially 265–266. Read 20 April 1807. Laplace was one of the referees appointed by the First Class for this paper; see *Procès-verbaux, 3,* 516 and 606–607 (20 April and 19 October 1807).

[54] Laplace, "Mémoire sur les mouvemens de la lumière dans les milieux diaphanes," *Mémoires . . . de l'Institut, 10* (1809), 300–342, especially pp. 302 and 309.

[55] *Ibid.,* pp. 301 and 303.

[56] *Ibid.,* p. 304.

lem, as he showed in his paper, and since he left no doubt as to his own belief in the physical reality of the molecular forces, it would have been an act of remarkable folly to attack the question set in December 1807 in any other way than Laplace's, and, as we should expect, Malus duly conformed, producing the vindication of the Laplacian position that was expected of him.[57]

As patron Laplace had been well served; specific problems had been answered for him, and the position of his program had been strengthened. And Malus had more than just his prize-winning paper to contribute to the Laplacian program. For example, after his discovery of the polarization of light in the autumn of 1808 he had given his now considerable authority to the view that the new phenomenon could not be explained by Huygens' wave theory, and instead had given an explanation in terms of the various forces which he supposed, in the best Laplacian fashion, to act on the particles of light.[58] In fact, Malus did so much for Laplacian physics in general and for the furtherance of the Laplacian program in particular that his premature death from consumption in February 1812, after some five years of intensive research, must have come as a grievous blow to Laplace.

However, there was no question of abandoning the program, and there were still outstanding issues to be settled. Foremost among these were the problems concerned with the behavior of elastic surfaces. Laplace had already stated that the theory of such surfaces might be established in terms of short-range intermolecular forces of repulsion,[59] and in 1809 a competition on the subject had been set by the First Class of the Institute.[60] Although the competition was stated to have been suggested by Napoleon, who had been greatly impressed by a demonstration of the experiments of Chladni, we may be sure that Laplace, whose zeal for his program was then at its height, had had a hand in the matter. But, presumably to his disappointment, by the closing date on 1 October 1811 no entry of sufficient merit had been received, and the competition had to be set twice more, with closing dates in October 1813 and October 1815, before the

[57]His paper was published in *Mémoires présentés . . . par divers savans*, 2 (1811), 303–508, with the title "Théorie de la double réfraction." For Malus' attempt to explain double refraction in terms of short-range forces of the Laplacian type see especially pp. 489–496.

[58]Malus, "Sur une propriété des forces répulsives qui agissent sur la lumière," *Mémoires de physique et de chimie de la Société d'Arcueil*, 2 (1809), 254–267, especially pp. 260–267.

[59]See the first passage quoted in note 35.

[60]*Mémoires . . . de l'Institut*, 9 (1808), 240–241 of the "Histoire de la Classe" for 1808.

prize was eventually awarded to Sophie Germain in January 1816.[61] This award represented something of a defeat for Laplacian interests, since Germain's approach was fundamentally different from that of Poisson, whose paper on elastic surfaces, read to the First Class of the Institute on 1 August 1814, used short-range forces in the orthodox Laplacian manner.[62] And, insofar as it was a defeat, it has significance as a mark of Laplace's declining influence and reputation after the downfall of Napoleon. But this is a point I shall return to in Section 3.

Another outstanding problem that was settled in the last years of Napoleon's rule, though this time with rather more success from the Laplacian point of view, concerned the theory of heat. Again the issue was raised in a prize competition of the Institute, set in January 1811. As was made clear by the committee that proposed the subject, it was hoped above all that the competition, which asked for a detailed experimental study of the specific heats of gases, would lead to a decision on an important point in the caloric theory.[63] Since the point was one that had to be resolved before even the simplest mathematical treatment of the theory could be undertaken, it was of obvious interest to Laplace, and naturally he sat on the committee that set the competition.[64] The aim was to decide whether it was possible for some caloric to exist in a body in a latent, or combined, state (i.e., without being detected by a thermometer) or whether all of the caloric was present in its "sensible" form and therefore as a contribution to the body's temperature. The issue, which had been very much a live one since the 1780's, though never more so than in the first decade of the nineteenth century, had divided calorists into two groups; the supporters of the former view looked chiefly to Lavoisier, Laplace, and Joseph Black as their authorities, while those who advocated the latter, such as Adair Crawford and John Dalton, followed the Scottish pupil of Black, William Irvine. Predictably enough, victory went, in January 1813, to two young men, François Delaroche and Jacques Étienne

[61] On the history of this competition see I. Todhunter, *A History of the Theory of Elasticity and the Strength of Materials from Galilei to Lord Kelvin*, 2 vols. (Cambridge, 1886–1893), *1*, 147–149.

[62] Poisson, "Mémoire sur les surfaces élastiques," *Mémoires . . . de l'Institut*, Pt. 2, *13* (1812), 167–225, especially pp. 171–172 and 192–225.

[63] *Mémoires . . . de l'Institut*, Pt. 2, *11* (1810), xcv of the "Histoire de la Classe" for 1810.

[64] See *Procès-verbaux, 4*, 399 (3 December 1810). He did not sit on the adjudicating committee but was well represented by Berthollet and Gay-Lussac; see *Procès-verbaux, 5*, 105 (12 October 1812).

Bérard, who had performed their experiments at Arcueil and who, by upholding the distinction between latent and sensible caloric, vindicated the position long favored by Laplace.[65] One cannot help feeling that the only other competitors, Nicolas Clément and Charles Bernard Desormes, who deviated from the Laplacian view, simply had no chance and were fortunate to receive even the "honorable mention" that was accorded them.

Despite a certain slackening of corporate research activity from 1812, Laplacian physics was still, to all appearances, in a strong position in France toward the end of the Napoleonic period. Certainly the fact that regular meetings of the Society of Arcueil stopped in 1813[66] did not augur well for the future. But Laplacian influence was still just as great in French scientific education as it had long been in research and, because of strong administrative centralization, it was just as easily exercised. An examination of syllabuses, textbooks, and sets of lecture notes of the period shows clearly that pure Laplacian physics was being taught as standard doctrine both in science courses in the *lycées*[67] and, what is even more important, in the courses that mattered most for the future of French physical science, those at the École Polytechnique. Here at the École Polytechnique, as we know from Hachette's handbook for students of 1809,[68] from the annually published outline syllabuses,[69] and even more clearly from some notes taken (by none other than Auguste Comte)

[65]The paper by Delaroche and Bérard appeared in *Annales de chimie et de physique, 85* (1813), 72–110 and 113–182, with the title "Mémoire sur la détermination de la chaleur spécifique des différens gaz." For a detailed discussion of the competition and the issues at stake in the caloric theory see Fox, *op. cit.* (note 8), especially pp. 25–32 and 104–150.

[66]Crosland, *op. cit.* (note 4), pp. 2–3.

[67]See, for example, R.J. Haüy, *Traité élémentaire de physique,* 1st ed. (Paris, an XII [1803]); 2nd ed. (Paris, 1806); 3rd ed. (Paris, 1821); all three editions are in two volumes. This excellent textbook was written at Napoleon's direction for the use of teachers in the *lycées*.

[68]J.N.P. Hachette, *Programmes d'un cours de physique; ou précis de leçons sur les principaux phénomènes de la nature, et sur quelques applications des mathématiques à la physique* (Paris, 1809), especially pp. 1–8 and 49–220.

[69]See, for example, *Programmes de l'enseignement de l'École Royale Polytechnique arrêtés par le Conseil de Perfectionnement, dans la session de 1815–1816* (Paris, 1816), pp. 34–40, where it is clear that even in 1816 heat, electricity, magnetism, and optics were still to be taught in terms of the appropriate imponderable fluids. On the changes in the published syllabus that began to appear in the volume for 1817–1818 see Section 3 and notes 141 and 142.

at Petit's lectures of 1814–1815,[70] the existence of the imponderable fluids—caloric, light, electricity, and magnetism—went virtually unquestioned, and other aspects of Laplacian physics, notably the treatment of capillary action, were given great prominence.

So this was the situation in French physical science up to the end of the reign of Napoleon. Laplace and Berthollet stood for and fostered a unified program for their disciplines, based on a coherent set of traditional doctrines that had originated in Newton's comments on matter and molecular forces in the *Opticks* and had then come down to them through the eighteenth century. And by their zeal and power within the scientific community of France they had established a situation in which they were able to give at least certain of the main branches of physics and chemistry a remarkable degree of uniformity.

Now it must be stressed that the uniformity imposed by the program was by no means complete. In the first place, there were those, outside the Arcueil circle and usually outside the Parisian "establishment" of science, who opposed Laplace. I have referred already to the "outsiders" Clément and Desormes, and in the next section I shall argue that Fourier's mathematical treatment of the distribution of heat in solids appeared as a major challenge as early as 1807. Moreover, by the time of the Bourbon Restoration, Fresnel was already working, in almost total isolation, toward his critique of the corpuscular theory of light. And there were many more whose research was not opposed to Laplacian principles but independent of them. For example, the work of Gay-Lussac and Thenard (both members of the Arcueil circle) on the alkali metals and electrochemistry, Gay-Lussac's experiments on the combining volumes of gases (though they had subversive implications), and J. P. Dessaignes' study of phosphorescence (which won the Institute's prize competition for physics in 1809)[71] simply did not bear on the Laplacian program or, in any direct

---

[70] The notes, in six notebooks bearing the heading "École polytechnique—Cours de physique de M$^r$. Petit—Comte," cover all the main branches of physics with the exception of light. Comte was in his first year at the École Polytechnique in 1814–1815, and light was always studied in the second-year physics course. The notes are now kept at the Maison d'Auguste Comte, 10 rue Monsieur le Prince, Paris 6$^e$. I am grateful to the resident archivist, D. Cantemir, for allowing me to examine the notes and for providing me with a copy of them.

[71] For accounts of this work see, in addition to the standard histories, Crosland, *op. cit.* (note 4), pp. 354–365, and, by the same author, "The Origins of Gay-Lussac's Law of Combining Volumes of Gases," *Annals of Science, 17* (1961), 1–26. Dessaignes' prize-winning paper appeared as "Mémoire sur les phosphorescences," in *Journal de physique, 68* (1809), 444–467, and *69* (1809), 5–35.

way, on the theories on which the program was based. The same may be said of the brilliant crystallography of this period, although the fact that Haüy, like Romé de l'Isle before him, chose to concentrate on the description and measurement of crystals, rather than on the theory of crystallization,[72] which could have included a study of the forces binding together crystals and their constituent molecules,[73] may be seen as a missed opportunity for Laplace and his program.

But, despite these deviations and independent traditions of work and despite Laplace's own occasional vacillation,[74] the uniformity in the physical science of Napoleonic France is striking. Even if in chemistry there had been little progress, the program in physics had been pursued for a decade with vigor and, to all appearances, success. And certainly in France at the beginning of 1815 there seemed no reason why the dominant orthodoxy that had emanated from Arcueil since the early years of the century should, at least in the foreseeable future, be abandoned.

## 3. THE REJECTION OF LAPLACIAN PHYSICS

Yet within about ten years, by the mid-1820's, the intricate structure of Laplacian physical science had collapsed, leaving just a few increasingly isolated diehards to pursue the chimera that the program and its attendant beliefs were then generally recognized to be. In these ten years of revolt against Laplacian orthodoxy, the tradition that had gone almost unchallenged in the physical sciences in the Napoleonic period was abandoned. To the men who led the revolt it undoubtedly seemed that a new and more glorious era was dawning. Indeed, it may lead us to see Napoleonic science in a somewhat less favorable light if we accept, as I believe we must, that these men shared much of that feeling of exhilaration and liberation of the intellect which Guizot, Edgar Quinet, Lamartine, and so many

[72]On the style of Haüy's work see Metzger, *op. cit.* (note 22), pp. 170–206, and Burke, *op. cit.* (note 22), pp. 78–106.

[73]For example, Guyton de Morveau had discussed the cause of crystallization at some length in the "Essai physico-chimique sur la dissolution et la crystallisation," in his *Digressions académiques, ou essais sur quelques sujets de physique, de chymie & d'histoire naturelle* (Dijon, 1762), pp. 271–359, and in his *Élémens de chymie théorique et pratique,* 3 vols. (Dijon, 1777–1778), *1*, 49–78. With acknowledgments to the work of Clairaut and Buffon, he treated the problem in terms of the same intermolecular forces by which he accounted for other chemical phenomena.

[74]See below, pp. 111 and 127, and notes 93 and 143.

others associated with the Bourbon Restoration.[75] The men of science may not have gone so far as to see the Empire as an intellectual "desert," as Quinet did,[76] but, contrary to general belief, I do feel that most of them participated fully in the new optimism which so many Frenchmen experienced in those early Restoration years. Sadly, this enthusiasm and spirit of optimism, which was to be so fruitful in literature and the arts, in science came to nothing. For, as we can now see, what emerged from the ruins of Laplacian orthodoxy was not the new, revivified physical science that the early years of the Restoration had seemed to promise, but only a burst of creativity whose duration was no less brief, and whose decline was even more drastic, than that of Napoleonic physical science.

The men chiefly responsible for the revolt of the decade 1815–1825 were Joseph Fourier, Pierre Dulong, François Arago, Augustin Fresnel, and Alexis Thérèse Petit. Of these only Fourier, born in 1768, was over thirty in 1815, so that, with this one exception, they had learnt their science and performed their earliest work in the period when Laplacian principles had enjoyed their greatest success in France. Dulong, Arago, Fresnel, and Petit had all been thoroughly indoctrinated with these principles as students at the École Polytechnique;[77] and Dulong and Arago had even been members of the Arcueil circle (though, significantly perhaps, only since about 1810), and both had benefited in their careers from Arcueil patronage.[78] Petit, by contrast, was not a member of the circle, but his brilliant doctoral thesis of 1811 on capillary action[79] and his first lectures as professor of physics at the École Polytechnique in the winter of 1814–1815[80] were as Laplacian as they could possibly have been.

[75] F.P.G. Guizot, *Mémoires pour servir à l'histoire de mon temps,* 8 vols. (Paris, 1858–1867), *1*, 27–58; E. Quinet, *Histoire de mes idées. Autobiographie,* 7th ed. (Paris, 1895) [vol. 15 of the *Oeuvres complètes d'Edgar Quinet*], especially pp. 177–187 and 239–247; A.M.L. de P. de Lamartine, *Des destinées de la poésie* (Paris, 1834), in *Oeuvres complètes de Lamartine publiées et inédites,* 41 vols. (Paris, 1860–1866), *1*, 30–32. In certain ways, notably in matters of religion, the Restoration did not bring greater freedom, but generally the characterization of the period by Guizot, Quinet, and Lamartine seems just.

[76] Quinet, *op. cit.* (note 75), p. 241.

[77] In, respectively, 1801–1802, 1803–1805, 1804–1806, and 1807–1809. Because of ill health Dulong failed to complete the course.

[78] See Crosland, *op. cit.* (note 4), pp. 315–318.

[79] Petit, "Théorie mathématique de l'action capillaire," *Journal de l'École Polytechnique,* cahier 16, *9* (1813), 1–40. On his continued support of the Laplacian theory after 1815 see note 141.

[80] See note 70.

It is probably no coincidence that the challenge to the prevailing orthodoxy was first raised by the two members of the anti-Laplacian group, Fourier and Fresnel, who spent the greater part of the Napoleonic period in provincial obscurity far from Paris and hence far from the center of Laplacian control.[81] Fourier was nearly twenty years older than any other member of the group, and even when teaching at the École Polytechnique soon after its foundation in 1794 he had affiliated more closely with Monge than with Laplace and Legendre. With time taken from heavy prefectural duties at Grenoble (imposed on him by Napoleon in 1802 soon after his return from distinguished service in Egypt), he prepared a massive treatise on the distribution of heat in solid bodies, which he read to the First Class of the Institute in December 1807.[82] In this the entire Laplacian machinery of derivation of the basic equations by Newtonian principles was ignored by Fourier, who concentrated instead on his own methods for their derivation and solution. In 1811 he took his work further when he submitted a revised version of the 1807 paper for a prize competition set by the First Class of the Institute, and in January 1812 he was awarded the prize. But, despite evidence that he was receiving some favor in the eyes of Laplace himself,[83] the challenge was premature. His 1807 paper was published only in the form of an abstract, drawn up by a less than enthusiastic Poisson;[84] and even his great prize-winning paper was criticized by the judges (Lagrange, Laplace, Legendre, Malus, and Haüy) and, apparently as a result of this criticism (for which Lagrange was chiefly responsible), did not appear in print until 1824–1826,[85] when

[81] For the relevant biographical details of Fourier and Fresnel see the article by J.R. Ravetz and I. Grattan-Guinness (on Fourier) and that by R.H. Silliman (on Fresnel) in C.C. Gillispie, ed., *Dictionary of Scientific Biography* (New York, 1972), *5*, 93–99 and 165–171; also I. Grattan-Guinness (in collaboration with J.R. Ravetz), *Joseph Fourier 1768–1830. A Survey of his Life and Work, based on a Critical Edition of his Monograph on the Propagation of Heat, presented to the Institut de France in 1807* (Cambridge, Mass., and London, 1972), pp. 14–25 and 441–459.

[82] *Procès-verbaux, 3,* 632 (21 December 1807). On the 1807 paper see J.R. Ravetz, "Preliminary Notes on the Study of J.B.J. Fourier," *Archives internationales d'histoire des sciences, 13* (1960), 247–251; I. Grattan-Guinness, "Joseph Fourier and the Revolution in Mathematical Physics," *Journal of the Institute of Mathematics and Its Applications, 5* (1969), 230–253; and, for a detailed study and critical edition, Grattan-Guinness, *op. cit.* (note 81).

[83] Discussed in Grattan-Guinness, *op. cit.* (note 81), pp. 444–452.

[84] [Fourier], "Mémoire sur la propagation de la chaleur dans les corps solides," *Nouveau bulletin des sciences par la Société Philomathique de Paris, 1* (1807–1809), 112–116 (in the issue for March 1808).

[85] Fourier, "Théorie du mouvement de la chaleur dans les corps solides," *Mémoires de l'Académie Royale des Sciences de l'Institut de France, 4* (1819–1820 [published

the whole spirit of French physical science was very different and when Fourier himself was a permanent secretary of the Academy of Sciences. So it was only when the sympathetic Arago became one of the joint editors of the reorganized *Annales de chimie et de physique* in 1816 that the public had the opportunity of learning any details of Fourier's achievement (by means of a lengthy summary that appeared in the *Annales*[86]).

It was about this time that Fresnel, too, began to make his mark on the Parisian scientific scene. In October 1815, having recently gained some months of leisure for research (a leisure that he owed incidentally to his expulsion from office for his royalist sympathies during the Hundred Days), he deposited his first paper on the diffraction of light at the Institute.[87] In this he gave powerful support to the wave theory of light and in doing so exposed serious shortcomings in the rival corpuscular theory. Immediately he won over Arago and Petit, hitherto good Laplacians, and by December 1815 these two new converts had even performed some experiments on refraction in gases which they interpreted in such a way as to support Fresnel.[88] Ampère, whose commitment to the anti-Laplacian cause became really apparent only in the early 1820's, had

---

1824]), 185–555, and 5 (1821–1822 [published 1826]), 153–246. On the criticism and delay in publication see G. Darboux's introduction to the *Oeuvres de Fourier*, 2 vols. (Paris, 1888–1890), *1*, vi–viii; also Arago's *éloge* of Fourier in *Mémoires de l'Académie des Sciences, 14* (1838), cxii–cxiii.

[86]"Théorie de la chaleur. Par M. Fourier. (Extrait)," *Annales de chimie et de physique, 3* (1816), 350–375. The volume from which the summary was made, described in a footnote as a quarto volume of 650 pp., never appeared. It would have been normal for Arago himself to prepare the summary, but it displays such familiarity with Fourier's work that Fourier himself was probably the author. This is the conclusion reached in Grattan-Guinness, *op. cit.* (note 81), p. 460n. If the summary was written by someone else, Sophie Germain may have been responsible, as Ravetz has suggested to me.

[87]Fresnel, "Mémoire sur la diffraction de la lumière, où l'on examine particulièrement le phénomène des franges colorées que présentent les ombres des corps éclairés par un point lumineux," *Annales de chimie et de physique, 1* (1816), 239–281. Presented to the First Class of the Institute on 23 October 1815 (*Procès-verbaux, 5*, 562).

[88]Arago and Petit, "Sur les puissances réfractives et dispersives de certains liquides et des vapeurs qu'ils forment," *Annales de chimie et de physique, 1* (1816), 1–9. Read to the First Class of the Institute on 11 December 1815. Two letters that illustrate Arago's enthusiasm for Fresnel's ideas during his period of conversion (both of them from Léonor Mérimée to Fresnel) are in *Oeuvres complètes d'Augustin Fresnel*, 3 vols. (Paris, 1866–1870), *2*, 831–833. According to Léonor Mérimée's letter of 20 December 1814 (*ibid., 2*, 830–831), Arago first learnt of Fresnel's work in December 1814. On the support that the work of Arago and Petit gave to Fresnel see Fox, *op. cit.* (note 8), pp. 202 and 233–234.

been won over by May 1816,[89] and even Berthollet's former *protégé* Gay-Lussac, now beginning to take on the mantle of his master as France's leading chemist, was sympathetic.[90] The interest in this challenge to the Laplacian position was enormous, and it was reflected most obviously in January 1817 in the decision of a committee of the Academy of Sciences, consisting of Laplace, Biot, Berthollet, Gay-Lussac, and the aged physicist J. A. C. Charles, to offer the prize in physics for a study of diffraction.[91] It seems clear that in this way the still powerful Laplacian party hoped to settle the issue finally in its own favor by bringing this important phenomenon of physical optics into line with polarization and double refraction, which had been explained so successfully in terms of the corpuscular theory. To Biot victory for a corpuscularian was an especially alluring prospect since, with the young C. S. M. Pouillet, he had recently been engaged in devising the corpuscular theory of diffraction which he described, with much other evidence likely to support the materiality of light, in his *Traité de physique* of 1816.[92] But the ruse—if such it was— backfired, for, despite the fact that among the five judges were Laplace himself and the two arch-Laplacians Biot and Poisson, Fresnel won the prize in March 1819 with a brilliant paper.[93]

[89] See Ampère's letter to Ballanche Fils, 19 May 1816, in *Correspondance du grand Ampère*, ed. L. de Launay, 3 vols. (Paris, 1936-1943), *2*, 511. Ampère was in no sense a typical or central figure in the anti-Laplacian group, but in his conflict with Biot in the early 1820's (see below, pp. 117) he attacked some of the fundamental beliefs of Laplacian physics. The central forces that were so important in his electrodynamic theory were decidedly, and significantly, not Laplacian in character, and a clear mistrust of Laplacian fluids can be seen in his *Théorie mathématique des phénomènes électro-dynamiques* (see below, pp. 117 and 128 and note 153). Moreover, in the 1820's Ampère experienced the direct opposition of Laplace concerning the possible identity of magnetism and electricity. In supposing the two to be identical Ampère was breaking with the view of Coulomb, which Laplace supported; see Ampère's letter to Davy, probably of 1825, in *Correspondance du grand Ampère, 2*, 680.

[90] See Arago, "Éloge historique de T. Young," *Mémoires de l'Académie des Sciences, 13* (1835), cii-civ.

[91] *Procès-verbaux, 6*, 138 (13 January 1817).

[92] Biot, *Traité de physique expérimentale et mathématique*, 4 vols. (Paris, 1816), *4*, 743-775. In this volume of the *Traité* Biot wrote at great length on polarization (pp. 254-600), which he felt to be adequately explained by his (corpuscularian) theory of mobile polarization. As Frankel has pointed out to me, the *Traité* has great importance both as a restatement of Laplacian doctrines, especially in optics, and as evidence of continuing work on the program after the death of Malus.

[93] Fresnel, "Mémoire sur la diffraction de la lumière," *Mémoires de l'Académie des Sciences, 5* (1821-1822 [published 1826]), 339-445. On the identity of the judges see *Procès-verbaux, 6*, 345 (27 July 1818). The other judges were Fresnel's good

However, on the question of the nature of light the Laplacians did not give up easily. In 1837 William Whewell raised the possibility that Laplace, Biot, and Poisson were chiefly responsible for a seven-year delay in the publication of Fresnel's prize-winning paper, and it seems not inconceivable that they even resorted to such underhand methods as mislaying some of his other papers.[94] But they were fighting a losing battle, as even Biot finally recognized when, in the early 1820's after some protracted and acrimonious debate with Arago, he retired from the Parisian scientific community (in particular, from the Academy of Sciences) for several years,[95] and so, at least in the eyes of his contemporaries, conceded victory to his adversary.[96]

The successful attack on the corpuscular theory of light helped to

friend Arago and Gay-Lussac who, despite his closeness to Berthollet and Laplace, had already shown some sympathy toward the wave theory, as we have seen. It is interesting to speculate on the course of the discussions that gave Fresnel his victory. Arago and presumably Gay-Lussac would have supported Fresnel, while Poisson, always the most orthodox of Laplacians, and Biot, whose acrimonious public debate with Arago was now imminent, would surely have opposed him. Perhaps, therefore, it was Laplace himself who swayed the decision. It becomes less difficult to imagine Laplace supporting anti-Laplacians when we note how in 1822 he was to vote for Fourier rather than Biot in the election for a new permanent secretary of the Academy of Sciences; see note 143. And already he had shown some favor to the work of Fourier when he might have been expected to support Poisson; see Grattan-Guinness, *loc. cit.* (note 83).

[94] For Whewell's somewhat speculative account see his *History of the Inductive Sciences,* 3 vols. (London, 1837), *2,* 408–411; also his recollection in his paper "Comte and Positivism," *Macmillan's Magazine, 13* (1866), 355–356, where it is stated that Arago had told Whewell that the Laplacian domination of French physical science had been so effective about 1815 that he had actually been afraid to voice his early support for Fresnel. The lengthy delays in the publication of the prize-winning papers by Fourier and Fresnel should, of course, be compared with the delay of little more than a year in the publication of the winning paper of Malus (see note 57), but it should also be noted that it was not only members of the anti-Laplacian group who suffered in this way. Cauchy, for example, had to wait more than ten years before his prize-winning paper of 1815 on water waves was published, with additions, in *Mémoires présentés par divers savans à l'Académie Royale des Sciences, 1* (1827), 3–312.

[95] The *Procès-verbaux* for the period show that Biot's appearances at the meetings of the Academy of Sciences were infrequent from the autumn of 1822 until the early 1830's. Between the end of January 1823 and the end of 1824 he was present on only three occasions. About this time, however, he was not inactive and was engaged, for example, in preparing the third edition of his *Précis élémentaire de physique* (note 108).

[96] Arago was left, as Guglielmo Libri put it in the *Revue des deux mondes,* ser. 4, *21* (1840), 799, "maître du champ de bataille." See the passage quoted on pp. 123–124.

create an atmosphere in which it was natural that other Laplacian beliefs should be subjected to a new scrutiny. Once action at a distance was discredited in one branch of the Laplacian program, it became far easier to attack it in other branches; and the program in its strict and complete sense naturally collapsed completely. Moreover, the threat to Laplace and his school was heightened by another challenge that achieved success almost simultaneously. This was the challenge of Sophie Germain, whose victory in the Academy's prize competition in 1816 was, as I have already mentioned,[97] both a blow to Laplacian interests, as represented above all by Poisson, and a sign of diminishing Laplacian control. Like the criticism of the corpuscular theory of light, Germain's treatment of elastic surfaces stimulated a prolonged controversy, which lasted far into the 1820's and engaged Poisson in a bitter debate with a group of critics inspired by Fourier.[98]

In such conditions of mounting criticism it seems plausible to interpret the attack on the caloric theory which accompanied Petit and Dulong's announcement of their famous law of atomic heats in 1819[99] as a natural product of a questioning mood that had come to prevail in French science since 1815. In fact, such an interpretation seems necessary. For, despite the confidence with which Petit and Dulong stated their criticism of caloric,[100] the justification for their attack in terms of experimental facts was far from conclusive. They brought forward virtually no new evidence, and the attack was one that could have been made equally well ten years earlier.[101] However, as we know, it was not made at that time—and this in itself is strong evidence that the general intellectual atmosphere of the Napoleonic period was very different from that which existed within five years of Napoleon's downfall.

Another illustration of the changing atmosphere may be found in chemistry, where, at precisely the same time as the first attacks on Laplacian physics were being launched, there was a similar turning away from related

[97]See above, p. 106.

[98]See below, pp. 118-119.

[99]Petit and Dulong, "Recherches sur quelques points importans de la théorie de la chaleur," *Annales de chimie et de physique, 10* (1819), 395-413, especially pp. 396-398 and 406-413.

[100]A confidence that is especially apparent in Dulong's letter to Berzelius, 15 January 1820, in *Jac. Berzelius Bref,* ed. H.G. Söderbaum, 6 vols. in 14 parts (Uppsala, 1912-1932), Pt. 1, *2,* 13-14.

[101]For an account of the criticisms by Petit and Dulong see R. Fox, "The Background to the Discovery of Dulong and Petit's Law," *The British Journal for the History of Science, 4* (1968-1969), 1-22, especially pp. 9-16.

principles that had gone virtually unchallenged in the Napoleonic period. In this challenge the break with the past was manifested not so much by an explicit, open attack on Berthollet's chemistry as by the gradual acceptance of Dalton's atomic theory, which directed attention away from molecular forces to combining weights. Again it is 1815, when France renewed close contact with Britain, which seems to be the turning point, for until that date the atomic theory, opposed by Berthollet, had made little headway in France.[102] Incidentally, I need hardly say that I consider it significant that the same man who appeared as the leading French critic of the caloric theory from 1819—Dulong—was also known, from 1816, as the most enthusiastic supporter of the atomic theory in chemistry.[103]

So the attack on the caloric theory in 1819 and the new support for the atomic theory both seem to reflect the critical spirit that was abroad in French science during the early years of the Restoration, insofar as neither depended essentially on any startling new discoveries or observations. Yet discoveries and experimental evidence did contribute to the weakening of the Laplacian position. It was a great blow to the corpuscular theory when, in 1819, experiment confirmed the prediction based on Fresnel's wave theory that there should be illumination at the center of the diffraction pattern of a small opaque disc,[104] and the discovery of Dulong and Petit's law did much to strengthen the atomists' case.

Perhaps the best illustration of the importance of a discovery in weakening Laplacian physics is in electromagnetism. Following Oersted's observation of the magnetic effect of a wire carrying an electric current in 1820, French physicists zealously engaged in the investigation of the new phenomenon, and Biot and Ampère were quickly among the most prominent of them. There were, of course, problems for the Laplacians. For example, electromagnetism introduced a rotational force which had no obvious connection with the central forces of Laplacian physics; and Coulomb, whose views on the electrical and magnetic fluids had become part of the Laplacian orthodoxy, had denied the possibility of an interaction between

---

[102]The early history of the theory in France is well described in M.P. Crosland, "The First Reception of Dalton's Atomic Theory in France," in Cardwell, op. cit. (note 32), pp. 274–287.

[103]See Fox, op. cit. (note 101), pp. 16–18.

[104]On this crucial experiment, which was suggested by Poisson in his capacity as one of the judges for the competition on diffraction but which did little to shake his confidence in the corpuscular theory, see Ronchi, op. cit. (note 49).

electricity and magnetism.[105] But Biot, then at his most belligerent, was undaunted, and inevitably, it seems, there was conflict.

Ampère's theory of electromagnetic interaction contained much that Biot found objectionable.[106] In particular, he protested at Ampère's attempt to reduce not only electromagnetic phenomena but even the forces between magnets to interactions between current-carrying conductors; magnetic forces, in his view, had been explained perfectly well in terms of Coulomb's two fluids of magnetism. And the fact that Ampère retained fluids of electricity was no consolation, for Ampère's fluids were thoroughly un-Laplacian and apparently had more in common with Fresnel's ether than with the fluids of Coulomb.[107] Between 1821 and 1824 Biot put forward his alternative explanation, while pursuing a policy of faint praise, misrepresentation, and open criticism toward the work of Ampère.[108] By 1824, when he published the third edition of his *Précis élémentaire de physique expérimentale,* he had developed fully a theory in which the forces of electromagnetism were explained in terms of magnetic interactions between tiny magnets which he supposed to be arranged in a circular fashion around the current-carrying wire.[109] For Biot, convinced of the correctness of Coulomb's explanation, the cause of magnetic interactions was, of course, not in doubt, so that his electromagnetic theory appeared to him a highly satisfactory one. But the model did not withstand the scrutiny of Ampère, who quickly demonstrated its weaknesses, while defending himself against the charges that his own theory was un-Newtonian.[110] So discredited, Biot's theory was soon forgotten, and the attempt to treat the exciting new phenomena in accordance with Laplacian principles had failed.

[105]See L.P. Williams, "Ampère's Electrodynamic Molecular Model," *Contemporary Physics,* 4 (1962), 113–114.

[106]For my treatment of Biot's response to the work of Ampère I am greatly indebted to E. Frankel, *Jean Baptiste Biot: The Career of a Physicist in 19th-Century France* (Univ. of Princeton Ph.D. thesis, 1972), of which the author has kindly allowed me to see the relevant chapters.

[107]See Williams, *op. cit.* (note 105), pp. 118–122.

[108]See especially the cursory treatment of Ampère's work in Biot's paper "Sur l'aimantation imprimée aux métaux par l'électricité en mouvement," *Journal des savants* (1821), pp. 221–235, and the overt criticism in his *Précis élémentaire de physique expérimentale,* 3rd ed., 2 vols. (Paris, 1824), *2,* 771–772.

[109]Biot, *Précis* (note 108), *2,* 766–771.

[110]See the many references to Biot in Ampère, *Théorie mathématique des phénomènes électro-dynamiques, uniquement déduite de l'expérience* (Paris, 1826), especially pp. 180–188.

By the mid-1820's, then, the position of the Laplacian orthodoxy had been gravely weakened. The attacks had been directed, for the most part, against established beliefs in various branches of physical science, but there is evidence of diminishing Laplacian authority in mechanics also. The relevant debate dates principally from the 1820's, although several of the issues had been raised some years earlier, notably in the prize competition won by Sophie Germain in 1816. It concerned the methods to be used in rational mechanics, particularly in the study of elastic media.[111] Underlying the debate, in which Fourier's *protégés* Navier and Germain were opposed most frequently by Poisson, there was a fundamental opposition between the "physical mechanics" (*mécanique physique*) advocated by Poisson and the style of the Fourier school, which Poisson described as "analytical mechanics" (*mécanique analytique*) and (incorrectly) associated with the name of Lagrange.[112] Although he had been using his style of mechanics as early as August 1814,[113] it was in a paper of April 1828 that Poisson stated its principles most clearly, when he supported it in the following terms:

> Let me add that it would be desirable for geometers to re-examine the leading problems of mechanics from this point of view, which is at once physical and consonant with nature. In order to discover the general laws of equilibrium and motion, it was necessary to treat them in a completely abstract manner; and, as far as treatments of this general and abstract kind are concerned, Lagrange went as far as anyone could imagine when he replaced the physical connections between bodies by equations relating the coordinates of the various positions they occupied. It is this that constitutes analytical mechanics. But besides this wonderful conception we can now establish physical mechanics, the sole principle of which is to reduce everything to the molecular actions which

[111]For a factual account see Todhunter, *op. cit.* (note 61), *1*, 133–160 and 277–285.

[112]For discussions of this opposition see P. Duhem, "L'évolution de la mécanique," *Revue générale des sciences* (1903), pp. 127–132; L. Brunschvicg, *L'expérience humaine et le causalité physique* (Paris, 1922), pp. 327–337; J.W. Herivel, "Aspects of French Theoretical Physics in the Nineteenth Century," *The British Journal for the History of Science, 3* (1966–1967), 121–125. In various ways Fourier and his associates, Navier and Germain, were related back to the Basel-St. Petersburg school of rational mechanics of the earlier eighteenth century, a school that embraced the Bernoullis and Euler. The line of descent to the nineteenth century touches Lagrange only incidentally and altogether bypasses Laplace.

[113]In Poisson, *op. cit.* (note 62).

convey from one point to another the effects of the given forces and are the agents maintaining the equilibrium between these forces. If we proceeded in this way, it would no longer be necessary to draw up special hypotheses when one wanted to apply the general rules of mechanics to particular questions. Thus, in the problem of the equilibrium of flexible strings the tension that is introduced to achieve a solution would be the direct result of the actions of the molecules on one another when they are displaced slightly from their natural positions. In the case of an elastic membrane, the bending moment of elasticity would be a consequence of these same actions, taken throughout the whole thickness of the sheet, and the expression for it would be established without any hypothesis. And, finally, the pressures exerted by fluids both internally and on the walls of the vessels containing them would also be the resultant of the actions of the molecules on the surface under pressure, or rather on an extremely thin layer of fluid in contact with each surface.[114]

In seeking to explain phenomena in terms of the attractive and repulsive forces operating on the molecular scale, Poisson was of course declaring his allegiance to those principles which had dominated the *Système du monde* and the *Mécanique céleste,* but by the late 1820's, with Laplace now dead, he was increasingly isolated. He had no school to support him, and through the 1830's the advocates of Fourier's style of mechanics, led by Lamé and encouraged by Comte, carried all before them.[115]

Given this evidence, it is probably not too much to say that by the early 1820's there had emerged in France certain anti-Laplacian principles, not only in physics but also in chemistry and mechanics, to which all critics of Laplacian science could subscribe. Of these, skepticism toward the traditional imponderable fluids, sympathy for Dalton's atomic theory, the new rational mechanics of Fourier and his followers, and Ampère's electrodynamics were the most obvious. That those who sought to break with Laplace and his school had so many shared beliefs and operated on such a broad intellectual front is striking. For instance, Petit, as well as evidently sharing Dulong's skepticism toward caloric and his enthusiasm for the atomic theory, was among the earliest supporters of Fresnel's wave theory,

[114]Poisson, "Mémoire sur l'équilibre et le mouvement des corps élastiques," *Mémoires de l'Académie des Sciences, 8* (1829), 361–362. Read 14 April 1828.
[115]Brunschvicg, *op. cit.* (note 112), p. 331.

as were Dulong and Ampère.[116] Fresnel, for his part, was a critic of the traditional caloric theory and influenced Ampère in his work on electro-magnetism,[117] and Arago not only championed Fresnel in his difficult early years after 1815 but also took a keen and highly favorable interest in the work of Petit and Dulong on heat.[118] Likewise, Fourier, whose role may be seen as that of a benign, influential, but rather detached patron of the new generation, expressed his support for the wave theory[119] and, by his extreme caution on the question of the nature of heat, notably in his *Théorie analytique de la chaleur* (1822), implied unmistakable criticism of caloric.[120] Such unanimity is, in fact, hardly surprising, for the mem-bers of the anti-Laplacian group were in close, almost daily contact in the scientific circles of Paris,[121] where they all lived and worked. Between some of them the relationship was especially close. Petit and Dulong were most intimate friends (until Petit's untimely death in 1820), and the same may be said of Ampère and Fresnel and of Arago and Fresnel. Arago, moreover, became Petit's brother-in-law when Petit married in November 1814.

Throughout the Restoration period the reaction of the Laplacian party to the growing criticism was complex. If we are to judge by Biot's response to Fresnel's wave theory, for example, the party felt the attacks keenly. But in their publications, at least, they gave the impression that little had changed. A comparison of the third edition of the *Précis élémentaire* (1824) with the *Traité de physique* (1816) shows that Biot was willing to make few concessions with regard to the imponderable fluids.[122] And

[116]See Petit and Dulong, *op. cit.* (note 99), p. 396; Dulong's letters of 15 January 1820 and 10 November 1825 to Berzelius, in *Berzelius Bref* (note 100), Pt. 1, *2*, 13 and 64; and his comment in *Annales de chimie et de physique, 31* (1826), 180–181. Also see above, pp. 112–113.

[117]See his "Complément au mémoire sur la diffraction," dated 10 November 1815, in *Oeuvres complètes d'Augustin Fresnel* (note 88), *1*, 59–60; also his letters of 5 July 1814 and 11 July 1814 to Léonor Fresnel, *ibid., 2*, 820–822 and 827–829. The connection between Fresnel and Ampère is discussed in Williams, *op. cit.* (note 105), pp. 118–120.

[118]See Fox, *op. cit.* (note 101), p. 2.

[119]In a report, written jointly with Ampère and Arago, on a paper by Fresnel on double refraction. See *Annales de chimie et de physique, 20* (1822), 337–344.

[120]The book began (on p. i) with the words: "First causes (*les causes primordiales*) are unknown to us; but they are subject to simple, unvarying laws which can be discovered by observation and the study of which is the object of natural philosophy."

[121]Fresnel is, in part, an exception since until 1818 his visits to Paris were re-stricted to periods of leave from the Corps des Ponts et Chaussées.

[122]Certainly, in the *Précis* (note 108), *1*, 466, and *2*, 2, Biot confessed ignorance

Laplace and the ever-loyal Poisson continued to work out their programs in accordance with the principles laid down two decades earlier.[123] Even in the fifth edition of the *Système du monde,* published in 1824, Laplace gave no indication that he had modified his view in any way,[124] and between 1821 and 1823 he confidently proceeded to devise and publish what was easily the most detailed of all versions of the caloric theory accounting for the physical and thermal properties of gases in terms of those short-range forces that he still supposed to govern all phenomena on the molecular scale.[125] Indeed, it was in a paper on the subject published early in 1822 that he first gave the classic statement of the Laplacian program, one version of which is reproduced at the head of this paper. In his work on caloric in the 1820's Poisson showed a similar disregard for the criticisms of Petit and Dulong (and of others, including that important ally of the anti-Laplacian cause Berzelius).[126] And even as late as

---

of the true nature of heat, electricity, and magnetism, but he denied that the corpuscular theory had been discredited and maintained that the evidence still favored it (*2,* 130–132 and 452–463). In his *Traité de physique* (note 92), *1,* 66–68, he admitted that the existence of a fluid of heat was not certain, but the existence of fluids of electricity and magnetism was "very probable" (*1,* 7–8), and the materiality of light was "beyond doubt" (*3,* 148–149). This confident statement concerning light conflicts with his assertion, in the dedication of the *Traité* to Berthollet (*1,* xx–xxiii), that it was impossible to know its nature "with certainty." The caution that Biot displays, even in the *Traité,* is striking and it has to be compared with his criticism of fluids, referred to in note 43. Having regard to his optical work and his vigorous defense of the corpuscular theory, however, I feel (with Frankel, *op. cit.* [note 106]) that his caution was formal and that it does not convey the true measure of his conviction which is apparent in his major interpretative papers.

[123]On Laplace's changing attitude to Fourier, however, see below, p. 127, and notes 93 and 143.

[124]See, for instance, the "Avertissement" to his *Exposition du système du monde,* 5th ed., 2 vols. (8vo) (Paris, 1824), *1,* v, where Laplace wrote that he intended to make molecular forces the subject of a special supplement. Work on this project was never completed, as we see from the "Avertissement" to the quarto version of the sixth edition, published posthumously in 1835, and in this edition a chapter on molecular attraction which had appeared on pp. 315–357 of the (quarto) fourth edition (Paris, 1813) was simply reinstated (as Chapter XVIII of Book IV, on pp. 323–364). The chapter did not appear in the octavo versions of the sixth edition published in Paris and Brussels in 1827.

[125]This theory appeared first in a series of papers in the volumes of the *Connaissance des tems* for 1824 and 1825 (published respectively in 1821 and 1822) and was given its definitive form in April 1823 in Book XII of the *Mécanique céleste* (note 1), *5,* 87–144.

[126]See, for example, his "Mémoire sur les équations générales de l'équilibre et du mouvement des corps solides élastiques et des fluides," *Journal de l'École Polytechnique,* cahier 20, *13* (1831), 1–174, especially pp. 4–8. Read to the Academy of

1835 we find him publishing a lengthy work, the *Théorie mathématique de la chaleur,* in which the existence of caloric and its traditional properties were taken as no less axiomatic than they would have been, say, thirty years before.[127] But by 1835 Poisson's book, although its author does not seem to have recognized the fact, was a relic of a bygone age, an anachronism in terms both of its physics and of its laborious and inelegant mathematics. And, to judge by the almost complete silence in which it was received, it was seen as such by his contemporaries.[128] By the 1830's Poisson was a lone, almost pathetic figure, clinging vainly to an ideal of a "physical mechanics," based on Laplacian principles, which was unrealizable. When he died in 1840, the mathematician Guglielmo Libri wrote of his funeral, in a notice of singular warmth and affection:[129] "Never, since the death of Cuvier, had anyone seen such general sorrow nor a cortège accompanied by so many demonstrations of grief of every kind."[130] But in reality there were few men of note to mourn him. He had no official *éloge,* and even the biographical memoir by the permanent secretary of the Academy of Sciences, Arago, who had been for so long the scourge of the Laplacian school, was never read in full.[131]

---

Sciences on 12 October 1829. On Berzelius as an ally of the cause see Fox, *op. cit.* (note 8), pp. 241–243 and 246–248.

[127]Poisson, *Théorie mathématique,* especially p. 7. The problem of heat diffusion in solids, which was treated in the *Théorie mathématique,* had been of great interest to Poisson for over twenty years. As is pointed out in Grattan-Guinness, *op. cit.* (note 81), pp. 466–470, his labored contributions on the subject are in sharp contrast with the elegant and incisive treatments of Fourier, and in a paper published in July 1823 Poisson did go so far as to acknowledge Fourier's priority with regard to most of his own results, though presumably with some reluctance; see his "Mémoire sur la distribution de la chaleur dans les corps solides," *Journal de l'École Polytechnique,* cahier 19, *12* (1823), 1–2. However, by way of justification of his own work, he stressed that his methods for deriving the results were different from Fourier's and that he had used Laplace's assumption that heat transfer within a solid was a short-range phenomenon (pp. 2–6).

[128]The rare comments which have been found, such as that by J.D. Forbes in his *Review of the Progress of Mathematical and Physical Science* (Edinburgh, 1858), p. 154, and the anonymous review in the Swiss *Bibliothèque universelle, 59* (1835), 144–166, are generally critical.

[129][Libri], "Lettres à un Américain sur l'état des sciences en France—III. M. Poisson," *Revue des deux mondes,* ser. 4, *23* (1840), 410–437.

[130]*Ibid.,* p. 429.

[131]And even when extracts from the memoir were read at the public meeting of the Academy, on 16 December 1850, Arago was absent; see the *Comptes rendus hebdomadaires des séances de l'Académie des Sciences, 31* (1850), 840. The whole memoir was printed in the *Oeuvres complètes de François Arago,* 17 vols. (Paris and Leipzig, 1854–1862), *2,* 593–689.

Naturally enough purely intellectualist factors were not alone in bringing about the move from Laplacian science. This was not simply a case of new principles being measured against old ones and being found superior, although there was something of this in the situation, especially with regard to the debate over the nature of light. Other relevant factors include the weakening of the authority of the Arcueil circle after regular meetings had ceased in 1813.[132] And possibly even the personal unpopularity incurred by Laplace in the early years of the Bourbon Restoration played its part. On this unpopularity, in which political considerations seem to have loomed large, Libri wrote (with reference to the debate between Biot and Arago on the nature of light):

M. Biot and M. Arago were among the first to participate. Unfortunately, instead of serving to strengthen the ties that bound them, the fact that they were engaged in the same field of study became the source of lively exchanges which culminated in a dramatic break between them; and the Academy was frequently moved by the strife between these two rivals who, in their heated debates, sometimes allowed themselves to be unduly carried away, especially when discussing questions of priority, which are always so delicate. Other *savants* joined in these discussions, and since Laplace, a man who wanted problems to be treated geometrically rather than in any other way, had appeared to take sides against Arago, enemies were raised to oppose him on every side; Legendre was put up deliberately as an adversary; the hand of friendship was offered to anyone who attacked the results contained in the *Mécanique céleste;* and all the liberal press was aroused and directed against those of whom we had once been so proud, men who, it was said, were now just old idols that had to be destroyed. Because the geometer Laplace had become the Marquis de la Place and on the pretext that some other academicians belonged to the Société des Bonnes Lettres,[133] these men were pro-

132On the decline of Arcueil, to the death of Berthollet in November 1822, see Crosland, *op. cit.* (note 4), pp. 395–428.

133The Société des Bonnes Lettres was a mainly literary society founded in the early years of the Restoration by Louis Fontanes and Chateaubriand, both champions of the Bourbons. Taking it as their aim "to revive the taste for good doctrines and good literature," most of the members supported traditional religion and monarchy, with the result that the society quickly became a byword for antiliberalism and hence the object of a good deal of popular suspicion. Under the influence of Chateaubriand and Charles Nodier, it helped to strengthen the early association between royalist sentiments and the new romanticism in literature. Among other leading members were the antiquaries Désiré Raoul Rochette and Quatremère de Quincy,

claimed ignoramuses, in the name of the Charter, in all the newspapers. It was then, as I have already said, that members of the public began to be admitted to the Academy,[134] and there they became the supporters of those who did not wish to excel solely by science. Laplace was put to silence, M. Biot stayed away from the Institute for several years, and M. Arago remained master of the battle field.[135]

Laplace's name, as Libri suggests here, seems to have become a byword for illiberalism in certain quarters (notably in the circle of the liberal writer P. L. Courier) in the early years of the Restoration, and it remained so until long after his death. Indeed, in the freer atmosphere of the Orléans monarchy, which did little to encourage restraint, criticisms of his "pliability" (*souplesse*) in political and personal matters and of his failure to defend the freedom of the press became common.[136] Perhaps the criticisms in his own lifetime were not so severe as to hasten his death, as the author of one standard biographical sketch maintained in 1834,[137] but there is sufficient evidence to dispel any image of Laplace living his last

---

the orientalists Antoine Léonard de Chezy and Jean Pierre Abel de Rémusat, and the writer Eugène Destains. The activities of the society, which included poetry readings by Victor Hugo, are best studied in the thirty-three volumes of its official publication, the *Annales de la littérature et des arts,* which appeared between 1818 and 1829. For a brief account see C. Dejob, *L'Instruction publique en France et en Italie au dix-neuvième siècle* (Paris, n.d.), pp. viii, 210–225, and 441–444. Dejob points out that the society was established as a royalist answer to the Parisian Athénée, founded in 1781 by Pilâtre de Rozier, where ideas more in keeping with the traditions of the eighteenth-century Enlightenment were discussed. Libri's comparison of Laplace with Legendre, who suffered, for political reasons, at the Restoration, was an obvious one to make.

[134]The ease with which journalists and the general public could gain access to the meetings of the Academy of Sciences remained a source of grievance long after this date; see, for example, Biot's comments in his *Mélanges scientifiques et littéraires* (note 43), *2,* 257–264 (first published in the *Journal des savants* for February 1837).

[135][Libri], "Lettres à un Américain . . . ," *Revue des deux mondes,* ser. 4, *21* (1840), 798–799.

[136]See, for example, the entry on Laplace in A. Rabbe, V. de Boisjolin, and Sainte-Preuve, *Biographie universelle et portative des contemporains,* 5 vols. (Paris, 1834), *3,* 151–153, especially p. 151. Valentin Parisot was equally critical in his article on Laplace in the *Bibliothèque universelle, ancienne et moderne,* 83 vols. (Paris, 1811–1853), *70* (supplément), 237–260, especially pp. 239–244. A most unflattering description of Laplace's shifting political views appeared in the article on him by E. Merlieux in the *Nouvelle biographie générale,* ed. F. Hoefer, 46 vols. (Paris, 1855–1866), *29,* cols. 533–534. Poisson's behavior was subject to similar criticism in the article on him in Rabbe, *et al., op. cit.,* *5,* 591.

[137]Rabbe, *et al., op. cit.* (note 136), *3,* 151.

years as a universally respected elder statesman of French science. By 1827 his reputation was severely tarnished.

And as Laplacian influence waned, so inevitably the leading members of the new anti-Laplacian generation were able, if only by virtue of age and seniority, to gain control of the still centralized scientific community of Paris. It was important, for example, that when the need for a wholesale reorganization of the *Annales de chimie* was felt, following the death of the secretary to the journal, Collet-Descotils, in December 1815, it was Arago (rather than, say, Biot) who became one of the two new editors.[138] Since this happened just after Arago's conversion to the wave theory of light and at a time when his relations with Biot were about to worsen rapidly, the appointment was crucial in the transfer of power from the Laplacian group. The publication of the work of Fourier and Fresnel, which followed with remarkable (and significant) rapidity,[139] soon gave a clear intimation of the changing allegiance of the *Annales* and, because of the established authority of the journal, did much to strengthen the anti-Laplacian position.

Almost as important as this new domination of the most prominent of the French research journals was the way in which critics of Laplace were able to exert influence at the École Polytechnique after 1815. Petit, for instance, had been made professor of physics there in 1814—as a good Laplacian and for reasons quite unconnected with the subsequent debate[140] —and he remained in the post until his death in 1820. Petit was followed in his turn by Dulong, who remained as professor until 1830, when he became Director of Studies for the École Polytechnique as a whole. The chief results of this sixteen-year tenure of the chair of physics by Petit and Dulong were, first, a marked rise both in the quality and the amount of physics taught and, second, some predictable changes of doctrine. In the published syllabus for 1817–1818, for example, the state-

---

138Crosland, *op. cit.* (note 4), pp. 404–406. Arago had special responsibility for physics, while Gay-Lussac, the other editor, was responsible for contributions on chemistry.

139Fresnel's first paper on diffraction appeared in the issue for March 1816 (see note 87), and the December issue contained the lengthy summary of Fourier's work cited in note 86. Moreover, the very first issue of the new series, in January 1816, began with an account of the recent experiments by Arago and Petit that strongly supported Fresnel; see note 88.

140The cause of Petit's promotion to the chair after some five years as a teaching assistant (*répétiteur*), first in analysis and from 1810 in physics, was the unsatisfactory standard of the teaching of J.H. Hassenfratz, who had been professor of physics since the foundation of the École in 1794; see Fox, *op. cit.* (note 8), pp. 231–232.

ment that light would be "treated as an emission from luminous bodies," which had appeared in earlier syllabuses, was omitted.[141] And in the syllabus for 1821–1822 all references to "caloric" (*calorique*) were eliminated and replaced by references to "heat" (*chaleur*).[142]

Changes that told against Laplacian interests also took place in the Academy of Sciences. Arago, then an orthodox Laplacian, had been elected back in 1809, and Ampère became a member in November 1814; but it was only after the final overthrow of the Empire that they were joined by the men who were to become their chief allies. Fourier, for example, was not elected to the place that he had so long deserved until 1816, and Dulong and Fresnel followed only in 1823, Navier in 1824. However, the really decisive election at the Academy dates from November 1822, when the anti-Laplacian cause gained its most glorious victory through the defeat of Biot by Fourier for the post of permanent secretary for the mathematical sciences.[143] The vote, thirty-eight to ten, was not overwhelming, but from that point Laplacian science was doomed, and the election of Arago to replace Fourier as permanent secretary in 1830 only sealed its fate, ushering in a period that sympathizers of Laplace seem to have resented bitterly.[144]

With the crumbling of the power of the Laplacian group, each of its members adopted his own strategy for survival. As has already been noted,

[141]*Programmes de l'enseignement de l'Ecole Royale Polytechnique, arrêtés par le Conseil de Perfectionnement, pour l'année scolaire 1817-1818* (Paris, n.d.), p. 35; cf. *Programmes . . . arrêtés . . . dans la session de 1815-1816* (Paris, 1816), p. 39. Naturally Petit did not effect a wholesale rejection of Laplacian doctrines, and in *Annales de chimie et de physique, 5* (1817), 404-406, he even defended Laplace against criticism of his theory of capillary action.

[142]*Programmes . . . arrêtés . . . pour l'année scolaire 1821-1822* (Paris, n.d.), pp. 31-32; cf. *Programmes . . . arrêtés . . . pour l'année scolaire 1820-1821* (Paris, n.d.), pp. 31-32. References to the fluid of electricity were far slower to disappear. In fact, it was only in *Programmes pour l'admission et pour l'enseignement à l'École Polytechnique, arrêtés par la commission nommée en exécution de la loi du 5 juin 1850, et approuvés par le Ministre de la Guerre* (Paris, n.d.), p. 93, that earlier references to "electric fluid" (*fluide électrique*) were replaced by references to "electricity" (*électricité*); cf. *Programmes pour l'admission et pour l'enseignement . . . arrêtés . . . pour l'année scolaire 1849-1850* (Paris, 1850), p. 29, where "electric fluid" is used.

[143]Arago was also a candidate in this election but openly gave his support to Fourier. It is interesting to note that, despite a show of strict impartiality, Laplace appears to have voted for Fourier rather than for Biot; see *Oeuvres complètes de François Arago* (note 131), *1*, 100-101; see also note 93.

[144]Libri, for example, launched a violent personal attack on Arago on pp. 796-812 of the first of his (unsigned) "Lettres à un Américain" of 1840 (cited in note 135). His main charge was that, as a result of Arago's consistent abuse of his position, the activities of the Academy of Sciences had become increasingly trivial.

Biot chose to retire from the scientific scene of Paris in the early 1820's, but in the 1830's he seems to have mellowed and he returned to resume a valuable career in which his patronage of Pasteur in his early researches on crystals was perhaps his most important contribution. Poisson, by contrast, remained stubbornly loyal to the doctrine of Laplace until his death in 1840. In fact, he seems to have pursued the program with even greater zeal than the master himself, who, at least on certain issues, showed some signs of trying to adjust to the winning side. For example, after Fourier had produced an estimate for the age of the earth from geothermal considerations in 1819, Laplace wrote of his work in a decidedly complimentary manner.[145] And we must not forget that it was apparently Arago rather than Biot who had Laplace's vote in the momentous election at the Academy of Sciences in 1822.[146] Laplace's support for Fourier and his behavior in 1822 could, of course, only serve to alienate Poisson, and in view of the shifting allegiances of the 1820's it is remarkable only that so many personal friendships survived.[147]

So by the mid-1820's the style of science that had appeared so right and unassailable in the Napoleonic period had been abandoned by the leading figures in a new generation; and the peculiar organizational structure centered on Arcueil, which had provided essential support for the old science, had collapsed, leaving power in new hands.[148]

## 4. THE NEW AGE

It remains now to examine what was built on the ruins of Laplacian physics. The problem is a difficult one and simple statements are not possible. For, despite the solidarity of those who turned against Laplace and his disciples in the years after 1815, there emerged no single well-defined new style of science that was capable of filling the gap left by the

[145] See especially Laplace, "Sur la diminution de la durée du jour par le refroidissement de la terre," *Annales de chimie et de physique, 13* (1820), 416–417.

[146] See note 143.

[147] For example, when Dalton visited Arcueil in July 1822 there was every sign of friendship in a gathering for dinner that included Berthollet, Laplace, Biot, Fourier, and Arago; see the accounts in H.E. Roscoe, *John Dalton and the Rise of Modern Chemistry* (London, 1895), pp. 178–181. This, of course, was some four months before the election for the new permanent secretary.

[148] Ravetz has pointed out to me that a similar transfer of power took place in the early 1820's in the Société Philomathique of Paris, with Poisson and Biot giving way to non-Laplacians, notably H.M.D. de Blainville (soon to become a follower of Comte) and Fresnel; see Fox, *op. cit.* (note 8), pp. 272–273.

old and of yielding a clear program for the future. And this should not surprise us, since a certain diversity of approach was a natural enough product of a period of reaction against the Laplacian orthodoxy, and diversity in any case reflects a more normal situation in science than the one that had prevailed under Napoleon.

It has been suggested (with an eye on Poisson's distinction between "physical mechanics" and "analytical mechanics") that what has here been described as Laplacian physics was followed by a turning toward a positivist approach, and the emergence of the positivist strain of the 1820's and 1830's onward has been cited as the beginning of the end of French theoretical physics.[149] Now Fourier's program for the science of heat, modeled on the traditional rational mechanics in which the causes are taken as given, could indeed be interpreted as positivist in the sense the term later acquired in the philosophy of Comte (although the program was conceived by 1807 and so was not truly Comtean in any sense[150]). Moreover, a mathematical study of heat transfer based on the principles laid down most prominently by Fourier in his *Théorie analytique de la chaleur* of 1822[151] did continue through the 1830's, with Lamé and Duhamel as its most distinguished exponents.[152] More evidence for a positivist trend in French physics is to be found in Ampère's refusal to discuss causes in his *Théorie mathématique des phénomènes électro-dynamiques, uniquement déduite de l'expérience* of 1826[153] and in his decision to present his theory in terms only of observed phenomena; i.e., in terms of forces such as those that were known from his own experiments to exist between two current-carrying conductors. And in any discussion of positivist science it is obviously impossible to omit Comte himself, who expressed the prevailing skepticism toward the Laplacian imponderable fluids in an extreme form when he wrote on the subject in the mid-1830's.[154]

---

[149]Herivel, *op. cit.* (note 112), especially pp. 121–132.

[150]On Fourier's work in 1807 see above, p. 111.

[151]The style of Fourier's treatment is conveyed in the opening words of the "Discours préliminaire" quoted in note 120.

[152]See G. Bachelard, *Étude sur l'évolution d'un problème de physique. La propagation thermique dans les solides* (Paris, 1928), pp. 89–132.

[153]See especially pp. 4–8 of the book. It is hardly necessary to point out that Ampère did not adopt this positivist stand in all his work. On the two faces of Ampère see L.P. Williams, *Michael Faraday. A Biography* (London, 1965), pp. 143–144.

[154]I.A.M.F.X. Comte, *Cours de philosophie positive,* 6 vols. (Paris, 1830–1842), 2 (1835), 438–445.

But positivism, with its variants, was not the only, or even the dominant, philosophy to gain favor, at least in the early years of the attacks on Laplacian science. It is important to observe that of the men who were most closely involved in the revolt of 1815–1820, Dulong, Arago, Fresnel, and Petit were emphatically not positivists, although they appear to have been no less concerned at the errors perpetrated by the Laplacians than were Fourier and Ampère. Certainly they advocated caution, and they rejected many Laplacian doctrines; but they all wanted to substitute new theories for the ones they were criticizing, and they championed their theories—the wave theory of light, the atomic theory, the vibrational theory of heat—with enthusiasm and utter conviction. Moreover, they provided the basis for research traditions that were anything but positivist. Perhaps the best example of such a tradition, which grew from the work of Fresnel, was the search for a model for an all-pervading fluid ether that possessed at once the high elasticity of a solid and also the capacity to allow solid objects, such as planets, to pass through it unhindered.[155] This problem, which quite defied solution until the work of Stokes in the 1840's, together with a number of related problems engaged some of the great men of nineteenth-century physics from the late 1820's until the rise of electromagnetic theory in the 1880's. With mathematical physicists of the stature of MacCullogh, Green, William Thomson, and Maxwell involved, the tradition was by no means exclusively French, but major French contributions were made by Navier and, more particularly, Cauchy.

So positivism was certainly not the one philosophy that rose to take the place of the Laplacian principles prevailing in the Napoleonic period; and still less was it a *cause* of the rejection of these principles. Positivism, in fact, did not emerge formally as a recognizable strain in French physical science until after the short period of creativity which itself followed the discrediting of Laplace and his school. It was at most a symptom, and not a cause, of the state of physics in France after the mid-1820's. And in any case, as I have argued, it did not have the philosophical field to itself, even by the mid-century.

Despite the confusing diversity that characterized French physics for several decades following the abandonment of Laplacian orthodoxy, one thing is clear: the enthusiasm, zeal, and confidence of the decade 1815–1825 were quickly lost. And it is in this loss of intellectual impetus, how-

155 On this work see E.T. Whittaker, *A History of the Theories of Aether and Electricity,* 2nd ed. (London, 1951), pp. 128–169.

ever caused, that I believe we must see one of the great turning points in the history of physical science in nineteenth-century France. In the last eighteen years of his life, for example, Dulong never again openly voiced his support for the modern vibrational theory of heat, despite the extreme confidence with which he had expressed it (and scorned caloric) in 1820.[156] There was no going back to caloric, of course, but, in the absence of the energy conservation principle, there was no going forward to a new theory of heat either. There was, in fact, widespread agnosticism, as is clear from the textbooks of the day.[157] By the mid-1830's the same was true of the atomic theory, which Dulong had championed so uncompromisingly as an anti-Laplacian doctrine some twenty years before. By this time and on this particular issue Dulong was not alone in his caution with regard to the physical reality of atoms, as we see from the guarded comments being made in the face of dauntingly complex problems concerning the determination of atomic weights by Jean Baptiste Dumas.[158] And there is a similar story of exasperation and unfulfilled hopes in the history of the wave theory of light, where the complex problems arose in the 1820's, 1830's, and 1840's in the search for a satisfactory model for the fluid ether.[159]

So the second quarter of the century in France seems to have been characterized by a failure to consolidate the gains of 1815–1825, and for a variety of reasons the men who once seemed so certain that they were retrieving the physical sciences from error and initiating a new golden age ceased to give French physical science the leadership it needed. Dulong, for one, was beset by frustrations and ill health and quickly lost heart for

[156]For evidence of Dulong's support for the vibrational theory see his letter of 15 January 1820 to Berzelius, cited in note 100 and quoted in Fox, *op. cit.* (note 101), p. 13, and *op. cit.* (note 8), p. 244.

[157]See Fox, *op. cit.* (note 8), pp. 275–277.

[158]J.B.A. Dumas, *Leçons sur la philosophie chimique* (Paris, 1837), pp. 231–290 (6th and 7th lessons). For accounts of the growing difficulties in the atomic theory and Dumas' mounting despair see G. Buchdahl, "Sources of Scepticism in Atomic Theory," *The British Journal for the Philosophy of Science, 10* (1959), 120–134, and Fox, *op. cit.* (note 8), pp. 282–295. As J.H. Brooke points out in his Cambridge University Ph.D. thesis "The Role of Analogical Argument in the Development of Organic Chemistry" (1969), pp. 61–68, the difficulties did not lead Dumas to positivism, even in the mid-1830's; indeed, Dumas can safely be described as a consistent realist with regard to chemical theory. But positivism did become prominent in French chemistry in the 1840's with the work of Charles Gerhardt; see Brooke, *op. cit.*, pp. 114–149.

[159]See note 155 for reference.

the struggle,[160] while Arago, like so many others, soon found the world of politics, in his case both academic and national, more alluring than the laboratory bench.[161] And, saddest blow of all, Petit, Fresnel, and Fourier were all dead by 1830; and Ampère died in 1836, just when Britain was beginning to assume European supremacy in the study of electricity and magnetism. Of these only Fourier had succeeded in establishing anything resembling a school of disciples to carry on the tradition of his work into the 1830's and beyond,[162] so that by the 1840's the thread of continuity with the early 1820's was tenuous indeed. It is significant in this respect that the most esteemed French physicist of the later period, Victor Regnault, had his intellectual roots not in the exciting years that followed the rejection of the Laplacian orthodoxy but in the subsequent period of diminishing impetus. In fact, the massive, dreary compilation of data which earned Regnault his high reputation and for which he is now best known[163] was begun in 1840 in answer to a plea from Dumas, who had urged a full experimental investigation of specific heats in an attempt to remove the notorious anomalies in current values for atomic weights.[164] Not surprisingly, the attitude to scientific investigation that Regnault's work reveals is strikingly similar to Dumas' at this time, being cautious but not truly positivist.

Regnault illustrates as clearly as any one man can the state of French physics at the middle of the century. Far from being an outsider like

[160]On Dulong's work between 1820 and 1838, when he died, see Fox, *op. cit.* (note 8), pp. 248-270.

[161]Arago was engrossed in his political activities, at the Academy of Sciences and as a liberal deputy, from 1830 until his death in 1853. Politics similarly enticed Dumas from science in later life, and Gay-Lussac and Thenard both gave much time to politics and public affairs. Among the less prominent men of science with strong political interests were Sadi Carnot, Charles Dupin, Galois, Desormes, Raspail, and Poncelet. The lure of public life in nineteenth-century France is discussed more fully in R. Fox, "Scientific Enterprise and the Patronage of Research in France 1800-1870," *Minerva, 11* (1973)

[162]See above, pp. 119 and 128.

[163]H.V. Regnault, *Relation des expériences entreprises par ordre de Monsieur le Ministre des Travaux Publics, et sur la proposition de la Commission Centrale des Machines à Vapeur, pour déterminer les principales lois et les données numériques qui entrent dans le calcul,* 3 vols. (Paris, 1847-1870). As well as being published separately in this form, the *Relation des expériences* also occupied almost the whole of three large volumes of the *Mémoires* of the Academy of Sciences (vol. 21, 1847; vol. 26, 1862; vol. 37, parts 1 and 2, 1868-1870). The pagination is identical in the two versions.

[164]On the work of Regnault and his debt to Dumas, see Fox, *op. cit.* (note 8), pp. 283-302 and 315-317.

Sadi Carnot, Galois, Laurent, or Gerhardt, he was in every sense a man of the scientific establishment, as the honor that was accorded him both inside France and, to a lesser extent, in the rest of Europe shows clearly enough;[165] and it is for this reason that a study of his career is unusually revealing. In nearly all respects he was ideally placed to participate in one of the most exciting developments in nineteenth-century physics—the discovery of the principle of the conservation of energy in the 1840's. Unlike many of his contemporaries in France, he had every material facility, in terms of laboratory equipment and assistance, that he could possibly have desired (because of generous government sponsorship), and by 1840, owing to his membership in the Academy of Sciences and his chair in chemistry at the École Polytechnique, he had the eminence and prestige to make his views felt. Moreover, he had the close familiarity with the operation of steam engines that seems to have been one of the most important elements in the intellectual makeup of the discoverers of the energy conservation principle.[166] Yet he failed; and he failed not only to make the discovery of the principle himself but also to appreciate its true significance when it had been made by others. Even by the mid-1850's Regnault recognized all too clearly the harm he had done himself by his preoccupation with experimenting, when he saw, sadly but too late, that the main course of physics had passed him by.[167] He was, I believe, a tragic figure, and he knew it only too well.

## 5. CONCLUSION

I have argued in this paper that between the end of the First Empire and the middle of the nineteenth century there occurred a highly significant change of style in French physical science. The change began, im-

[165]See Fox, op. cit. (note 8), pp. 299–300; also my article on Regnault in a forthcoming volume of the Dictionary of Scientific Biography (note 81). Regnault's was one of the few laboratories in France to attract students from abroad about the middle of the century. In addition to the students listed in Regnault, op. cit. (note 163), 2, ix, the young William Thomson worked there in 1845; see S.P. Thompson, The Life of William Thomson, Baron Kelvin of Largs, 2 vols. (London, 1910), 1, 122–133.

[166]See T.S. Kuhn, "Energy Conservation as an Example of Simultaneous Discovery," in M. Clagett, ed., Critical Problems in the History of Science (Madison, 1959), pp. 329–336.

[167]His disappointment can be observed in his comments in Regnault, op. cit. (note 163), 2, iii and iv. Here, as also in vol. 1, p. 12, it is apparent that Regnault had seriously underestimated the magnitude of his task. His tone was certainly not that of someone content with his achievements.

mediately after 1815, with a sharp reaction against the leading tradition of the Napoleonic era. This reaction seems to have stimulated rather less than a decade of great creativity in physics, in which period scientists, along with many other French intellectuals of the day, apparently breathed more freely than they had done before 1815. But, in a way that remains to be analyzed in detail, enthusiasm and excitement were quickly dissipated and, despite the initial high promise, consolidation of the achievements of the first ten years of the Restoration period was not achieved.

This interpretation of the course of French physics in the first half of the nineteenth century leads naturally to a somewhat equivocal view of the achievements of the Napoleonic period. Of course, it is impossible to discredit completely an approach to physics that was capable of stimulating equally experimental work (such as Delaroche and Bérard's determination of the specific heats of gases, which remained standard until the 1820's), the highly sophisticated theoretical studies of Biot, Poisson, Malus, and Laplace himself, and at least one major discovery (polarization). Nor can it be doubted that these achievements owed much to the effectiveness of the highly centralized organizational structure that was developed in the period and that allowed Laplace, Berthollet, and their *protégés* to work together as one of the most closely knit schools in the whole history of science. But by the same token we must also observe certain grave weaknesses both in the content and in the strategy of Laplacian physics, as this was pursued under Napoleon. These weaknesses are to be seen in the excessively firm adherence to doctrines which, because their basic principles were open to such serious objection, were almost bound to be attacked and discredited once the influence of the Arcueil group waned. Certainly to scientists working during the First Empire, as to Pasteur a half century later, the years of Napoleonic rule were glorious ones for science.[168] But the historian, I believe, must take a different view. For he would merit no charge of writing Whig history if he were to assess many of the theoretical studies of the great mathematical physicists of the school of Laplace as little more than spectacular *tours de force* based on models that had largely outlived their usefulness. In fact, I would maintain that, far from being uniformly glorious, the period of Laplacian domination was

[168]The point cannot be missed in, for example, the annual reports on the work of the First Class of the Institute, published in the *Mémoires* of the Class. And it is explicit in J.B.J. Delambre, *Rapport historique sur les progrès des sciences mathématiques depuis 1789, et sur leur état actuel* (Paris, 1810), especially pp. 1–3 and 40–42, and in Cuvier's companion volume for the *sciences naturelles,* also published in 1810, especially pp. 389–394.

one in which French physics (and to a lesser extent chemistry) suffered from the imposition of theories, notably the theories of imponderable fluids, which were not only incapable of internal development but also quite inappropriate for the stimulation, or even the effective study, of the new experimental results that were transforming the physical sciences in the early years of the nineteenth century. It is worth noting, for example, that although, over a forty-year period that embraced the First Empire, Coulomb and Poisson between them were able to formulate the classic theories of static electricity and dipole magnetism, thereby completing a characteristically eighteenth-century research tradition, the exciting new field of electrochemistry had its origins not in France but in Britain, Germany, and Scandinavia. Significantly, too, it was in England that the freer, if less stimulating, intellectual climate allowed serious criticism of the imponderables of heat and light to get under way by the first years of the nineteenth century (in the writings of Rumford, Davy, and Young).

Hence I would suggest that the physical scientists of Napoleonic France had their notable successes when grappling with the outstanding problems of the eighteenth century. In the newer fields of research, by contrast, it is the paucity of their contributions that is remarkable.

In later life Arago recalled how the orthodoxy at Arcueil had been so rigid that at first he had not even dared to voice his support for the wave theory of light.[169] And in his biographical sketch of Gay-Lussac, read in 1851, he said of the Arcueil circle:

> For young men beginning in science it was a distinctly flattering situation to have, as the first judges and advisers in their work, men of European renown, such as Laplace, Berthollet, Humboldt, etc. But could one be sure that some preconceived ideas, which the best minds adopt more readily in what I may term an intimate gathering than before a large audience, were not such as to stifle the spontaneity of genius and to limit research to generally agreed problems? Also, was it not inevitable that the wish to display a fertile mind in the presence of the most famous *savants* of the day would sometimes lead men of lively intellect to commit themselves to rash theories?[170]

These comments, like much that Arago wrote, have a strong element of contentiousness and they cannot be accepted uncritically as reliable evidence. They ignore some of the great strengths of Arcueil. There were

[169]See note 94.
[170]*Oeuvres complètes de François Arago* (note 131), *3*, 33–34.

great leaders (albeit leaders steeped in the traditions of an age that was rapidly coming to a close), and under them there was a distinguished school of young men whose common objective gave their work at least coherence and momentum. But, in pointing to the way in which exclusiveness could lead all too easily to the perpetuation of "preconceived" doctrines that inhibited new research, Arago surely identified the Achilles' heel of Napoleonic science.

Of course, the weaknesses were not evident in the years of the Empire. The long-acknowledged distinction of Laplace and Berthollet, their influence, and their considerable personal fortunes (for which they had Napoleon, above all others, to thank[171]) allowed their control over teaching, research, and the careers of the rising generation to go unchecked and gave them every opportunity to pursue their own ambitions in science and to create an indebtedness and natural allegiance on the part of the young men who formed their school. But the situation in which they held such power, both directly (by the provision of research facilities at Arcueil) and indirectly (by their ability to manipulate the Institute and teaching institutions for their own advantage), was an unstable one, as was proved when, from 1815, the authority of the Arcueil school was seriously challenged for the first time.

In its suddenness and in its effectiveness the challenge of the years immediately after 1815 was remarkable, and it can only be explained by reference to a quite fortuitous combination of circumstances. I have referred already to Laplace's personal unpopularity following the Restoration; and the diminished income of the masters of Arcueil also had an effect, in that it made private patronage of research on a large scale impossible.[172] But perhaps the most important changes that accompanied

[171]On the incomes of Laplace and Berthollet, which exceeded 50,000 francs p.a. during the Empire, see Crosland, *op. cit.* (note 4), pp. 69–74. This figure should be compared with the 6000 francs paid to the permanent secretaries of the First Class of the Institute and to professors at the École Polytechnique. According to a letter cited in J.B. Morrell, "Science and Scottish University Reform: Edinburgh in 1826," *The British Journal for the History of Science,* 6 (1972–1973), 51 (note 54), John Leslie was impressed to find Laplace and Berthollet with incomes of between £5000 and £6000 each when he visited Paris in 1814. At the current rate of exchange, this suggests an income in each case of over 100,000 francs p.a. Salaries paid to them as Senators (positions accorded them by Napoleon in 1799) were their chief source of income.

[172]By February 1816 Berthollet's income was reduced to 24,000 francs; see Crosland, *op. cit.* (note 4), p. 400. For a comment on the lack of research schools after the Restoration see note 115 of Fox, "Scientific Enterprise and the Patronage of Research" (note 161).

the Restoration were those that resulted simply from the passage of time. From 1815, when he was sixty-six, until his death in 1822, Berthollet increasingly felt the burden of old age and ill health;[173] and time had the even more important effect of bringing maturity, status, and the possibility of independent thought and action to men who once would have seen the favor and patronage of Arcueil as the surest way to success in research and in their careers as teachers.

However, even these changed conditions would not have sufficed to cause the sudden rejection of Laplacian orthodoxy. For this overthrow to come about, the old order had to be tested, and it was unfortunate for Laplace and his remaining disciples that so many major issues arose over such a short period of time. It was quite by chance, of course, that Fresnel emerged from isolation just when influential encouragement and a sympathetic audience were awaiting him in Paris. And the discovery of Dulong and Petit's law and Oersted's discovery of the magnetic effect of an electric current were likewise chance events which could easily have occurred before 1815 but which then would not have had the corrosive effect that they did have between 1815 and 1825.

So it was that one of the most distinguished schools in the history of physical science collapsed. As a research school it was impressive both for the boldness of the program that gave it coherence and purpose and for the enterprise with which its leaders sought to give it institutional strength. As an illustration of the power of "totalitarianism" in science, it is perhaps without equal, and for the historian seeking to explain, for example, why the French persisted so long and so keenly in their adherence to the theories of imponderable fluids, it displays the dark side of totalitarianism. For in the perpetuation of ideas that were kept immune from rigorous criticism at a time when reappraisal could have been beneficial there lay the dangers of the orthodoxy that Laplace and his followers tried to impose on French science.

[173]Crosland, op. cit. (note 4), pp. 398–401. See also Berthollet's letters to Berzelius, dated 20 December 1819 and 4 September 1820, in Berzelius Bref (note 100), Pt. 1, 1, 70 and 73.

# Fresnel and the Emergence of Physics as a Discipline

BY ROBERT H. SILLIMAN*

"I think I have proved that light is propagated by the undulations of an infinitely subtle fluid diffused in space, and it is to the demonstration of this great principle that I have been particularly attached. It is the end towards which I have directed all my efforts."[1] In lines concluding an early paper on diffraction, the French engineer Augustin Jean Fresnel sounded the theme of his brief but brilliant career in science. From his first optical experiments in 1815 to his death twelve years later, the problem of the nature of light was his foremost concern. Ignorant of the findings of Thomas Young, he embarked on his investigations with a mere *aperçu* that light is undulatory. Step by step he elaborated this simple surmise into a comprehensive mathematical theory confirmed by experiment. Unlike the polymath Young, Fresnel put all his intellectual resources into the development of wave optics. His success, moreover, owed much to his intense concentration and singleness of purpose.

This is not to say that Fresnel's career is significant for the history of optics alone, even though when viewed in this limited context his work is sufficiently important to merit more detailed study than it has received.[2] Here I want to consider Fresnel's optics in a wider frame of reference, in its relationship to the whole of physics. Sloughing off the conventions of natural philosophy, physics in the first half of the nineteenth century emerged as a unified, autonomous discipline and acquired the status of a profession. Fresnel's career coincided with an early stage of this revolutionary development and affords an instructive vantage point for examining certain of its features. His scientific concerns testify to the role of theoretical and methodological factors in the rise of the physics discipline. Because of the meagerness of surviving biographical details, his career does

*Department of History, Emory University, Atlanta, Georgia 30322.

[1] Augustin-Jean Fresnel, "Supplément au deuxième mémoire sur la diffraction," *Oeuvres complètes d'Augustin Fresnel,* eds. Henri Senarmont, Emile Verdet, and Léonor Fresnel, 3 vols. (Paris, 1866–1870), *1,* 169–170.

[2] The most comprehensive treatment is Emile Verdet's excellent introduction to the collected works, *ibid.,* pp. ix–xcix. Additional references are cited in Robert H. Silliman, "Fresnel, Augustin Jean," *Dictionary of Scientific Biography,* ed. Charles Coulston Gillispie (New York, 1972 -), *5,* 171.

not greatly illuminate the part played in the rise of the discipline by social and institutional factors such as the growth of the physics community, the expansion of educational and employment opportunities for physicists, and the appearance of specialized physics journals and associations.[3] Although these "external" factors would need to be considered in a full assessment of the transformation of physics, I will not discuss them here. Without minimizing their importance, I would suggest that conceptual factors—changes in theoretical orientation and methodological standards— merit special attention. Had these changes not occurred, there would still have been a community of physicists, but physics itself would have been something less than a distinct specialty based on common interests, common conceptual commitments, and common procedures.[4]

The developments in question can be briefly summarized. At the end of the eighteenth century physics was still an immature, undisciplined pursuit with indefinite limits and little cohesiveness among its various concerns. The main source of disunity was the unequal development of its two chief divisions: general physics, equivalent to mechanics, and particular physics, embracing the study of heat, light, electricity, magnetism, and other special properties of matter. Whereas the former was a coherent, exacting, quantitative science, the latter, otherwise referred to as experimental physics, was essentially a miscellany of empirical findings joined to a loose array of speculative theories. Physics emerged as a discipline when these two components came into closer accord, facilitated by two significant developments within particular physics. First, there was a gain in methodological sophistication, entailing improved experimental design, wider, more intensive use of mathematics, and greater philosophical astuteness in matters of theory construction and verification. As a result, particular physics was lifted above the level of mere empiricism and was submitted to standards of rigor comparable to those of mechanics. The second development, not unrelated to the first, was the rise of the ideas of energy and energy conservation, which allowed the theories of particular physics to be related to one another and to the laws of mechanics. Through these and other devel-

<hr>

[3] As far as I know, there are no studies devoted to the rise of the international physics community in the nineteenth century. One recently published source that might be used in such a study is L. Pearce Williams, ed., *The Selected Correspondence of Michael Faraday*, 2 vols. (Cambridge, 1971).

[4] This is the meaning I attach to the term "discipline." On the relationship of a scientific community to its paradigms, see Thomas S. Kuhn, *The Structure of Scientific Revolutions*, 2nd ed. (Chicago, 1970), pp. 176–181, especially the remark (p. 179) that there was no physics community before the mid-nineteenth century.

opments the old disparities were sharply reduced, and physics coalesced into a mature, unified science.

In the context of these developments Fresnel's work acquires broader significance. From the start of his career his scientific interests centered on particular physics, and his reform of optics was undertaken out of dissatisfaction with the whole scheme of imponderable fluids that supplied its theoretical foundations. As his research proceeded, he continued to believe that a demonstration of the wave nature of light would lead to a fundamental reordering of physics. Dissatisfied with the theoretical content of particular physics, he was also critical of its methods and approach. His own investigations, taking the form of a continuous interplay between observation and theory and effectively balancing mathematics with experiment, set a new standard. As he had clearly foreseen, the establishment of the wave theory of light stimulated a reevaluation of other classes of physical phenomena. Heat and electromagnetism came to be seen as due to vibrations or undulations. Most important, the new emphasis on motion at the expense of matter helped set the stage for the development of the energy concept. Wave optics, of course, was not the only factor in this development; other factors included German nature philosophy and work in mechanics, heat, and physiology, especially the contributions of Joule, Mayer, and Helmholtz. Moreover, in assessing Fresnel's contribution, it is important to note that the energy concept matured two decades after his death and that his role in its formulation was indirect. With the wave theory of light, Fresnel made the first successful assault on the physics of imponderables and inaugurated the new physics of vibrations, and that is his notable contribution.[5]

## 1. PHYSICS IN THE EIGHTEENTH CENTURY

In assessing physics at the beginning of the nineteenth century, one should begin with the history of the term itself. In its origins "physics" meant simply the knowledge of natural things or the study of nature. Closely associated with Aristotle's treatise of that name, the term retained its broad meaning through the seventeenth century Scientific Revolution;

[5] That wave optics had a major impact on scientific thought in the early nineteenth century has been noted previously. See, for example, Stephen G. Brush, "The Wave Theory of Heat: A Forgotten Stage in the Transition from the Caloric Theory to Thermodynamics," *British Journal for the History of Science*, 5 (1970), 145–167; and Joseph Agassi, "Sir John Herschel's Philosophy of Success," *Historical Studies in the Physical Sciences, 1* (1969), 1–36.

and as late as the middle of the eighteenth century the narrowing of its scope had hardly begun. A brief entry in the first edition of the *Encyclopaedia Britannica* in 1771 read: "Physics, a denomination sometimes given to natural philosophy."[6] If the British preferred to speak of natural philosophy and the French of *la physique,* the terms were strictly equivalent. As characterized by d'Alembert in his article on physics in the *Encyclopédie,* "this science, which is sometimes also called *natural philosophy,* is the science of the properties of natural bodies, their phenomena, and their effects, as well as their different affections, motions, etc."[7] In both French and English this usage continued well into the nineteenth century.

Meanwhile, increasing specialization within science began to promote a more restricted conception of physics. It might be supposed that the new conception followed from a consolidation of those concerns that we now allot to physics. In part this was the case, but other developments were no less important. Other sciences were becoming specialized and breaking away from natural philosophy; physics was simply what remained. The evolution of the French *physique* illustrates the specialization process. The delimitation of the term seems to have begun when the subjects belonging to natural history were excluded from its scope. Devoted to the three "kingdoms" of nature, natural history was not a unified, coherent discipline, and yet, due to the popular writings of Linnaeus, Buffon, and others, it attracted special attention and acquired an independent standing. Generally it did not figure in definitions of physics by the end of the eighteenth century. Monge and his fellow academicians who published their *Dictionnaire de physique* in 1793 found a curious way to advertise the new conception.[8] At the very beginning of the dictionary they entered two articles, on *abdomen* and *abeille,* merely to point out that subjects belonging to anatomy or natural history have no place in a work on physics; indeed, except for these two articles, they did not include any biological subjects.

The *Dictionnaire* does include chemical topics, and not surprisingly. Indeed, for several more decades chemistry continued to be classed under

[6] *Encyclopaedia Britannica,* 3 vols. (Edinburgh, 1771), *3,* 478.

[7] Jean Lerond d'Alembert, "Physique," *Encyclopédie, ou Dictionnaire raisonné des sciences, des arts et des métiers, par une société de gens de lettres. Mis en ordre et publié par M. Diderot; et quant à la partie mathématique, par M. d'Alembert,* 36 vols. (Lausanne and Berne, 1780–1782), *25,* 701.

[8] Gaspard Monge, Jean-Dominique Cassini, Pierre Bertholon, *et al., Dictionnaire de physique* (Paris, 1793). This was the first volume on physics for the *Encyclopédie Méthodique;* three subsequent volumes listing Monge as the principal author and bearing the title *Encyclopédie Méthodique. Physique* appeared over the years 1816–1822.

physics, at least where formal definitions were concerned. Philosophers of science sought a logical basis on which to establish the autonomy of chemistry, but without conclusive success. The problem was still unresolved when Comte took it up in 1835 in the second volume of his *Cours de philosophie positive*.[9] In fact it was the practical considerations of chemists that proved decisive; through the efforts of Lavoisier and his associates, chemistry became an independent science. In actual usage *chimie* was dissociated from *physique*.

*Physique*, then, came to denote all the scientific concerns outside the province of natural history and chemistry. But what essentially was physics? French discussions of the question attached fundamental importance to the distinction between *physique générale* and *physique particulière*. Considered formally, the first science was concerned with the properties belonging to all bodies; namely, extension, impenetrability, mobility, inertia, and gravity. The second science was concerned with the properties or effects distinguishing bodies from one another such as hardness, opacity, and magnetism.[10] In the practical sense *physique générale* meant Newtonian mechanics or rather the whole legacy of mathematical science derived from the *Principia*, whereas *physique particulière* had a special relationship to Newton's *Opticks*. The approach of *physique particulière* was experimental and hypothetical, and the broad scope of its subject matter matched that of the "Queries" of the *Opticks*. Initially chemistry and natural history belonged to *physique particulière;* and long after the word "physics" was understood in a more limited sense, the designation "physical sciences" was applied, within the Paris Academy of Sciences, to chemistry, mineralogy, anatomy, and zoology, recalling their earlier affiliation. Under the narrower conception, *physique particulière* usually brought to mind the study of sound, heat, light, electricity, and magnetism.

Although the branches of what we have come to understand as "physics" were marked off toward the end of the eighteenth century, physics was not yet a well-integrated scientific specialty. Above all, the division between general physics and particular physics presented a divergence of outlook and approach, and until the two were brought into closer relationship there was little sense of a unified discipline. Resting on a few fundamental principles and elaborated in a rigorous fashion, mechanics stood at a high level of development and was regarded as a model science. Clearly

[9] Auguste Comte, *Cours de philosophie positive*, 5th ed., 6 vols. (Paris, 1907–1908), 2, 203–208.

[10] See, for example, Denis Diderot, "Explication détaillée du système des connoissances humaines," *Encyclopédie, op. cit.* (note 7), *1*, xcv.

changes had to occur within particular physics or, as it was more commonly called, experimental physics, a weak partner to mechanics.

The immaturity of experimental physics was not due to lack of effort on the part of physicists. Throughout the eighteenth century experimental physics had its dedicated practitioners and enthusiastic public following. In France the vogue of experimental physics began early in the century when a rather feeble native tradition in experimental science was reinforced by influences from England and Holland.[11] Inspired particularly by the Dutch Newtonians, a succession of French scientists led by the Abbé Nollet applied themselves to experimental physics, and interest grew rapidly.[12] Popular surveys, dictionaries, and manuals were published in great numbers; chairs were established in colleges and universities, and informal lecture series were available to the public. Judged by its scope alone, the attention devoted to experimental physics was impressive. Yet in terms of significant contributions to scientific advance, the results were disappointing; and toward the end of the century some of the interest in experimental physics seems to have fallen off.

Among French scientists the declining situation in experimental physics became a matter of concern. In 1785 the chemist Lavoisier charged that experimental physics was "almost entirely neglected."[13] Distressed that it had never been represented in the organization of the Academy of Sciences, he led the reform that introduced it; but his efforts did little to allay the prevailing uneasiness. Ironically, the decline in experimental physics was commonly attributed to chemistry's monopoly of scientific talent. As Delambre wrote in 1808 in his report on the mathematical sciences, "the revolution occurring in chemistry during our time could not have taken place without diverting our physicists somewhat from their usual investigations, since they saw a career opening up in a neighboring science which promised more numerous discoveries."[14] More encouraging was Cuvier's complementary report on the natural sciences, which covered various aspects of experimental physics under the heading of general chem-

---

[11] Pierre Brunet, *Les physiciens hollandais et la méthode expérimentale en France au XVIIIè siècle* (Paris, 1926).

[12] Jean Torlais, "La physique expérimentale," *Enseignement et diffusion des sciences en France au XVIIIè siècle,* ed. René Taton (Paris, 1964), pp. 619–645.

[13] Antoine-Laurent Lavoisier, "Notice relative à l'Académie des Sciences," *Oeuvres de Lavoisier,* ed. Jean-Baptiste Dumas and Edouard Grimaux, 6 vols. (Paris, 1862–1893), *4,* 559.

[14] Jean-Baptiste-Joseph Delambre, *Rapport historique sur les progrès des sciences mathématiques depuis 1789 et sur leur état actuel* (Paris, 1810), pp. 31–32.

istry.[15] But this connection of physics and chemistry gave another reason for concern. In the view of Libes, a professor in the *écoles centrales* of Paris, a clear indication of the weakness of physics was that its proper sphere had been divided up among chemists and mathematicians.[16] He said that without spurning the aid of chemistry and mathematics, physicists should take the work of physics back into their own hands. He hoped in this way that they would be more adept with it than they had been in the past.

For Libes, Nollet symbolized what had gone wrong with physics. Although Nollet had performed a positive service in substituting experimental physics for the speculative physics of Descartes, he had been overzealous. Hasty and uncritical, neglecting mathematics, he had built nothing solid. Under the "perfidious name of experimental physics," physics had become the "plaything of childhood and the instrument of charlatanism."[17] In reviving physics, a more rigorous approach and more attention to theory were needed. Libes wrote in 1801:

> Let us add a word in favor of theories, which certain physicists still dare to present as invincible obstacles to the discovery of truth. It is incontestable that experience and observation ought to serve as the basis of our physical knowledge. But without the help of theory the most well-certified experiments, the most numerous observations will be only isolated facts in the hands of the physicist, isolated facts which cannot serve for the advancement of physics. The man of genius must seize upon these scattered links and bring them together skillfully to form a continuous chain. This continuity constitutes the theory, which alone can give us a glimpse of the relations which bind the facts to one another and of their dependence on the causes which have produced them.[18]

In its consideration of "imponderables," experimental physics did concern itself with theory. By the end of the eighteenth century the sensible effects of heat, light, electricity, and magnetism were generally referred to the action of distinct, imponderable fluids. Endowed with forces of attraction and repulsion, these fluids had an obvious analogy with ordinary ponderable matter. With the development of this "materialist" analogy the

---

[15] Georges Cuvier, *Rapport historique sur les progrès des sciences naturelles depuis 1789 et sur leur état actuel* (Paris, 1810), pp. 16–67.

[16] Antoine Libes. *Traité élémentaire de physique*, 3 vols. (Paris, 1801), *1*, v.

[17] *Ibid.*, p. viii.

[18] *Ibid.*, p. xii.

doctrines of the *Opticks* and the *Principia* were brought together in a comprehensive, harmonious conception of the natural world.[19] In view of their role in a broad Newtonian conception, the fluid theories had an understandable appeal; and in specific instances they proved their value in guiding research and correlating disparate experimental facts.

Yet, on the whole, the scheme of imponderables testifies to a certain immaturity of physics. By this I mean that the imponderable theories, by being imprecise and largely gratuitous, fell short of the scientific standards even of the eighteenth century. Hypothetical fluids were multiplied to explain an ever-widening circle of phenomena. Analogous modes of action gave them a resemblance to one another, but their multiplicity conflicted with the presumed unity and simplicity of nature. Moreover, any individual fluid theory tended to explain too much; it was formed by transferring to the fluid the properties of the sensible bodies it was supposed to account for, and it grew in complexity with the addition of ad hoc hypotheses. There were still other difficulties; typically the theory was incapable of making predictions and was subject to no precise tests; and quantification was limited. A recognition of these deficiencies was an important motivation behind the reordering of physics early in the nineteenth century.

## 2. THE ORIGINS OF FRESNEL'S WAVE THEORY OF LIGHT

If Fresnel took pride in the general quality of the education he received at the École Polytechnique, he had good reason to be dissatisfied with his preparation in physics.[20] Physics rated low in the educational priorities of the school and was accorded none of the attention lavished on mathematics, mechanics, and chemistry. In contrast with the strong offerings in these subjects, physics was represented by a single and rather ineffectual course. Taught by the veteran chemist Hassenfratz, the course extended

[19] On the meaning of "materialist" as applied to eighteenth-century natural philosophy, see Robert E. Schofield, *Mechanism and Materialism. British Natural Philosophy in an Age of Reason* (Princeton, 1970). A comparable work on France is needed.

[20] For bibliographic references to the École Polytechnique, see Frederick B. Artz, *The Development of Technical Education in France, 1500–1850* (Cambridge, Mass., 1966), p. 152, n. 66. Other useful studies for the period include W.A. Smeaton, "The Early History of Laboratory Instruction in Chemistry at the École Polytechnique, Paris, and Elsewhere," *Annals of Science, 10* (1954), 224–233; and L. Pearce Williams, "Science, Education and Napoleon I," *Isis, 47* (1956), 369–382. Fresnel attended the École Polytechnique from 1804 to 1806. Details on his life are sparse; the fullest biographical account is still Arago's *éloge*, in *Oeuvres complètes d'Augustin Fresnel, op. cit.* (note 1), *3*, 475–526.

over two years and covered a miscellany of topics: the general properties of bodies, heat, meteorology, electricity, and magnetism in the first year; and light, sound, and "the system of the world" in the second.[21] The course was elementary in content, loosely organized, and poorly taught.[22]

The treatment of optics in particular seems to have been rudimentary and incoherent. Hassenfratz used as text La Caille's old *Leçons élémentaires d'optique* (1750), haphazardly revised by "several students" of the Polytechnique and reissued in 1802.[23] Conceived with practical emphasis, the text is brief in scope and empirical in orientation. In its treatment of optics, it stresses geometrical optics, vision, and optical instruments, and pays scant attention to chromatic phenomena. In a note to the text the problem of the nature of light is posed, but left unresolved; elsewhere the corpuscular hypothesis is presupposed.[24] For optical theory, students depended on Hassenfratz' lectures, which inculcated an orthodox Newtonian viewpoint. A notebook dating from 1813–1814, eight years after Fresnel took the course, indicates that Hassenfratz explained refraction in terms of the attraction of luminous corpuscles, explained the phenomena of colored rings by Newton's theory of fits, and explained polarization effects by the polarity or "sidedness" of light particles.[25] He showed that double refraction was accurately represented by Huygens' construction employing

[21]*Correspondance sur l'École Polytechnique, 1* (1804), 5. Jean-Henri Hassenfratz (1755–1827) had figured in the Revolution as a radical Jacobin and member of the Paris Commune and was known primarily for his work in metallurgy and mineralogy. Further details on the contents of his course are given in a speech he delivered at the beginning of classes in the winter of 1799: *Journal de l'École Polytechnique, 2*, cahier 6 (1799), 236–242. See also, Etienne Barruel, *La physique réduite en tableux raisonnés, ou programme du cours de physique fait à l'École Polytechnique* (Paris, 1799).

[22]The ineffectiveness of Hassenfratz as a teacher seems to have been absolute. See the comments of François Arago, "Histoire de ma jeunesse," *Oeuvres de François Arago*, 12 vols. (Paris, 1854–1859), *1*, 12–13; Jean-Louis Rieu, *Mémoires* (Geneva and Basle, 1870), p. 19; and Auguste Comte, quoted in Henri Gouhier, *La jeunesse d'Auguste Comte et la formation du positivisme. I. Sous le signe de la liberté* (Paris, 1933), p. 99.

[23]Nicolas-Louis de La Caille, *Traité d'optique par Lacaille. Nouvelle édition, revue, corrigée et augmentée, particulierèment de la marche des images dans les instruments d'optique, des lunettes acromatiques et de l'iris; par plusieurs élèves de l'École Polytechnique* (Paris, 1802).

[24]*Ibid.*, p. 20.

[25]André Chappert, "L'introduction des vibrations transversales dans l'oeuvre de Fresnel" (Unpublished study submitted for the Diplôme d'Études Supérieures de Philosophie, University of Paris, 1966), pp. 20–21. Chappert does not further identify the notebook, which is in the manuscript collection of the École Polytechnique. See also the references to optics in Hassenfratz, *loc. cit.*, and Barruel, *op. cit.* (note 21).

spherical and ellipsoidal waves, but he emphasized that the geometry alone was valid, not the physical hypothesis. What Fresnel made of such incongruities is unknown, but later he remarked that his doubts about the corpuscular theory began at the École Polytechique.[26]

For about eight years he apparently made no serious effort to resolve these doubts. Commissioned an engineer in the Corps des Ponts et Chaussées and assigned to road construction in the provinces, he could devote only spare hours to science. Over the years he took up a variety of scientific and technical problems, but in one inquiry after another his hopes of making a significant discovery were frustrated. After trying chemistry he finally fixed his attention on the problem of the nature of heat and light. In a letter to his brother in July 1814 he announced his new interest and his dissent from established views. Attacking the materiality of both heat and light, he suggested an alternative view that embraced heat and light and hopefully more:

> I tell you I am very tempted to believe in the vibrations of a special fluid for the transmission of light and heat. One would explain the uniformity of the speed of light as one explains that of sound; and one would perhaps see in the derangements of the equilibrium of this fluid the cause of electric phenomena. One would easily conceive why a body loses so much heat without losing its weight, why the sun has illuminated us for so long a time without diminishing in volume, etc.[27]

This bare suggestion immediately engrossed Fresnel's attention and started him on his optical investigations.

It seems likely that his reasons for questioning the scheme of imponderables went beyond his stated objections. Explicitly he cited as evidence against the imponderable theories only the above commonplace observations, plus one or two others associated with the quantities of heat and light released during chemical combustion. In all this there was nothing especially novel or decisive. He might in addition have been influenced by the more substantial evidence against the imponderables recently advanced by Rumford, Herschel, Young, and others; but he gave no indication he was familiar with their work, and his admission of ignorance about the meaning of "polarization" in another letter in 1814 shows how little he knew of current scientific developments.[28] Nor apparently was he in-

---

[26]Fresnel to Léonor Fresnel, 5 July 1814, *Oeuvres, op. cit.* (note 1), *2*, 820.

[27]*Ibid.*, pp. 821–822.

[28]On 15 May 1814 he wrote to his brother Léonor: "Je voudrais bien avoir aussi des mémoires qui me missent au fait des découvertes des physiciens français sur la polarisation de la lumière. J'ai vu dans le Moniteur, il y a quelques mois, que Biot

debted to German nature philosophy, another possible ground for opposing the imponderable fluid theories.[29] Although there are a few hints—his
"spiritualist" position in psychology and his friendship with Ampère—that
he may have had some interest in German idealism, that interest left no
trace on his physics.[30]

What his physics does show is his commitment to the philosophy of the
Enlightenment. Combining English empiricism and Cartesian rationalism,
his approach to physics followed the tradition of the *Discours préliminaire*.
Like d'Alembert he believed that scientific knowledge must be rooted in
experience, but again like d'Alembert he was haunted by the ideal of a universal deductive science in which all particulars are logically subordinated
to the fewest and most general principles possible.[31] His Cartesianism may
have predisposed him to take an anti-Newtonian stand in physics; undoubtedly the Cartesian ideal of the unity of knowledge supplied a basis
for his dissent from the scheme of imponderables.

One thing Fresnel learned at the École Polytechnique was an appreciation for theory. In sharp contrast with the radical empiricists he regarded
theory as the proper goal of science and as an indispensable instrument for
scientific progress. Mere observation plus sagacity may lead to important

---

avait lu à l'Institut un mémoire fort intéressant sur la *polarisation de la lumière*. J'ai
me casser la tête, je ne devine pas ce que c'est" (*ibid.*, p. 819). Two months later he
still knew nothing about polarization. Frantic with curiosity, he issued another plea
for information (*ibid.*, pp. 826–827).

[29] For the relationship between *Naturphilosophie* and the physical sciences, see
L. Pearce Williams, *Michael Faraday. A Biography* (New York, 1965), pp. 60–73, and
*The Origins of Field Theory* (New York, 1966), pp. 32–63; and Gerhard Hennemann,
*Naturphilosophie im 19. Jahrhundert* (Freiburg and Munich, 1959). Some cautions to
be observed in attributing scientific influences to Romanticism have been discussed by
D.M. Knight, "The Physical Sciences and the Romantic Movement," *History of
Science, 9* (1970), 54–75.

[30] Around 1811 Fresnel drafted an essay on psychology. While it has not survived,
his brother Léonor reported that it "développe les principaux arguments sur lesquels
se fonde la doctrine spiritualiste, dont il fut toujours ardent défenseur" (*Oeuvres,
op. cit.* [note 1], *2*, 811, n. b.). The allusion is quite vague, but it may be that
Fresnel's spiritualism had affinities with the voluntarism of Maine de Biran and
Ampère, which owed a debt to Kant and German philosophy. See André-Marie
Ampère and Jean-Jacques Ampère, *Philosophie des deux Ampère*, ed. J. Barthélemy
Saint-Hilaire (Paris, 1866); and L. Pearce Williams, "Ampère, André-Marie," *Dictionary of Scientific Biography, op. cit.* (note 2), *1*, 140–142. The relationship between Fresnel and Ampère was close at both the personal and scientific level. See
especially the references to Fresnel and his brother Fulgence in the *Correspondance
du Grand Ampère*, ed. Louis de Launay, 3 vols. (Paris, 1936–1943), *passim*.

[31] Thomas L. Hankins, *Jean d'Alembert. Science and the Enlightenment* (Oxford,
1970), esp. chap. 5.

discoveries, but the more complex or singular laws of nature will remain hidden without the guidance of theoretical ideas.[32] Of course everything depends on the truth of the theory, and Fresnel scattered many remarks on this subject throughout his papers.

His criteria of theoretical truth were founded ultimately on a basic belief about nature, a belief he epitomized in his prize memoir on diffraction as *Natura simplex et fecunda*.[33] Nature is economical, striving to do much with little, to produce the maximum number of effects with a minimum number of causes:

> It is doubtless quite difficult [he writes] to discover the bases of this admirable economy, that is, the simplest causes envisioned under such a broad point of view. But if this general principle of the philosophy of the physical sciences does not lead immediately to knowledge of truth, it can, nevertheless, direct the efforts of the human mind by banishing systems that relate phenomena to an excessive number of different causes and by making it adopt by preference those which, supported by the fewest hypotheses, are the most prolific in consequences.[34]

Here Fresnel was concerned specifically with the theoretical foundations of optics, but there was no reason for him not to have considered a broader application of the principle of simplicity. Undoubtedly the principle prompted his general dissatisfaction with the fluid theories. The Newtonian scheme as a whole was incohesive, and its component theories constructed around individual fluids were overly complex. Any scheme or individual theory relating phenomena to so many causal factors was inherently improbable.

The weight Fresnel gave to such formal considerations is evident from his extended criticism of the corpuscular theory of light. The complexity of the corpuscular theory always bulked large in his criticism; particularly damaging were the multiple, independent hypotheses bolstering the central concept of luminous molecules. It was unsatisfactory that optical effects were explained by ascribing appropriate hypothetical characteristics to the corpuscles, every new phenomenon requiring a new hypothesis. He preferred a simpler theory, one correlating the most diverse phenomena under a general principle.

---

[32] Fresnel, "Second mémoire sur la double réfraction," *Oeuvres, op. cit.* (note 1), *2*, 484–485.
[33] Fresnel, "Mémoire sur la diffraction de la lumière," *ibid., 1*, 247.
[34] *Ibid.*, p. 249.

In adopting a wave theory of light as an alternative to the corpuscular, Fresnel's understanding of the nature of theory was again important. Prior to any detailed investigation, a theory treating light as the vibrations of a universal fluid promised to be simpler.[35] The corpuscular theory necessitated ad hoc hypotheses because the light corpuscles were autonomous and had limited potential for diversity. Aside from possessing a motion of translation, they could be thought of as rotating and as having different faces or poles; but other characteristics were difficult to imagine. A wave hypothesis, however, had a simple basis for diversity in the varied modifications that could be given a fluid composed of interdependent particles.

Fresnel suspected that the vibrations of the universal fluid—which he called caloric—had "a great influence on all the phenomena embraced by physics and chemistry."[36] Here his belief in the economy of nature was carried to its logical conclusion; he glimpsed a new unified physics in which heat, light, and other imponderable agents were only different modes of motion within a universal fluid. Such a physics would be far more credible than the Newtonian scheme with its multiplicity of independent fluids. Although Fresnel was absorbed with optics throughout his brief career, he kept abreast of developments in other branches of physics and carried out a few minor investigations of heat, electricity, and magnetism.[37] Focused on the interactions between the various imponderable agents, these researches show that he never abandoned his youthful vision of a new, unified physics. At the end of his life, when the wave theory of light was gaining support and vibratory conceptions figured prominently in interpretations of heat, electricity, and magnetism, he was able to witness a partial realization of what he had worked for.

[35] Ibid., p. 250.

[36] Fresnel, "Complément au mémoire sur la diffraction," ibid., 1, 60.

[37] Fresnel, "Note sur la répulsion que les corps échauffés exercent les uns sur les autres à des distances sensibles," ibid., 2, 667–672; "Note sur des essais ayant pour but de décomposer l'eau avec un aimant," ibid., pp. 673–676; "Notes relatives aux expériences d'Arago concernant l'influence exercée par un anneau ou disque de cuivre sur les oscillations de l'aiguille aimantée," ibid., pp. 677–680; "Comparaison de la supposition des courants autour de l'axe avec celle des courants autour de chaque molécule," Collection de mémoires relatifs à la physique, publiés par la Société Française de Physique. Tome II, Mémoires sur la électrodynamique, 2 vols. (Paris, 1885–1887), 1, 141–143; and "Deuxième note sur l'hypothèse des courants particulaires," ibid., pp. 144–147. The last two notes, which Fresnel did not publish, proposed a hypothesis that would become the basis of Ampère's electrodynamic molecular model. A passage in the first of the two notes indicates that Fresnel barely missed the discovery of electromagnetic induction.

## 3. FRESNEL'S SCIENTIFIC METHOD

It was one thing to surmise that light is undulatory; it was another to develop mathematically the hypothesis and demonstrate its conformity with experience. To accomplish this task Fresnel set himself a research agenda and worked systematically through the various classes of optical phenomena: diffraction, colored rings, reflection and refraction, polarization, double refraction, and dispersion.[38] The single question of the nature of light gave purpose and direction to his investigations; his goal was clear and his methods carried him far. Between rationalism and empiricism, the two extremes of French physics in the past, he charted a middle course. His study of light was a dynamic interplay between theory and observation, mathematics and experiment.

In the eighteenth century the universally acknowledged ideal of scientific practice was the method of analysis. Knowledge of the physical world was to be built up from experience; beginning with observations or experiments the investigator decomposed complex appearances into their simplest elements and from these proceeded inductively to a general principle. The principle was tentative; but if logical consequences drawn from it could be shown by additional experiments to conform with experience, it became more certain. The discoveries of the law of gravity and of the composition of white light by the method of analysis seemed proof of its efficacy, and Newton's authority assured the method a prominent place in eighteenth-century philosophy of science. Educated in this Enlightenment tradition at the École Polytechnique, Fresnel regarded the nature of light as a problem for analysis.

Although continually under the sway of his theoretical *idée fixe,* Fresnel had a deep respect for facts, for the test of experience. He opened and closed every phase of his study of light with experiments; he devoted more time to experimental investigations than to any other. Whenever his professional duties denied him access to a laboratory, he grew restless and badgered his superiors for leave. An ingenious and resourceful experimenter, he improvised his apparatus from odds and ends when instruments were lacking. He found new ways to display phenomena and devised new techniques of observation.[39] Careful and exacting, he focused his attention

---

[38] Fresnel made some efforts to develop a mathematical theory of dispersion at the end of his career but did not get beyond a few suggestive hypotheses, which Cauchy made use of in working out his theory. See Fresnel, "Second supplément au mémoire sur la double réfraction," *Oeuvres, op. cit.* (note 1), *2,* 438.

[39] An example is his basic innovation in diffraction experimentation. He first replaced the traditional receiving screen with a plate of ground glass and observed the

on effects that could be measured; he used the micrometer as routinely as Lavoisier used the chemical balance.

To show how Fresnel proceeded from experiment to theory, I will briefly discuss his study of diffraction. In attempting to establish a vibratory theory, diffraction phenomena were of particular interest. If it could be shown that light deviates from a rectilinear course in bending around obstacles, a major objection to the wave conception would be removed. An examination of the shadows cast by hairs, threads, and other narrow objects seemed likely to exhibit this attribute of light.

Beginning his diffraction experiments in the summer of 1815, Fresnel noted the appearance of colored fringes inside and outside the shadow.[40] The fringes had been seen before and were not in themselves decisive for or against the wave hypothesis.[41] Fresnel probed further; seeking to isolate the factors that determine the appearance of the bands, he screened the light from one side of a wire diffracter by attaching to its edge a slip of black paper. The internal fringes on both sides of the shadow disappeared; when the paper was removed, they reappeared. He concluded that the internal fringes depend on a crossing of rays inflected into the shadow from both edges of the diffracter. Since the fringes outside the shadow on the side opposite the attached paper remained, external fringes apparently arose from a crossing of rays proceeding directly from the light source and, by reflection, from one edge of the diffracter. Aided by an acoustical analogy, he now took the short step to the idea of interference. Young had come to interference by the same experiment, but Fresnel seems to have made the discovery independently. Interference gave Fresnel a conceptual device for analyzing various classes of optical phenomena, and whenever he applied it successfully he obtained new evidence for the wave nature of light. The basis for his confidence in interference was firmly established during the first phase of his investigation of diffraction.

Fresnel's interpretation of the diffraction bands in terms of the construc-

---

bands from behind it with a strong lens. Then, trying a glass plate of which only half the surface was frosted, he noted that the effects seen through his lens were the same for both halves. The glass apparently served no purpose, and thereafter the effects could be studied directly with the lens, with a considerable gain in convenience. The experimenter no longer needed to be concerned about obstructing the rays of light with his head and could make observations up to the edge of the diffracter itself. See Fresnel, "Premier mémoire sur la diffraction," *ibid., 1,* 13.

[40] *Ibid.,* pp. 9–33.

[41] Not long before, Henry Brougham had offered an interpretation of diffraction bands in terms of the corpuscular hypothesis. See his papers in *Phil. Trans., 86* (1796), 227–278, and *87* (1797), 352–384.

tive and destructive interference of waves remained inconclusive until he had put it to quantitative test. To facilitate such a test he derived simple algebraic formulas giving the positions of the internal and external bands as a function of the path differences of convergent rays of monochromatic light.[42] By the principle of interference bright bands would occur where the path differences were any even number of half wavelengths, and dark bands where the path differences were any odd number. Determining his wavelengths from Newton's intervals of successive fits of easy reflection or easy transmission and supposing the diffracter and receiving screen set at different distances from the light source, Fresnel computed theoretical values for the positions of the bands relative to the shadow. These values were in close agreement with the positions of the bands as he actually observed them.

Fresnel was gratified. He transmitted his findings to the Academy of Sciences, explaining to Delambre:

> The theory of Newton is still generally accepted. I know of no work in which it is directly attacked or where one gives, as I have done, the formulas for calculating the width of the colored fringes of the shadows. These formulas, joined to the observations by which I have verified their exactitude, appear to me to augment very much the probabilities in favor of the system where one considers light as resulting from the vibrations of caloric.[43]

The equations were suggestive indeed, but they gave Fresnel less than a complete theory of diffraction. His indiscriminate use of the terms "rays," "vibrations," "inflection," and "diffraction" indicated a residue of corpuscular influence and was symptomatic of a lack of precision in his formulation. The need for further refinement was brought home to him by the following troublesome point: the formulas, which posited rectilinear "rays" and referred path measurements to the very edge of the diffracter, predicted band positions, but only on the assumption that the rays that were turned aside at the diffracter lost a half wavelength. Without this assumption the bright bands occurred where dark ones were predicted and vice versa. Deeply committed to the simplicity principle, Fresnel was not satisfied with his ad hoc hypothesis and set out to eliminate it. The elimination entailed a major revision of his theory.

---

[42] Fresnel, "Premier mémoire sur la diffraction de la lumière," Oeuvres, op. cit. (note 1), 1, 16-19, 24.
[43] Fresnel to Delambre, 15 October 1815, ibid., p. 9.

In the next phase of his study of diffraction, Fresnel cast around for new theoretical concepts. He began by rejecting his original view "that the center of the undulation of inflected light was always at the very edge of the opaque body [the diffracter] or, in other words, that inflected light could proceed from rays that have touched its surface."[44] The alternative view was that "inflected rays take their source in direct light at a sensible distance from the opaque body." This simple introduction of new path differences in the calculation of distances to the shadow eliminated the problem of the reversal of fringes and opened the way to an explanation of diffraction that was free of arbitrary assumptions. The question he now faced was: what basis is there for believing that inflected light originates at some lateral distance from the edge of the diffracter?

Seeking an answer, Fresnel hit on the bold idea of combining Huygens' principle with the principle of interference.[45] He applied the combined principles to diffraction by supposing that elementary waves arise at every point along the arc of the wave front and, passing the diffracter, mutually interfere. The problem, then, was to determine the resultant vibration produced by all the wavelets reaching any point behind the diffracter. The mathematical difficulties were formidable. Resorting to crude approximations, Fresnel found in his first attempt that the overall effect of the mutual interference of wavelets was equivalent to an inflected ray originating at a definite distance from the edge of the diffracter and traversing a path a quarter wavelength longer than that of a ray proceeding from the edge itself. Although this hypothesis of "efficacious rays" reduced by half the discrepancy between theory and observation, Fresnel was not yet satisfied; in the paper of 15 July 1816 in which he reported the investigation he begged the critics at the Institut to treat with indulgence "his essays on such a difficult theory."[46]

Not until the spring of 1818 was he able to reach his goal. Throughout the previous year he had been concerned with polarization, but the need to cope with the periodic effects of chromatic polarization immediately reintroduced the basic mathematical problem from the study of diffraction: "calculating the influence of any number of systems of luminous waves on one another." He was now working outside the laboratory, wholly concerned with theoretical ether mechanics. Aided by an analogy

[44] Fresnel, "Supplément au deuxième mémoire sur la diffraction," *ibid.*, pp. 158–159.
[45] *Ibid.*, pp. 160–161.
[46] *Ibid.*, p. 169.

between the oscillations of an ether molecule and those of a pendulum, his analysis reached a decisive stage in his derivation of a general expression for the velocity of ether molecules set in motion by a wave.[47] Considering next the combined effect of multiple waves, he worked through to the following important result: just as a force can be resolved into perpendicular components, so the amplitude of the oscillations imparted by a wave can be reduced to the amplitudes of two superimposed waves following one another at an interval of a quarter wavelength. To find the net effect of multiple waves, then, it was sufficient to reduce each to its two components, to add like components, and to recombine the sums. Applying this result to diffraction, Fresnel derived two integrals expressing the effect at any point of the wavelets proceeding from the wave front intercepted by the diffracter.[48] The square root of the sum of their squares gave the amplitude of the resultant vibration at the point, while the sum of their squares measured the observable light intensity. This result essentially completed Fresnel's study of diffraction. The theory was now unified and coherent, requiring no auxiliary ad hoc hypotheses and meeting every test of experience.

Fresnel entered his new theory in the Academy's competition on diffraction in 1819, winning the prize. During the judging his theory received a dramatic and unexpected confirmation. One of the commissioners, Poisson, deduced from it the seemingly improbable consequence that the center of the circular shadow cast by a small diffracting disc should be brightly illuminated.[49] Fresnel carried out an experiment to test the deduction and confirmed it exactly. For him the prediction of such hidden and singular consequences was one of the clearest marks of a true theory.

Fresnel's manner of investigating diffraction was typical of his whole approach to optics. He held a preconception about the nature of light that informed all his research and that he never questioned; at the same time he observed rigorous empirical standards in developing and demonstrating his theory. Characteristically, he began with experiments that served to establish the phenomena and suggest theoretical ideas. He then cast his ideas in

---

[47] Fresnel, "Mémoire sur la diffraction de la lumière, couronné par l'Académie des Sciences," *ibid.*, pp. 286–293.

[48] *Ibid.*, pp. 313–316.

[49] François Arago, "Rapport fait par M. Arago à l'Académie des Sciences, au nom de la commission qui avait été chargée d'examiner les mémoires envoyés au concours pour le prix de la diffraction," *ibid.*, pp. 236, 245–246. The theoretical basis of Poisson's prediction is discussed by Fresnel in an appendix to the prize memoir (*ibid.*, pp. 365–372).

mathematical form and drew from them precise consequences. Finally, he verified the consequences by measuring observed effects. In his studies of diffraction and of double refraction, he moved between observation and theory many times, continually reformulating and refining the theory to give it a closer fit with experience and greater generality. Typically, his theoretical inquiries extended back to ether mechanics, which facilitated quantification and supplied mechanical underpinnings for his theory. From the point of view of method, his investigations extended from the manual operations of the laboratory to the most abstract mathematical analyses. Few physicists since Newton had been so versatile.

## 4. FRESNEL'S WAVE THEORY AND THE RISE OF ENERGETICS

In a resume of his theory published in 1822 Fresnel remarked that "for the progress of optics and everything related to it, that is to say, the whole of physics and chemistry," it was important to know whether light consists of corpuscles or the vibrations of a universal fluid.[50] A decade later, after both Young and Fresnel had died, the question of the nature of light was a prominent issue among scientists. By 1832 Fechner could say that "the undulatory theory, particularly after the development it has received from Fresnel, is beginning to win ascendancy over the emission theory."[51] If conversion to the new optics was not always acknowledged in explicit terms, the assumption of the wave theory as a framework for optical research became increasingly common. Foucault's "crucial experiment" in favor of the wave theory in 1850 merely confirmed what scientists generally believed. Developments after Fresnel validated his contention that a decision on the nature of light would have implications extending far beyond optics: apart from the influence of the wave theory in stimulating investigations of the principles of elasticity, the theory also played an important role in the general reorientation of physics associated with the rise of energetics.[52]

When Fresnel took up his first optical experiments in 1815, the shift

[50] Fresnel, "De la lumière," *ibid.*, *2*, 6. The essay appeared in a supplement to the French edition of Thomas Thomson's *System of Chemistry* (Paris, 1822).

[51] G.T. Fechner, quoted in Ferdinand Rosenberger, *Die Geschichte der Physik*, 3 vols. (Hildesheim, 1965), *3*, 188.

[52] Economy of expression has prompted me to use the term "energetics," which I will employ in a broad and somewhat unconventional sense to denote the view that heat, light, electricity, and magnetism are forms of energy and that energy is conserved.

away from the imponderable fluids had already begun. Rumford had challenged the caloric theory of heat, and Young the corpuscular theory of light. Discoveries in the new science of electrochemistry had cast doubt on the simple fluid theory of electricity.[53] As well as questioning the individual fluids, scientists had devoted more attention to the relationships between the fluids; and the laboratory had supplied evidence of previously unsuspected relationships. If Oersted's dramatic revelation of the magnetic effects of an electric current was still a few years off, investigations by Herschel and Ritter on the solar spectrum had already weakened the belief in the individuality and separateness of the fluids. Indeed, there had been widespread speculation about the underlying unity and interconvertibility of physical forces, a speculation incompatible with materialist fluid theories. Forces could undergo transformations and appear in different forms, which specific kinds of matter could not.

Fresnel's advocacy of a wave concept of light may be regarded as just another manifestation of the embryonic movement away from the physics of fluids. In a number of ways, however, his achievement appears distinctive. Where a major theoretical issue was concerned, no one before Fresnel had undertaken a direct assault on Newton and made it effective. Unlike Young, who deferred to Newton's optical authority, Fresnel denounced the *Opticks* as error-laden and superficial.[54] Although his condemnation was intemperate, Fresnel was correct in thinking that physics would benefit by liberating itself from the sway of Newton. Of course, his real quarrel was not with Newton but with the Newtonians; among the early critics of the scheme of imponderables, Fresnel was the most penetrating and thorough. He challenged corpuscular optics at all points, developing a comprehensive alternative and securing its acceptance. The establishment of the wave theory of light was the first substantial setback of the Newtonian system.

The conversion to wave optics did not merely presage the more general theoretical shift away from fluid theories; wave optics provided a powerful model for reforming the other branches of physics. By 1830 dissatisfaction with the fluid theories was widespread, and perplexed physicists were ready to give serious thought to alternatives. Since evidence of intimate relations between the various classes of physical phenomena had also grown, physicists inevitably came to focus their attention on the new theory of

[53] L. Pearce Williams, *Michael Faraday, op. cit.* (note 29), pp. 55–59.
[54] Fresnel, "Second mémoire sur la double réfraction," *Oeuvres, op. cit.* (note 1), 2, 485, n. 1.

light. Substituting process for substance, motion for matter, and continuity of action for action at a distance, the wave theory sanctioned general conceptions that could be applied elsewhere. The full extent to which wave optics influenced the development of energetics is difficult to gauge with precision, but its influence was considerable. It acted as a major stimulus in two areas of strategic importance in the energetics movement: thermodynamics and electromagnetism.

Despite the attempts of Rumford, Davy, and Young to revive the mechanical theory of heat at the turn of the century, the theory began to make significant headway only after 1830.[55] The fact that the wave theory of light was becoming established around 1830 was more than coincidence. William Herschel had noted in his paper on infrared radiation in 1800: "For, in what manner soever this radiance may be effected, it will be fully proved hereafter, that the evidence, either for rays, or for vibrations which occasion heat, stands on the same foundation on which the radiance of the illuminating principle, light, is built."[56] If light were undulatory, then heat would have to be undulatory as well. When Fresnel's theory was accepted, this argument retained its force. It appeared decisive even to Carnot, who presupposed the fluid concept of heat in his *Réflexions sur la Puissance Motrice du Feu:*

> We may be allowed to express here a hypothesis concerning the nature of heat.
>
> At present, light is generally regarded as the result of a vibratory movement of the etherial fluid. Light produces heat, or at least accompanies the radiant heat and moves with the same velocity as heat. Radiant heat is therefore a vibratory movement. It would be ridiculous to suppose that it is an emission of matter while the light which accompanies it could only be a movement.
>
> Could a motion (that of radiant heat) produce matter (caloric)?
>
> Undoubtedly no; it can only produce a motion. Heat is then the result of a motion.
>
> Then it is plain that it could be produced by the consumption of motive power and that it could produce this power.[57]

[55] Thomas S. Kuhn, "Energy Conservation as an Example of Simultaneous Discovery," *Critical Problems in the History of Science,* ed. Marshall Clagett (Madison, 1959), p. 340.

[56] William Herschel, "Experiments on the Solar, and on the Terrestrial Rays that Occasion Heat," *Phil. Trans., 90* (1800), 284.

[57] Sadi Carnot, *Reflections on the Motive Power of Fire,* ed. E. Mendoza (New York, 1960), p. 63. The quotation is from an undated manuscript.

Once the wave concept of light had helped restore prominence to the general view of heat as motion, Fresnel's theory provided guidance for a detailed exploration of the parallels between light and heat. During the 1830's Melloni and others showed that radiant heat is subject to interference, polarization, and double refraction.[58] Even the problematic transversality of light waves seemed to have a parallel. Obtaining circularly polarized heat by Fresnel's procedure for obtaining circularly polarized light, Forbes remarked: "With such evidence before me I cannot for a moment doubt that the waves (if such there be either in light or heat) produced by non-luminous hot bodies are *identical in character* with those producing light, *that is—that the vibrations are transversal.*"[59] From clues provided by Fresnel's wave optics, a comprehensive theory of radiant heat was built up in a relatively short time.

In turn, as Brush has recently demonstrated, the wave theory of heat played an important part in the establishment of the first law of thermodynamics.[60] Since the wave theory characterized heat as the vibrations of the luminiferous ether, it was not the same thing as the mechanical theory of heat, which appealed to molecular motions; but historically the wave theory served as a transition to the mechanical theory of heat. Widely adopted in the decade and a half preceding the full statement of energy conservation, the wave theory became a general theory of heat; the qualifying adjective "radiant" was dropped, habituating scientists to think of heat as motion rather than matter. In the case of Helmholtz and a few other discoverers of the principle of energy conservation, the influence of the wave theory is clear.[61]

In a less decisive way, wave optics also figured in the development of electromagnetism. Again the undulatory view of light was an inspiration for those who searched beyond the imponderables for a new type of scientific explanation. One of the searchers was Ampère, who was already a convert to Fresnel's theory when Oersted's discovery stimulated his interest in electricity. Extending Oersted's results, he first showed that current-carrying wires attract one another if the currents are in the same direction and repel if in opposite directions. This result confirmed his

[58] E. Scott Barr, "The Infrared Pioneers—I. Macedonio Melloni," *Infrared Physics, 2* (1962), 67–73; Ernst Mach, *Die Principien der Wärmelehre historisch-kritisch entwickelt* (Leipzig, 1896), p. 129.

[59] James D. Forbes, "Note respecting the Undulatory Theory of Heat, and on the Circular Polarization of Heat by Total Reflexion," *Phil. Mag., 8* (1836), 248.

[60] Brush, *op. cit.* (note 5).

[61] *Ibid.,* pp. 161–164.

surmise that current electricity is the cause of magnetism, and it supplied the factual foundation on which he built his mathematical theory of electrodynamics.

Ampère then proceeded to give his theory a basis in physics.[62] Previously he had held to Volta's contact theory of the pile, interpreting electricity as the flow of positive and negative fluids in opposite directions. This view of electricity appeared to be refuted by the new electrodynamic phenomena. Seeking an alternative view, he seized upon the ether Fresnel had introduced as a basis for the vibrations of light. Adapting the ether to his own purposes, Ampère supposed it to consist of negative and positive electricity. When a current is produced, the two electricities are separated and proceed in opposite directions. Flowing along a closed circuit, they meet and recombine; recombination is followed by decomposition, and the process continues. Accompanying the translation of electric fluids, a series of vibrations is propagated into the space surrounding the wire. If these vibrations are in phase with like vibrations sent out by a neighboring wire, the two wires will attract each other; if out of phase, they will repel. Ampère thus accounted for the magnetic effects of electric currents.

To sustain his view of the identity of electricity and magnetism, Ampère also needed to explain permanent magnetism. Here the wave theory of light could offer no assistance. Initially Ampère had decided that all the effects of permanent magnetism would be accounted for if electrical currents were imagined to circulate around the axis of the magnet. At this point Fresnel himself contributed a valuable suggestion. He recognized that the heat that one would expect to be associated with Ampère's coaxial currents was undetectable, since in general a magnet is not hotter than its surroundings. He proposed to Ampère the hypothesis that electric currents circulate around each molecule of the magnet. The hypothesis was equivalent to Ampère's in its ability to account for magnetic effects and was also consistent with the absence of heating effects.

> I will add [Fresnel remarked] that the fact that a magnet is not hot, although apparently it should be according to the hypothesis of currents around its axis, is not a difficulty in the hypothesis of currents around molecules. If a current, in traversing a mass of molecules of a conducting

---

[62] Details in the following account of Ampère's physical theory of electromagnetism are documented in L. Pearce Williams, "Ampère's Electrodynamic Molecular Model," *Contemporary Physics, 4* (1962-1963), 113-123. See also Theodore M. Brown, "The Electric Current in Early Nineteenth Century French Physics," *Historical Studies in the Physical Sciences, 1* (1969), 61-103, esp. 82-89.

body, heats it, there is no necessity to believe that currents around the molecules of a similar mass should also heat it: the circumstances are no longer the same. We know too little of the cause of heat developed by an electric current, and our ideas on the constitution of bodies are too incomplete for us to know whether electricity ought to produce heat in this case.[63]

Eagerly adopting Fresnel's idea, Ampère now had a solution to the problem of permanent magnetism and with it a comprehensive model for interpreting electromagnetic effects.

One of the critics of Ampère's theory was Michael Faraday. Since Faraday had already dismissed the imponderable fluids as an adequate explanation of electromagnetic phenomena, he was alert to new theoretical ideas. Just before his discovery of electromagnetic induction, he encountered the wave theory of light. The mathematics of the theory were a stumbling block for him, but an authoritative, nontechnical account of wave optics was available in Fresnel's "De la lumière," translated by Young in the *Quarterly Journal of Science* in 1827–1829; Faraday read the article and expressed great admiration for it.[64] He was also struck by certain passages in John Herschel's *Preliminary Discourse on the Study of Natural Philosophy* that touched on the analogies between sound and light. From Fresnel and Herschel, Faraday was led to the idea that light, sound, and electricity were analogous.

Motivated by the analogies Faraday set out to detect the electric wave. This search seems to have been the stimulus for his famous induction ring experiment carried out in August 1831.[65] The momentary deflection of the galvanometer in the secondary coil when contact between the battery and the primary coil was made or broken suggested to him that the electric wave was "apparently very short and sudden." A few months later Faraday found that electricity could be induced by simply thrusting a bar magnet in and out of a wire helix. He then succeeded in producing a steady current by rotating a conductor between the poles of a magnet.

Faraday remained convinced of the wave nature of electricity. All electrical action was bound up with the imposition of an intermolecular strain, which he called the "*electro-tonic* state."[66] In metals, which are

[63] Fresnel, "Deuxième note sur l'hypothèse des courants particuliers," *loc. cit.* (note 37), p. 144.
[64] Williams, *Michael Faraday, op. cit.* (note 29), pp. 176–177.
[65] *Ibid.,* p. 182.
[66] *Ibid.,* pp. 198–200.

little able to bear the strain, the electrotonic state is unstable, collapsing and being restored in rapid succession. The collapse and restoration of strain produce a wave of force, and the wave constitutes an electric current. Those materials that are better able than metals to sustain the strain are poor conductors. The electrotonic state gave way to the field concept, but an important idea was retained. The propagation of electric action still took the form of a wave, though now the cause was the collapse and restoration of the field and not a material strain in the conductor. The field theory, which Faraday worked on some thirty years, established links between light, electricity, and magnetism and prepared the way for Maxwell's electromagnetic theory of light.

The stimulus of wave optics in the rise of energetics was considerable, but no single factor can fully account for this unusually complex phase in the history of science. To a degree each area of experimental physics seems to have moved independently in the same direction. In addition there were multiple cross influences within physics and a variety of exchanges with other disciplines. Currents of thought from many different quarters joined to promote the ideas of energy and energy conservation. If the various contributory factors proceeded from a common base, that base must be sought in the general cultural environment of the early nineteenth century. The influence of the cultural environment may have taken diverse forms. Does the rise of energetics reflect the practical concerns with power associated with industrialization? Does it have a foundation in the idealistic and anti-Newtonian tendencies of the Romantic movement? Or was energetics simply bound to emerge once the outlook and methods of science had acquired a certain level of maturity?

Whatever its causes there can be little doubt that the energetics movement represents a critical stage in the history of physics. In itself the introduction of the energy concept was not as sweeping and radical a change as the theoretical innovations associated with the revolutions of the seventeenth and twentieth centuries. This early nineteenth-century revolution had, however, another important dimension: it marked the consolidation of physics and its emergence as an autonomous discipline with rigorous, exacting methods.

From beginning to end the revolution spanned more than five decades. Its origins date from the late eighteenth century when the subject matter of physics was delimited, other subjects being removed from the general province of natural philosophy and assigned to specialized sciences. Although its content was now less far-ranging and disparate, physics was not

yet a unified specialty owing to the divisions between mechanics and experimental physics. Whereas the coherence and rigor of mechanics made it
a model science, experimental physics was held in low regard for the
weakness of its theoretical structure. The weakness became increasingly
evident and intolerable through the disclosure of inexplicable new laboratory findings early in the nineteenth century. The need to construct more
adequate theories stimulated an improvement in methods that transformed
experimental physics into a more precise, quantitative, theoretical under-
taking. Worked out in the decades following 1820, the new theories had a
common basis in their commitment to the primacy of motion, process,
and continuity of action. With the formulation of the law of energy conservation in the 1840's, the theories of experimental physics were brought
into direct relationship with one another and with the laws of mechanics.
The distinction between general physics and experimental physics was now
only academic. A physicist engaged in a mathematical study of ether
mechanics or an experimental investigation of the mechanical equivalent
of heat was simply doing physics. By 1850 the methods of physics were
much more uniformly rigorous and its theoretical structure far more
tightly knit than had been the case a half century earlier. For the first
time physicists could feel they were engaged in a common enterprise.

Against the broad definitions of physics from the eighteenth century, I
will oppose a definition from the end of the nineteenth:

> The science of physics, in addition to the general laws of dynamics and
> their application to the interaction of solid, liquid, and gaseous bodies,
> embraces the theory of those agents, which were formerly designated as
> imponderables—light, heat, electricity, magnetism, etc; and all these are
> now treated as forms of motion, as different manifestations of the same
> fundamental energy.[67]

The career of Fresnel coincided with the transition to the new physics,
and his work pointed to the direction the science would take.

[67]John Bernhard Stallo, *The Concepts and Theories of Modern Physics*, 4th ed.
(1900), quoted in *The Oxford English Dictionary*, ed. James A.H. Murray, 13 vols.
(Oxford, 1933), *8*, 808–809.

# Gustave LeBon's Black Light: A Study in Physics and Philosophy in France at the Turn of the Century[1]

BY MARY JO NYE*

One of the most difficult problems in studying the development of scientific ideas lies in analyzing the interaction of scientific thought with its concomitant intellectual and social milieu. There can be little doubt that both the timing and substance of the theoretical structure of science at any given moment are related to a climate of opinion extending far beyond the laboratories, classrooms, and professional journals of the scientists. The relation is most untidy and too often conjectural; here lies, of course, one of the most pressing problems for the historian of ideas.

Certain situations in the history of science strike the observer as peculiarly indicative of the complex relationship; one is the late nineteenth century "discovery" of a new radiation by the Frenchman Gustave LeBon. His radiation, paradoxically christened "black light," entered the memoirs of the French Academy of Sciences alongside Roentgen's X rays and Becquerel's uranium rays; his explanation of the relation between his rays and those of his more illustrious colleagues was to excite vehement controversy for a decade. LeBon himself was a rank amateur—a man outside the system of universities and lycées of France—who began his first experiments in physics after thirty years of popular writing on medicine, anthropology, and psychology. Yet his experiments and ideas were taken quite seriously by many members of the French scientific elite and by scientifically inclined members of the intellectual elite. Why did this occur?

The answer, I believe, demonstrates clearly the influence on scientific development of factors extrinsic as well as intrinsic to the events and logic

*Department of the History of Science, University of Oklahoma, Norman, Oklahoma 73069.

[1] Materials for this study were gathered coincidentally to two major projects, one a 1968-1969 study of Jean Perrin (*Molecular Reality. A Perspective on the Scientific Work of Jean Perrin* [London and New York, 1972]), the other a 1969-1970 study of the philosophy of science in France during the Third Republic. Both projects were carried out under the financial sponsorship of the National Science Foundation. I should like to thank Sabetai Unguru, Russell McCormmach, and especially Robert A. Nye for their helpful reading and criticisms of the manuscript.

163

of experiment and theory. The scientific hearing LeBon received was in part the result of the internal upheaval in physical theory at the end of the nineteenth century and the ease of experimental work in the new field of cathode rays and other radiations. It was in part, too, because of his friendship with certain members of the Academy, men with whom he shared political and philosophical, rather than scientific, views. Most important, his success in science lay in his interpretation of black light and other radiations, including those associated with radioactivity, in terminology that drew on the prevalent intellectual and philosophical trends of his time: an antirationalism and, particularly, an antimaterialism that emphasized intuition, spontaneity, evolution, and action at the expense of the traditional emphasis in science on mechanism, determinism, and materialism.

I will first examine the prevailing moods in intellectual France in the last decade of the nineteenth century. Then I will examine the early extrascientific publications of LeBon, as well as his contacts with members of the intellectual community; my purpose will be to ascertain his philosophical predilections and his reasons for turning to scientific pursuits. After examining his experiments and his interpretation and reinterpretation of them in light of their immediate reception, I will assess the ways in which the fate of his scientific work was entwined with factors extrinsic as well as intrinsic to the scientific enterprise.

In tracing the intellectual climate in France through the last decades of the nineteenth century, one is immediately struck by its increasingly antirational and antiintellectual character.[2] The decades were later seen as marking a philosophical revolution in France;[3] the most important factor in the revolution was the meteoric rise of the irrationalist, intuitionist philosophy of Henri Bergson. Fundamentally opposed to Descartes and Comte, Bergson stressed that although the systematic, rational intellect

[2]Certainly this was not a French phenomenon alone. The German philosopher Friedrich Nietzsche was well known for his criticism in the late 1880's of the excessive development of man's rational faculty at the expense of his instinct and will. Yet as the French novelist André Gide remarked, "the influence of Nietzsche preceded with us the appearance of his work; it fell on soil already prepared . . . ; it did not surprise but confirm." (Roland N. Stromberg, "The Crisis of European Thought: 1880–1914," in his European Intellectual History Since 1789 [New York, 1968], pp. 145–190, on p. 157.)

[3]See Jules Sagaret, La Révolution philosophique et la science (Paris, 1924); Jean Jacob, "La philosophie d'hier et celle d'aujourd'hui," Revue de métaphysique et de morale, 6 (1898), 170–201; and Léon Brunschvicg, "La philosophie nouvelle et l'intellectualisme," ibid., 9 (1901), 433–478.

was an efficient and practical tool, man's intuition alone could lead him to reality and truth. Bergson's "mysticism and impressionism"[4] was the leading philosophical expression in France of the broader European neo-idealist reaction.[5] Impressionism and cubism in art and decadence and symbolism in literature were other manifestations of the emphasis on intuition, spontaneity, and action. Mysticism and religion were in vogue again,[6] and the political corollary of utilitarianism and positivism—nineteenth century liberalism—lost ground against the rising tide of the politics of nationalism, myth, and action.[7]

The implications for French science of these general movements were striking. In summary, they were an antiscientism directed at the scientific community, an epistemological conventionalism within the philosophy of science, and an ethical and physical antimaterialism that, when applied to intrascientific ideas, pitted continuum against particles and process against substance.

The antiscientism and ethical antimaterialism were in large part a reaction against the apparent failure of the early years of the Third Republic to rebuild "moral fiber" and provide national direction after France's defeat by Bismarck's armies and the social disturbances of 1870–1871. With his peculiar Lamarckian bias in looking at the problem of the "races,"[8] the Frenchman feared that his countrymen lacked the essential will (volonté) and force necessary to compete successfully with France's neighbors. His conclusion was that the French volonté had been undermined by a too stringent reliance on intellectualism and by a materialism

[4] Jacob, loc. cit.

[5] See Antonio Aliotta, The Idealistic Reaction against Science, trans. A. McCaskill (London, 1914); Dominique Parodi, La Philosophie contemporaine en France, 2nd rev. ed. (Paris, 1920); and Leszek Kolakowski, The Alienation of Reason, trans. N. Guterman (New York, 1969).

[6] See Auguste-Théodore-Paul de Broglie, Le Présent et l'avenir du catholicisme en France (Paris, 1892); R. Eucken, "La rélation de la philosophie au mouvement religieux du temps présent," Rev. met. et morale, 5 (1897), 399–418; and Clarisse Coignet, De Kant à Bergson. Reconciliation de la religion et de la science dans un spiritualisme nouveau (Paris, 1911).

[7] On the disillusionment with liberalism and the new European-wide emphasis on "force" in politics, see Benedetto Croce, History of Europe in the Nineteenth Century, trans. H. Furst (New York, 1933), pp. 255–259.

[8] The French reception of Darwin's theory was much slower and more complex than the English or German. The theories of Lamarck and Darwin were taught together, and the greatest French popularizer of biological evolution, Félix LeDantec, was a thoroughgoing Lamarckian. See Raymond Lenoir, "La philosophie biologique de Le Dantec," Revue philosophique, 88 (1919), 386–446.

that deified science and technology.[9] Some charged that science was a
bankrupt enterprise; science, the Sorbonne literary historian Ferdinand
Brunetière asserted, does not give us the means to live morally.[10] Like the
intuitionist Bergson, antiscientist critics granted that the scientific enterprise was efficacious, but felt that efficacy was its total value. Georges
Sorel and Maurice Blondel asserted that scientific knowledge is justified
only as an instrument of action, and that as a moral imperative it is use-
less: "The clear idea is inert; as people say, a man dies only for a belief."[11]
These charges against science were repeated by a number of French
literary figures.[12] The seriousness with which antiscientism was regarded is
illustrated by the speech of Henri Brisson, president of the Chamber of
Deputies, at a state banquet honoring the chemist Marcelin Berthelot and
attended by forty senators and seventy deputies. Brisson warned that the
issue of the bankruptcy of science was not an esoteric philosophical dispute, but an attack upon republican politics; science, he said, was the
basis of republicanism and free thought.[13] The antiscientist critique
clearly had both intellectual and political import.

The intuitionist movement and the rising bias against scientific "truth"
were significant for the philosophy of science. The new emphasis was on
the role of individual freedom and creativity in formulating scientific law
and theory. As early as 1874, Émile Boutroux departed from his Kantian
bias to argue the "contingency of natural laws," and Gaston Milhaud
argued that there is no logical necessity in nature or in the corresponding

[9] Édouard LeRoy, the conventionalist and pupil of and later successor to Bergson at
the Collège de France, deplored materialism and the exaggerated faith in science.
(Édouard LeRoy, "Science et philosophie," *Rev. met. et morale,* 7 [1899], 375–425,
503–562, and 708–731, on p. 711.)

[10] See Ferdinand Brunetière, "Après une visite au Vatican," *Revue des Deux Mondes,*
127 (1895), 97–118; also A. Darlu, "Réflexions d'une philosophe sur une question du
jour: science morale et religion," *Rev. met. et morale, 3* (1895), 239–251, on p. 248.
Brunetière only reiterated earlier criticisms of Elme Caro that the Comtian positivistic
approach had failed to show that science can provide man with ideals (*Revue des
Deux Mondes, 51* [1882], 35, 37; quoted in D.G. Charlton, *Positivist Thought in
France During the Second Empire. 1852–1870* [Oxford, 1959], p. 70). See the analy-
ses of Reino Virtanen, "Marcelin Berthelot. A Study of a Scientist's Public Role,"
*University of Nebraska Studies,* new ser., No. 31 (April, 1965); and of Harry W. Paul,
"The Debate over the Bankruptcy of Science in 1895," *French Historical Studies, 5*
(1968), 299–327.

[11] See Dominique Parodi, pp. 302–306, 311–314; also Georges Sorel, "Vues sur les
problèmes de la philosophie," *Rev. met. et morale, 18* (1910), 581–613, on p. 589;
and Maurice Blondel, *L'Action* (Paris, 1893), p. 108.

[12] They included Paul Bourget, François de Curel, and Joris-Karl Huysmans.

[13] See Paul, p. 300; Virtanen, p. 38.

laws of nature.[14] Henri Poincaré, Pierre Duhem, and Édouard LeRoy laid down the principles of what came to be called French conventionalism: they argued that scientific propositions are in large part artificial creations, that the experimental facts on which the propositions depend are interpreted by criteria of convenience, utility, or aesthetic appeal.[15] Here, too, the emphasis was on the individual and his intuition, on movement and action. Boutroux wrote that "the laws of nature participate in a double mobility, a mobility in things themselves and in our minds";[16] Poincaré commented on the "ephemeral nature of scientific theories [that] takes by surprise the man of the world."[17] The evanescence of theories and their dependence upon the subjective intelligence reassured man of his primitive, fundamental freedom of decision and action in the world: even in formulating scientific laws, "man is the maker both of his character and of his destiny."[18]

The intellectual and philosophical movement, which concentrated on individual will, action, and freedom, came to involve an antimaterialism that was not only ethical in the sense of denying man's subjugation to "material" factors, but also physical in the sense of denying the existence of an unchanging mechanical substratum underlying the physical world. Here again, physical antimaterialism rested on the assertion that reality lies in process or action.[19] According to Bergson there are no stable entities, but only action, since "tout est devenir."[20] Historicism and evolution pervaded this new approach to essence and reality, due in large part

[14]Émile Boutroux, *The Contingency of the Laws of Nature*, trans. F. Rothwell (Chicago, 1920); Gaston Milhaud, *Essai sur les conditions et les limites de la certitude logique* (Paris, 1894).

[15]Poincaré emphasized that what scientists obtain is not knowledge of the reality of things but of the relationships between things. Duhem argued that the complexity of conceptual systems is so great that an *experimentum crucis* is impossible. LeRoy, the most radical of the group, doubted that facts themselves are more than conventions. See Henri Poincaré, *Science and Hypothesis*, trans. W.J. Greenstreet (New York, 1952), p. 139; Pierre Duhem, *The Aim and Structure of Physical Theory*, trans. P. Wiener from 2nd French ed. (Princeton, 1954), p. 21; also D.H. Mellor, "Models and Analogies in Science: Duhem versus Campbell," *Isis, 59* (1968), 282-290; and LeRoy, pp. 514-518.

[16]Quoted in Parodi, p. 184.

[17]Poincaré, *Science and Hypothesis*, p. 160.

[18]Boutroux, pp. 166-167; see also Léon Brunschvicg and E. Halévy, "L'année philosophique 1893," *Rev. met. et morale, 2* (1894), 563-590, on p. 577.

[19]This assertion is Hegelian; see Herbert Marcuse, *Reason and Revolution. Hegel and the Rise of Social Theory* (Boston, 1960), p. 144.

[20]See Sageret, pp. 9-10.

to the immersion of French philosophers in English evolutionary thought. One contemporary analyst noted that the evolutionary approach was Spencerian, retaining Spencer's respect—akin to Lamarck's—for the obscure notion of force.[21]

Evolutionary antimaterialism inspired a critique of the billiard-ball, atomistic view of nature associated with classical mechanics. Boutroux wrote that "It is not . . . the nature of things that should be the final object of our investigations; it is their history."[22] In asserting that existence is not static, Bergson denied the tenets of rigorous reversibility and predictability in classical mechanics.[23] Agreeing with Bergson, LeRoy concluded that the atom can be neither solid, liquid, nor gas; nor can it be elastic or nonelastic, limited or infinite. It is a center of forces; as Bergson said, "modern science is oriented towards the reestablishment of continuity in the universe."[24] Alfred Fouillée, author of the influential psychology of the "idées-forces," asserted the formula "continuité, c'est réalité," as did the Sorbonne philosopher Arthur Hannequin.[25] Both Henri Poincaré and Pierre Duhem were at this time dubious about the existence of an atom as a material-mechanical reality.[26] It was the period of the rise of the "energetics" system of Wilhelm Ostwald and Georg Helm, a system which many contemporaries regarded as metaphysical. In France, as elsewhere, energetics was often interpreted as the assertion of the primacy of energy over matter, with energy connoting will (*Kraft* or *énergie-volonté*).[27] Jules Sageret later wrote that Albert Einstein unwittingly contributed in the early years of the twentieth century to the revolt against nineteenth century rationalism by his demonstration of the reciprocity of matter and energy. Such an idea, Sageret argued, suggested that matter and energy

[21] Jacob, p. 177; see also Brunschvicg and Halèvy, p. 478, who conclude that it is necessary to take evolutionism as the point of departure for the new philosophical movement.

[22] Boutroux, p. 166.

[23] Sageret, p. 59.

[24] LeRoy, pp. 384–385.

[25] Hannequin, who wrote *Essai critique sur l'hypothèse des atomes dans la science contemporaine,* 2nd ed. (Paris, 1899), argued that reality is defined by "the incessant act of change" (Jacob, p. 191).

[26] See Henri Poincaré, "Sur la théorie cinétique des gaz," *Revue générale des sciences, 5* (1894), 513–521; Abel Rey, *La Philosophie moderne* (Paris, 1908), p. 137; and Duhem, pp. 98–99.

[27] The chemist Henry LeChatelier pointed out the vulnerability of the term *énergie* to "amphibologies." (LeChatelier, "Les phénomènes de combustion et la production de la puissance mécanique, de la chaleur et de l'électricité," *Revue scientifique,* 4th Ser., *9* [1898], 225–231, on p. 227.)

undergo perpetual transformation and, indeed, that "substance is only history."[28]

That the writer and amateur scientist Gustave LeBon clearly saw himself as participating in the new philosophical trend that emphasized intuition, action, and antimaterialism and that he sought a "scientific" verification of the new philosophy can, I think, be clearly demonstrated. Only one of many indications is his correspondence with Albert Einstein in 1922. If Sageret attributed a blow against philosophical determinism and materialism to Einstein for his demonstration of the reciprocity of matter and energy, LeBon assuredly believed the credit for the demonstration was *his* due, and he so informed Einstein.[29] Einstein's failure to see grounds for priority in the publications LeBon cited is indeed part of the problem with which I shall be dealing.[30]

At the time of his first publication on the new black light, Gustave LeBon[31] had already written the book that was to give him a legitimate place in the history of the social sciences.[32] The *Psychologie des Foules* (1896) characterized the mentality of crowds as nonrational and nonquantifiable (as more than the sum of its parts), and it popularized, if not actually introduced, the concept of "mental contagion" as an involuntary and unconscious process by which a crowd acquires an active, collective will. Used later by Benito Mussolini and Adolf Hitler[33] as a valuable tool

[28] Sageret, p. 12.

[29] This correspondence consists of letters from LeBon to Einstein (7 June 1922 and 7 July 1922); and from Einstein to LeBon (19 May 1922, 18 June 1922, 30 June 1922, and 13 July 1922). The letters are in a private manuscript collection belonging to Madeleine Caillon, whose aunt was LeBon's secretary at the time of his death. I am indebted to Madeleine Caillon for allowing me to consult the letters.

[30] Einstein wrote that he could find no mathematical or experimental verification of the idea of mass-energy equivalence in LeBon's work. (Einstein to LeBon, 18 June 1922, Caillon Collection.)

[31] LeBon was born in 1841 into a petit-bourgeois family of the Beauce. He died in 1931.

[32] See the unpublished dissertation by Robert A. Nye, *Gustave LeBon; A Study of the Development and Impact of a Social Scientist in His Historical Setting* (Madison, Wisconsin, 1969; Ann Arbor, Michigan [University Microfilms], 1969). See also Otto Klineberg, preface to *Psychologie des Foules* (Paris, 1963); Harry Elmer Barnes, "A Survey of the Contributions of Gustave LeBon to Social Psychology," *American Journal of Psychology, 31* (1920), 333–369; and E. Dupreel, "Y-a-t-il une Foule Diffuse?" in *La Foule*, ed. Georges LeFebvre (Paris, 1954), p. 110.

[33] See Pierre Chanlaine, *Les Horizons de la Science* (Paris, 1928), p. 7; and an interview with Chanlaine cited in R. Nye, pp. 319–320. See also Alfred Stein, "Adolf Hitler und Gustave LeBon," *Geschichte in Wissenschaft und Unterricht, 6* (1955), 362–368.

for learning the art of manipulating the masses, LeBon's book was implicated in the political irrationalism of the twentieth century.

Although most of his influential publications, such as *Lois psychologiques de l'évolution des peuples* (1894), *Psychologie du socialisme* (1898), and *Psychologie de l'éducation* (1901), were in the social sciences, LeBon's education in the 1860's had been at the Faculté de Médecine, followed by internship at the Hôtel Dieu. He never practiced medicine, but wrote several books on human physiology; and for a number of years, he ran a small chemical laboratory in which he tested clinical specimens for sugar, albumin, and phosphates. He became a close friend of the psychologist Alexandre Ribot in the 1870's and was a regular contributor to Ribot's journal, the *Revue philosophique*. He joined the Paris Society of Anthropology in 1878 and made several field trips for sociological-anthropological studies, including ones to India and the Arabian peninsula, financed in part from the sales of his books and in part by the government.

Throughout his life, LeBon utilized medical and biological conceptions and terminologies such as "mental contagion" regardless of the context in which he was working. In his youth he was strongly influenced by the lectures of Claude Bernard and by his reading of Herbert Spencer; it was Spencer's ideas that dominated his thought in later years. LeBon's two-volume *L'Homme et les Sociétés* (1881) marked the apex of his orthodox positivism and materialism.[34] By the 1880's he had already begun to doubt the associationist conception of knowledge and to picture the mind as a battleground between intelligence and "sentiment"; he indicated that it was shortsighted and perhaps impossible to educate the intelligence alone.[35]

His writings began to emphasize more and more the role of sentiment and emotion, both in individuals and in societies. He retained the earlier Spencerian conception of society as an organism participating in universal organic evolution, but his approach to evolution was that of Lamarck, not Darwin. Like Spencer, LeBon did not visualize a progressive or unidirectional evolution of man and society, but a delicate equilibrium of forces "more or less unstable. . . . Diverse influences, notably that of the milieu, are able to easily upset it . . . ascendant evolution is replaced by a descendant evolution—regressive as the physiologists say."[36] His pessimism was part of the widespread discontent that led to the search for a new

---

[34] R. Nye, p. 105.
[35] R. Nye, p. 88.
[36] LeBon, *L'Homme et les Sociétés, 1,* 62; cited in R. Nye, p. 107.

philosophy at the end of the nineteenth century; his reliance on Spencer and his whole intellectual development reflected his epoch.

LeBon not merely reflected but helped shape that epoch. Indeed if we look at his friends and companions in the 1890's and if we examine his correspondence, we see among his confreres some of the leading figures of the philosophical revolution in France. In 1892 LeBon and Ribot established a group that dined monthly in a suburb near Paris; among its regular members was Henri Poincaré,[37] whose articles espousing the new conventionalism began to appear at this time. That LeBon was fully acquainted with Poincaré's ideas is clear; it was in fact LeBon who, as editor of the "Bibliothèque de philosophie scientifique" for the publishing firm of Flammarion, commissioned Poincaré to assemble his epistemological ideas in *La Science et l'Hypothèse*.[38]

LeBon knew or was in communication with many of the leaders of the new philosophical trends. Émile Boutroux, Poincaré's brother-in-law, was in correspondence with him, as was Gaston Milhaud. Henri Bergson considered himself one of LeBon's most valued friends and was later one of his strongest supporters for a seat in the Institute. Georges Sorel acknowledged an intellectual relationship, if not a debt, to LeBon, in particular in the discipline of collective psychology. Although there are no letters extant from Édouard LeRoy to LeBon, LeRoy was Bergson's pupil, and LeBon and LeRoy traveled in the same social circles. Denys Cochin, a right-center parliamentarian, on at least one occasion invited LeBon to a small dinner party at which LeRoy was to be present.[39]

Denys Cochin was only one of LeBon's friends among the conservative political and military elite of the Third Republic who spoke avidly of the need to reactivate the French national will against foreign military and

[37] LeBon, "Les Déjeuners du Mercredi de Gustave LeBon," *Revue politique et littéraire, 66* (1928), 508–509.

[38] LeBon, "Henri Poincaré," *L'Opinion, 1* (1908), 13–14. All of Poincaré's books on the philosophy of science were first published in the "Bibliothèque de philosophie scientifique" series. LeBon shared many of Poincaré's ideas, but he had greater hope than Poincaré for the certitude of scientific knowledge. (LeBon, "L'Edification scientifique de la Connaissance," *Revue scientifique, 81* [1908], 176; cited in R. Nye, p. 201.)

[39] Correspondence between these men and LeBon is in a private manuscript collection belonging to Pierre-Sadi and Lucie Carnot, who generously allowed me to consult it. The Carnots are cousins to LeBon; LeBon left his personal library and manuscripts to Pierre-Sadi and Lucie Carnot's father. On Sorel and LeBon, see Robert A. Nye, "Two Paths to a Psychology of Social Action: Gustave LeBon and Georges Sorel," *Journal of Modern History, 45*, No. 3 (September 1973).

economic forces. Besides Cochin, the dining group included Aristide Briand, Louis Barthou, Raymond Poincaré, Édouard Herriot, Gabriel Hanotaux, and Generals Mangin, de Maud'huy, and Gascouin.

Prominent scientists, too, belonged to the group. When LeBon and Ribot had a falling-out in 1902, the monthly sessions were transformed into weekly ones hosted jointly by LeBon and Albert Dastre, a pupil of Claude Bernard and a Sorbonne physiologist. There is no doubt that science as well as politics and philosophy was a topic of conversation at the dining sessions. The mathematician and perpetual secretary of the French Academy Émile Picard was often present, as was his predecessor as secretary, Roland Bonaparte. The physicist Daniel Berthelot (the son of Marcelin Berthelot), the astronomer Henri Deslandres, and the geographer Charles Lallemand also attended.[40] And since LeBon himself had been interested not only in chemical analysis, but in electrical apparatus since the late 1870's,[41] it is not surprising that physical experiments were demonstrated at the meetings in the 1890's. Experiments with the new cathode rays were a focal point of discussion and demonstration,[42] and within a few years the new phenomenon of X rays was to join and even surpass them in interest. In 1896 LeBon spoke to the dining group of a new radiation that he himself had discovered.

The first photographs utilizing W. C. Roentgen's X rays had been shown to the French Academy in late January of 1896,[43] and it was Henri Poincaré who suggested that since it was the phosphorescent point of a cathode ray tube that emits X rays, it might be fruitful to investigate phosphorescent substances to ascertain if they also emit an invisible radiation similar to X rays.[44] Heeding this suggestion, Henri Becquerel re-

[40] See LeBon, "Les Déjeuners du Mercredi"; and Ernest Flammarion, ed., *Les Déjeuners de Gustave LeBon* (Paris, 1928). The correspondence in the Caillon and Carnot manuscript collections also indicates the participation of these men.

[41] LeBon published chemical studies on tobacco in 1880 (*La Fumée du Tabac. Recherches Expérimentales* [Paris, 1880]). He also displayed equipment for the timing of physiological reactions at the Paris exposition of 1878 (R. Nye, *op. cit.* [note 32], p. 13). Articles in the *Revue scientifique* in this period indicate his general interest in thermodynamics and sources of energy.

[42] In an undated letter to LeBon in the Carnot Collection, Henri Poincaré agrees to help LeBon with the demonstration of an experiment regarding the nature of cathode rays.

[43] See the captioned photograph in *Comptes rendus, 122* (1896), 150.

[44] Henri Poincaré, "Les rayons cathodiques et les rayons Roentgen," *Revue générale des sciences,* 7 (1896), 52–59.

ported in late February that phosphorescent crystals of potassium uranium sulfate do indeed emit radiations that affect photographic plates; at first he assumed that these radiations were similar to X rays.[45]

LeBon, interested like many other amateurs in cathode rays, X rays, and radiations of electrical or chemical origin, made a report to the Academy in late January of 1896 on experiments he had made in the small laboratory at his flat in the rue Vignon. He claimed to have found that ordinary light from an oil lamp produces invisible radiations as it impinges upon a closed metal box and that these radiations affect a photographic plate inside the box, producing an image of another plate in the box. He called this new radiation "black light," deeming it some sort of extraordinary vibration capable of penetrating opaque objects and intermediate in nature between light and electricity.[46] He believed that this radiation was different from cathode rays, as it could not be deviated in a magnetic field.[47] He believed, too, that it was different from X rays;[48] he found that an electric charge was associated with it, since it discharged the leaves of an electroscope.[49] In 1896 the Academy heard fourteen papers devoted to LeBon's rays and three to Becquerel's, while Roentgen's predominated with approximately one-hundred.[50] Over the next few years each radiation remained subject to considerable controversy, since the various experiments reported to the Academy either seemed to contradict each other or suggested that the radiations themselves possessed contradictory properties.[51]

[45] Even when successive experiments demonstrated that incident sunlight was unnecessary for the emission of these uranium-salt radiations, Becquerel at first persisted in his belief that the phenomenon was merely a long-lived form of phosphorescence. (Lawrence Badash, "Becquerel's 'Unexposed' Photographic Plates," Isis, 57 [1966], 267-269.)

[46] LeBon, "La lumière noire," Comptes rendus, 122 (1896), 188-190.

[47] LeBon, "La photographie à la lumière noire," Comptes rendus, 122 (1896), 233-235.

[48] LeBon, "La nature et les propriétés de la lumière noire," Comptes rendus, 122 (1896), 387.

[49] Ibid., p. 388.

[50] X-rays were widely publicized and debated; Roentgen's German biographer O. Glasser, (Wilhelm Conrad Röntgen, 2nd ed. [Berlin, 1959], p. 318), writes that within the first year of his discovery, no fewer than 49 books or pamphlets and 1044 papers appeared on Roentgen's rays. See also George Sarton, "The Discovery of X-Rays," Isis, 26 (1937), 349-369, on p. 356.

[51] From the outset, Roentgen was uncertain how to characterize X rays, since they eluded his initial efforts to demonstrate reflection, refraction, or polarization (Sarton, loc. cit.). Becquerel at first claimed success in polarizing the radiations emitted by uranium salts, indicating that he thought they were light waves; but he later retracted

Confirmation of LeBon's experiments was reported to the Academy by H. Armaignac of Bordeaux, Henri Murat of Havre, and F. Braun of Paris.[52] Although Ulric Draussin, Armaignac, and Murat all personally wrote LeBon of their success in duplicating his experiments,[53] LeBon received a series of letters from Auguste Lumière of the Lumière Brothers' photographic equipment company protesting the validity of his discovery. The Lumière brothers had already reported to the Academy that they were unable to reproduce LeBon's results,[54] and Auguste Lumière now wrote:

> Every day someone submits to us some cases of this kind; we have by the hundreds cases of a partial or total clouding of photographic plates, of impressions produced in extraordinary circumstances, without intervention of light, or without apparent intervention. In most of these cases which are submitted to us constantly, we have almost always been able to find the cause of these phenomena, after a study—albeit sometimes very lengthy—of each of them.[55]

Lumière indicated that exposure of LeBon's photographic plates was due to the high sensitivity of the emulsion used in the firm's plates, and that the phenomenon could be produced without the intervention of sunlight and could be varied at will by modifying the preparation of the emulsion. Lumière further informed LeBon that he had successfully repeated Bec-

---

these claims ("Sur les propriétés différentes des radiations invisibles émises par les sels d'uranium, et du rayonnement de la paroi anticathodique d'un tube de Crookes," *Comptes rendus, 122* [1896], 762-767; "Note sur quelques propriétés du rayonnement de l'uranium et des corps radio-actifs," *ibid., 128* [1899], 771-777, on p. 772). That Becquerel rays could be bent in a magnetic field suggested a possible relationship with cathode rays, which J.J. Thomson was demonstrating in 1897 to be negatively charged particles. Both kinds of rays seemed related to the phenomenon of ionization, a topic of study at the Cavendish. Rutherford and Thomson established in 1897 that ionization was a process occurring in the atom itself and not between the components of the complex molecules; but the nature of the atom, the manner in which it was deprived of electric charge, and the way in which it produced the new radiations remained in great dispute. See J.J. Thomson, "Cathode Rays," *Philosophical Magazine, 44* (1897), 293-316; and *A History of the Cavendish Laboratory* (London, 1910), pp. 159-194.

[52] Arsène d'Arsonval, "Observations au sujet de la photographie à travers les corps opaques," *Comptes rendus, 122* (1896), 500-501.

[53] Letters from Ulric Draussin to LeBon, 28 February 1896 and 5 March 1896; H. Armaignac to LeBon, 13 February 1896 and n. d. (probably March 1896); Henri Murat to LeBon, 15 February 1896 and n. d. (Carnot Collection).

[54] See Auguste Lumière and Louis Lumière, "À propos de la photographie à travers les corps opaques," *Comptes rendus, 122* (1896), 463-465.

[55] Letter from Auguste Lumière to LeBon, 6 June 1896 (Carnot Collection).

querel's experiments and that "it is indisputable that uranium salts have a special action."[56] LeBon's black light, he insisted, was on the contrary entirely of chemical origin.[57]

In 1897 LeBon published a partial reassessment of his earlier experiments, stating that when light strikes an ordinary body it engenders two kinds of "obscure" radiations, each with its own effect. The first effect is a residual electric charge that remains on the illuminated body, whereas the second is what he had previously called black light. In particular, LeBon described an experiment in which metal letters are separated from a partially exposed photographic plate by a sheet of ebonite; after developing the plate, he found an intense, black impression of the letters on a grey background. According to LeBon the obscure black light is produced as light impinges on the metal letters.[58] Reaction to this new contribution was instantaneous; Perrigot suggested that only a certain brand of Lumière plates successfully showed the effects of black light, and further that the ebonite sheet that LeBon used to screen his photographic plates was not really opaque to ordinary white light.[59] Becquerel, who had investigated spectroscopic lines in the near infrared in studying phosphorescence-related phenomena, argued that LeBon's results were due not to white light, but to the less refrangible red and infrared rays that ebonite transmits; and at the Academy he demonstrated this fact for Arséne d'Arsonval, Gabriel Lippmann, and Henri Poincaré.[60] At the session of the Academy following Becquerel's demonstration, Perrigot agreed with Becquerel's explanation, as did Pierre Curie in 1900.[61] LeBon was to admit eventually that the presence of infrared radiations had confused him at the time of his first reports.

That LeBon's "discovery" received the due consideration of the Academy in 1896 cannot be denied. D'Arsonval, professor of physiology at the Collège de France and director of its biophysics laboratory, who together with Henri Poincaré had presented LeBon's papers to the Academy, duly warned LeBon of impending opposition.[62] In a letter of

[56] Letter from Auguste Lumière to LeBon, 11 June 1896 (Carnot Collection).

[57] Letter from Auguste Lumière to LeBon, 19 June 1896 (Carnot Collection).

[58] LeBon, "Nature des diverse espèces de radiations produites par les corps sous l'influence de la lumière," *Comptes rendus, 124* (1897), 755-758.

[59] M. Perrigot, "Sur la lumière noire," *Comptes rendus, 124* (1897), 857-859.

[60] Henri Becquerel, "Explication de quelques expériences de M.G. LeBon," *Comptes rendus, 124* (1897), 984-988, on p. 985.

[61] Pierre Curie, "Remarques à propos d'une note récente de M.G. LeBon," *Comptes rendus, 130* (1900), 1072-1073.

[62] Apparently d'Arsonval's first acquaintance with LeBon was not friendly, but

1 February he wrote LeBon that one of Lippmann's students had failed to obtain LeBon's first results and that d'Arsonval would gladly communicate to the Academy further details from LeBon at the same time as he submitted the student's note.[63] Lippmann, who was director of physical researches at the Sorbonne, wrote LeBon a number of questions regarding his experiments and assured him of his high consideration.[64]

Certainly the most striking of LeBon's sympathetic listeners was Henri Poincaré. Poincaré made a number of salient suggestions of ways in which LeBon might clear up doubt about the validity of his experiments.[65] He

---

polemical. In an article written in 1881 ("Sur l'utilisation des forces naturelles et leur transport," *Revue scientifique*, 3rd. Ser., *2* [1881], 269–272) LeBon wrote that compressed gases would be "la force motrice de l'avenir." D'Arsonval felt on the contrary that the motive force would be electricity. He also seriously questioned LeBon's competence in electricity, despite LeBon's display of electrical devices at the Paris Exposition ("Utilisation des forces naturelles par l'électricité," *Revue scientifique,* 3rd. Ser., *2* [1881], 550–556, 603). Louis Chauvois, one of d'Arsonval's biographers, characterizes LeBon as a man "qui eut toute sa vie une puissante envergure intellectuelle, embrasse des champs d'activité étendus et divers, mais n'eut pas toujours, sur tous les chapitres qu'il aborda, la 'solidité de base' que le pur savant de Science est en droit de réclamer" (Chauvois, *D'Arsonval. Soixante-cinq ans travers la Science* [Paris, 1937], pp. 195–196). Why d'Arsonval presented LeBon's experiments to the Academy is not clear, although one must assume a detente had occurred between them in the meantime.

[63] Letter from Arsène d'Arsonval to LeBon, 1 February 1896 (Carnot Collection). The student was most probably G.H. Niewenglowski, who in his report to the Academy stated that LeBon's results could be obtained without the intervention of sunlight; he argued instead that the results must be due to a phosphorescence of the gelatin emulsion coating the two photographic plates that LeBon used in his first experiment. (Niewenglowski, "Observations à propos de la note de M.G. LeBon," *Comptes rendus, 122* [1896], 232.)

[64] Letter from Gabriel Lippmann to LeBon, 11 March 1897 (Carnot Collection).

[65] Poincaré's first suggestion was that LeBon should rid his initial 1896 experiment of the plate (*cliché*) resting on the photographic plate; he, like Niewenglowski and Lumière, thought that the *cliché* might well account for LeBon's observations, invoking phosphorescence or some chemical process. He also insisted that LeBon should vary the distance of the photographic plate from the top of the metal box and should attempt to set up an artificial pinpoint from which the radiations produced in the metal proceeded. He warned LeBon to check for spurious contacts between parts of the apparatus that might result in electrical effects. These suggestions were made in three letters from Poincaré to LeBon, all undated but probably falling in 1896 (Carnot Collection). LeBon nevertheless continued to maintain that chemical effects were not involved, arguing that even when the two plates were used the exposure of the sensitive plate occurred only following the action of light on the metal, and that exposure occurred regardless of whether the *cliché* or photographic plate was in contact with any metal (LeBon, "La photographie à la lumière noire," *Comptes rendus, 122* [1896], 233–235).

also questioned LeBon regarding his 1897 distinction between two forms of "obscure light," and he inquired if all bodies, or only fluorescent bodies, possess the property of storing up light. He invited LeBon to the Academy in order to avoid "all equivocation" on the new topic of "obscure light."[66] There is no indication that LeBon came.

Within the next couple of years LeBon changed the direction of his thought as well as his interpretation of his original observations. He had always associated some sort of electrical effect with his black light and "obscure radiations," and in a new note on electrical properties he concluded that all bodies struck by light produce electricity.[67] In the years succeeding Becquerel's discovery of uranium radiations, LeBon followed closely the publications not only of Becquerel and the Curies, but also those of Rutherford and of the Cavendish workers under J. J. Thomson. He noted the experiments in which Marie Curie tested a large number of elements to determine if they emitted rays analogous to Becquerel's, and he came to disagree with her conclusion that among the traditional elements only thorium produced an effect comparable to that of uranium.[68] He immediately took issue with Becquerel's contention that uranium rays, like light, could be polarized,[69] and he felt vindicated in this by Rutherford's similar conclusion.[70]

Becquerel had already remarked that uranium rays were absorbed unequally, and in 1899 Rutherford suggested that one component of the

[66] Two further letters from Henri Poincaré to LeBon, undated (Carnot Collection).

[67] LeBon, "Sur les propriétés électriques des radiations émises par les corps sous l'influence de la lumière," Comptes rendus, 124 (1897), 892–895.

[68] Marie Curie, "Rayons émis par les composés de l'uranium et du thorium," Comptes rendus, 126 (1898), 1101–1103. This investigation led to her recognition of the existence of two new elements, polonium and radium, which she termed "radioactive." She had coined the term "radioactivity" when it became apparent that the element thorium emitted spontaneous rays like those of uranium. She termed "radio-elements" those chemical substances which, like uranium and thorium, had this kind of "radiance." (Eve Curie, Madame Curie, trans. V. Sheean [New York, 1967], p. 164.)

[69] LeBon cites himself in "La lumière noire et les propriétés de certains radiations du spectre," Revue scientifique, 4th Ser., 7 (1897), 689–691, on p. 691; and in "La luminescence invisible," Revue scientifique, 4th Ser., 11 (1899), 106–109, on p. 108.

[70] Rutherford demonstrated in 1899 that the radiation could not be reflected, refracted, or polarized. He concluded that nothing stood in the way of identifying uranium rays with X rays except for the different ways they were emitted. (Rutherford, "Uranium Radiation and the Electrical Conduction Produced by It," Philosophical Magazine, 47 [1899], 109–163; cited in John L. Heilbron, "The Scattering of $\alpha$ and $\beta$ Particles and Rutherford's Atom," Archive for History of Exact Sciences, 4 [1967–1968], 247–307, on p. 250.)

rays might be analogous to X rays and another to secondary, "soft" X radiation. In the following year, Rutherford discarded this interpretation after recognizing that the first component was deviated by a magnet and thus must be a stream of charged particles. By using a very strong radium source in an intense magnetic field, he found in late 1902 that the nondeviating α component could in fact be bent. By 1903 α rays were accepted as charged particles, although a third component, γ rays, discovered by Pierre Villard in 1900, had not been deviated experimentally. In attempting to explain the nature and mechanism of radioactivity, both Rutherford and J. J. Thomson pictured the radioactive atom as an assembly of rings of electrons and α particles, which suddenly expelled some of its components due to uncompensated radiation of energy.[71] But radioactivity remained a puzzle, and on the whole the experimentalists were reluctant to propose encompassing theoretical explanations.

LeBon, however, was not reluctant; it was not his way to be cautious or timid. In the spring of 1900, he published an article in which he once more reinterpreted his earlier observations, admitting that he had incorrectly identified effects produced by infrared light and phosphorescence as black light. Nonetheless, an invisible radiation had been produced in his experiments, the nature of which he now fully understood. When light impinges on any material, especially a metal, it produces a radiation that affects photographic plates and discharges electroscopes; and this radiation is another form of the radiations investigated by Becquerel and the Curies. It cannot be polarized since it is composed of charged particles, not waves. Where magnetic deviation of the electric stream cannot be detected, LeBon argued that it is because the particle velocity is too low. Are cathode rays, X rays, Becquerel rays, and black light all related? LeBon was certain they are. All are products of a dissociating atom, and each form of radiation corresponds to a different degree of dissociation.[72] Radioactivity is a general property of matter, triggered by any disturbance of equilibrium within the chemical atom; the quality of incident energy rather than its quantity determines the nature of the effect. LeBon saw radioactivity as an illustration in the physical world of that delicate equilibrium of forces that Spencer recognized in the organic world.

[71] See Heilbron, pp. 247–257; see also Rutherford, "Radioactivity," *Encyclopedia Britannica*, 11th ed. (Cambridge, 1911), pp. 793–802; and Aaron J. Ihde, *The Development of Modern Chemistry* (New York, 1964); pp. 487–492.

[72] LeBon, "La transparence de la matière et la lumière noire," *Revue scientifique*, 4th Ser., *13* (1900), 449–458.

Chemical "species," once believed to be immutable, are in fact as variable as biological species.[73]

In the next years LeBon elaborated his interpretation of matter, attracting the attention of readers of the *Revue scientifique* by dramatic titles such as "The Materialization of Energy," "The Dematerialization of Matter," and "The Intermediary World between Matter and the Ether." He repeated his interpretation in his 1905 bestseller *The Evolution of Matter* and again in his 1907 *Evolution of Forces.*[74] "Matter is not eternal and can vanish without return," he announced. The atom is a reservoir of forces more immense than any we know. Matter has an "aptitude to disaggregate [sic] by emitting effleuves [sic] of particles analogous to those of cathode rays, having a speed of the same order as light." Almost any source of energy—sunlight, lamplight, chemical reactions, electric discharge—can cause effluvia to appear. Substances such as radium or uranium that are called radioactive simply manifest in a higher degree an activity that all matter possesses. Further, matter does not consist of atoms in the final analysis; matter, by passing through successive phases that gradually deprive it of its material qualities, returns to the imponderable ether where it originated. Matter is a stable form of intraatomic energy, nothing more. The classical duality of matter and energy disappears: heat, electricity, and light represent the last stages of matter—of energy—before its disappearance into the ether.[75]

Before dealing with the reception of LeBon's theoretical conjectures, it will be helpful to examine the status of the amateur physicist at the end of the nineteenth century. By this time the physical sciences had become highly specialized and mathematical, and it seemed that the amateur and the layman could at best only follow their philosophical implications. But

---

[73] LeBon, "L'uranium, le radium, et les émissions métalliques," *Revue scientifique,* 4th Ser., *13* (1900), 548–552; and "La variabilité des espèces chimiques," *Revue scientifique,* 4th Ser., *14* (1900), 769–780.

[74] LeBon, "L'énergie intra-atomique," *Revue scientifique,* 4th Ser., *20* (1903), 481–499, 513–519, 551–559; "La matérialisation de l'énergie," *ibid.,* 5th Ser., *2* (1904), 481–495, 609–617; "La dematérialisation de la matière," *ibid.,* pp. 641–651, 737–740; and "Le monde intermédiaire entre la matière et l'ether," *ibid.,* pp. 776–783; *L'Évolution de la Matière* (Paris, 1905); *L'Évolution des Forces* (Paris, 1907). *L'Évolution de la Matière* sold 44,000 copies and went through twelve editions; *L'Évolution des Forces* sold 26,000 copies (according to a letter to R. Nye from René Hess of the publishing firm Flammarion, 9 January 1969).

[75] LeBon, *Evolution of Matter,* trans. F. Legge from the 3rd French ed. (London, 1911), pp. 1, 6, 7, 9, 12.

the experimental discoveries of cathode rays, X rays, and radioactivity allowed the amateur and layman once again to have the sense of following, even participating in, the advance of the physical sciences. To give one example: the N rays reported by the physicist René Blondlot in 1904[76] were the subject of amateur experiments and of much publicity in the popular press.[77]

Another example is LeBon's black light. LeBon was an amateur, studying radiations by the use of simple electrical equipment; his results seemed plausible in the context of other early work on various radiations. The physical chemist Jean Perrin referred to LeBon's experiments as "an extraordinarily confused mélange both of errors and of accurate results."[78] Rutherford and J. J. Thomson referred to LeBon's observations and theories in their writings on radioactivity,[79] both to clear up his mistakes and to report on his results.

In several ways LeBon's experimental work touched on the concerns of the professional physical scientists. The darkening of photographic plates and discharge of electroscopes by radiation were being studied at this time.

[76] In 1903 Blondlot reported to the Academy that he had successfully polarized X rays emanating from a Crookes tube, but later reported that he had discovered a new species of light, which he called by the initial of his city and university. Augustin Charpentier of the Medical Faculty at Nancy announced in late 1903 that N rays issued from the muscle and nervous tissue of the living organism as well as from a Crookes tube or Nernst filament. M.E. Meyer, professor of physiology at Nancy, communicated to the Academy in early 1904 his discovery of the emanation of N rays from vegetables. The Johns Hopkins physicist R.W. Wood visited the Nancy laboratory and reported in *Nature, 70* (1904), 530–531, that the experimenters claimed to have seen a spectrum of the rays even when he clandestinely removed the prism. After the Sixth International Congress of Physiology rejected the possibility of an emission of N rays by organic substances, Augustin Waller was heard to remark that the rays of Nancy should in fact be called "rays de la suggestion," alluding to the famous "School of Nancy" and their psychological studies on suggestion (Edouard Toulouse, "Les rayons N existent-ils?" *Revue scientifique,* 5th Ser., *2* [1904], 545–552, on p. 548). The Academy devoted approximately 150 papers to N rays and awarded Blondlot the LeConte Prize. See also Ian Firth, "N-Rays—Ghost of Scandal Past," *New Scientist, 44* (1969), 642–643.

[77] The *Revue scientifique* polled leading scientists on their judgment of the existence of N rays, which led Henri Moissan of the Sorbonne to ask angrily if scientific questions could now be resolved by plebiscites. ("Enquête: Les Rayons N existent-ils?" *Revue scientifique,* 5th Ser., *2* [1904], 590–591, 620–625, 656–660, 682–686, 718–722, 752–755, 785–786; Moissan's remark is on p. 657.)

[78] Jean Perrin, "Les Arguments de M. Gustave LeBon," *Revue du Mois, 4* (1907), 729–732, on p. 731.

[79] Ernest Rutherford, *Radioactivity* (Cambridge, 1904), pp. 5, 9, 372; and J.J. Thomson, *Conduction of Electricity through Gases,* 2nd ed. (Cambridge, 1906), p. 425.

So was the discharge of negative surfaces when light impinges on metals,[80] as was the action of metals and organic bodies on photographic plates.[81]

LeBon's theoretical notions were also represented in current arguments over the nature of radioactivity. One, for example, was his emphasis on the appearance and disappearance of radioactivity under changing conditions. William Crookes found in 1899 that upon purifying uranyl nitrate, the uranium apparently became inactive, whereas an impurity, "uranium X," was strongly radioactive; he suggested that the radioactivity of uranium might be due to the impurity. Becquerel also discovered that uranium lost its activity when barium sulfate was precipitated from a solution containing uranium salts, and Rutherford and Soddy reported similar results with thorium in 1902. It was only after it was shown that thorium recovered its activity that physicists were convinced that radioactive radiations were permanent features of certain elements and not affected by chemical conditions.[82]

LeBon used two particular examples to illustrate the disappearance and reappearance of electrical charge—which he associated with radioactivity—with changing physical or chemical conditions. He demonstrated in 1900 that certain salts produce varying conductivity in a surrounding gas by their dehydration and hydration.[83] Pierre Curie informed the Academy that he and Giesel had already reported on this property of luminous barium bromide.[84] One of Rutherford's students, Fanny Cook Gates, investigated LeBon's analogous findings for quinine sulfate, concluding that the electrical effects were due not to "radioactivity" but to the ionization of the gas close to the surface of the salt or to a chemical action taking place at the surface.[85]

---

[80]This was the photoelectric effect, which had been intensively studied since Hertz's pioneering experiments nearly ten years before LeBon's first experiments.

[81] The action was generally regarded as chemical in origin; e.g., W.J. Russell attributed the photographic action of certain organic bodies to their absorption of oxygen while acting as chemically reducing substances. In the case of both organic substances and metals, he assumed that a vapor emitted by the active body was involved. (Russell, "Further Experiments on the Action Exerted by Certain Metals and Other Bodies on a Photographic Plate," Bakerian Lecture, *Proceedings of the Royal Society (London), 63* [1898], 102–112.)

[82]See Rutherford, "Radioactivity," *loc. cit.*

[83] LeBon, "La transparence de la matière et la lumière noire."

[84]Pierre Curie, *loc. cit.* (note 61).

[85]Fanny Cook Gates, "On the Nature of Certain Radiations from the Sulphate of Quinine," *Physical Review, 18* (1904), 135–145, on p. 144; and Rutherford, *Radioactivity* (1904), pp. 9, 372. Rutherford points out that LeBon's effect was neither spontaneous nor permanent.

Even as LeBon's experiments on the "decay" and "recovery" of electrical effects had a familiar ring to those studying the properties of radiations, so did his rejection of the notion that radium and polonium were distinct elements. Noting that the spectral evidence was inconclusive on this point, he argued that the only evidence that radium and polonium differ from barium and bismuth—their nearest neighbors on the periodic table—is their radioactivity. He thought that when barium and bismuth compounds were properly purified, their "radioactive" effects would disappear.[86] LeBon was not alone in this opinion; as late as 1906 Kelvin continued to question the existence of radium, thinking that what was termed "radium" was a compound of some metal, possibly lead, with helium, and that if the metal could be reduced from its salt it would lose all its "radioactive" properties.[87]

Similarly LeBon was not alone in doubting the "dogma of the invariability of chemical species."[88] In this connection he cited Wilhelm Ostwald, who was attempting to purge the physical sciences of their mechanical and atomistic hypotheses and to refound the sciences on the descriptive laws of thermodynamics. LeBon also shared Ostwald's hostility to the dualism of matter and energy. Ostwald's resolution of the dualism was through his "energetics";[89] however, even though LeBon often sounded like an Ostwald-type energeticist, his main inspiration came from Spencer.[90]

Even LeBon's view that all elements were radioactive was a respectable speculation at the time. William Ramsay's experimental work seemed to

---

[86] LeBon, "L'uranium, le radium, et les émissions métalliques," pp. 550–551.

[87] See A.S. Eve, *Rutherford* (Cambridge, 1939), pp. 140–142. When Rutherford offered his opinion at the Southport Meeting of the British Association in 1903 that the energy of radium originated inside the atom, Oliver Lodge communicated a written statement from Kelvin maintaining that radium received its energy "by absorption of ethereal waves." Kelvin's statement also suggested that although beta rays were indeed electrons, gamma rays were radium vapor and alpha rays were atoms of radium or radium bromide. H.E. Armstrong agreed that chemists certainly had "no evidence of atomic disintegration on the earth" (Eve, p. 97).

[88] LeBon, "La variabilité des espèces chimiques," p. 778.

[89] See Wilhelm Ostwald, "Elements and Compounds," in *Faraday Lectures 1869–1928*, ed. C.S. Gibson and A.J. Greenaway (London, 1928), pp. 185–201; and "La déroute de l'atomisme contemporain," *Revue générale des sciences*, 6 (1895), 953–958. See also Niles R. Holt, "A Note on Wilhelm Ostwald's Energism," *Isis, 61* (1970), 386–389. Ostwald's collaborator Georg Helm wrote the fundamental statement of energetics: *Die Energetik nach ihrer geschichtlichen Entwicklung* (Leipzig, 1898).

[90] LeBon talked of thermodynamics, but knew very little about the discipline. Here his lack of a mathematical background was especially debilitating.

support this view.[91] So did that of R. J. Strutt, especially his 1903 measurements of the ionization of gases placed in various metal and glass vessels and his 1906 examination of a large number of rocks for traces of radium.[92] Strutt found radium in all of the rocks of his samples, which led the *Athenaeum* to speak of the "evidence for the radioactivity of all matter—first announced by LeBon and since affirmed by the Hon. R. J. Strutt."[93] J. J. Thomson reported in 1902 that he had found radium and its emanation to be widely diffused in nature; he detected it in Cambridge tap-water, as well as in various sands, gravels, clays, and even in wheaten flour.[94] Julius Elster and Hans Geitel detected radioactivity in soil and abnormally strong ionization in cellars and caves.[95] Robert Campbell treated the subject of the universality of radioactive properties exhaustively in a paper in the *Jahrbuch der Radioaktivität* in 1906.[96]

Scientists were only beginning to realize that uranium, thorium, and other long-lived radioactive elements are thinly spread through the rocks and soil of the earth's crust and that these elements together with cosmic rays contribute to a constant background radiation. Thus J. J. Thomson could write in 1906 that a large amount of evidence had recently been collected "in favour of the view that this property [radioactive radiations] is possessed to some extent by all bodies, although there seems to be a great gap between the amount of radiation emitted by the least active of the recognized radioactive elements and the most active of the others."[97] This is exactly what LeBon was saying.

[91] See William Ramsay, "Chemical and Electrical Changes Induced by Ultraviolet Light," *Philosophical Magazine*, 12 (1906), 397–418, especially p. 402. Ramsay repeated some of LeBon's experiments with positive results, indicating that zinc under the influence of ultraviolet light loses some of its electrons, and that what is left is no longer zinc. This seemed to imply that ultraviolet light acted as a detonator, producing the disintegration of matter.

[92] See R.J. Strutt, "Radio-activity of Ordinary Materials," *Nature*, 67 (1903), 369–370; and "On the Distribution of Radium in the Earth's Crust, and on the Earth's Internal Heat," *Proceedings of the Royal Society (London)*, Ser. A, 77 (1906), 472–485.

[93] "Research Notes," *Athenaeum*, 3 December 1904, pp. 768–769.

[94] J.J. Thomson, "Experiments on Induced Radioactivity in Air, and on the Electrical Conductivity Produced in Gases when They Pass through Water," *Philosophical Magazine*, 4 (1902), 352–367.

[95] Julius Elster and Hans Geitel, *Physikalische Zeitschrift*, 4 (1903), 526; cited in J.J. Thomson, *Conduction of Electricity through Gases*, note 412.

[96] Robert Campbell, "Die Radioaktivität als allgemeine Eigenschaft der chemischen Elemente," *Jahrbuch der Radioaktivität und Elektronik*, 3 (1906), 434–462.

[97] J.J. Thomson, Chapter 13, "The Power of the Elements in General to Emit Ionising Radiation," in *Conduction of Electricity through Gases*, pp. 410–419, on p. 410.

Finally, LeBon's imaginative hypothesis that matter is slowly disappearing into the ether had parallels in the contemporary scientific literature. His conception of the atom and its properties was drawn in particular from J. J. Thomson's writings—writings that were later summarized in *Electricity and Matter*—and from Rutherford's *Radioactivity* and Larmor's *Ether and Matter*. LeBon compared the atom to a solar system, "a comparison at which several physicists have arrived by different roads";[98] but he preferred to think of the atom as a vortex phenomenon. He approved of Larmor's view that the ether probably formed small vortices when it originally condensed, and that the vortices constitute electrons.[99] Following Larmor, he regarded matter as a structure in the ether rather than the ether as a material structure. For LeBon an electron was an intermediate transition stage between matter and ether, and in support of his view he pointed to Kaufmann's and Abraham's demonstration that an electron's inertia is not constant, but varies with speed.[100] He agreed with Lorentz' electron theory in which vibrating electrons produce light waves and with the general view that accelerating electrons must lose their energy and the stable atom must collapse. He concluded that the collapsing atom generates waves in the ether which at length disperse, leaving the ether in repose in its primitive state.[101]

The widespread appeal of LeBon's "scientific philosophy"[102] in *Evolution of Matter* and *Evolution of Forces* was rooted in the intellectual and philosophical trends at the turn of the century. Just as the philosophical thought of his time was characterized by a mood of rebellion, so was his own thought. Just as evolutionary thought was still a dominant theme in biological, sociological, historical, and philosophical writings, so it was in LeBon's writings. In a period when fear of social disorder was paramount, when religious values had renewed attractiveness, and when intuition, force, and action were advocated for a French national revival, LeBon's

[98] LeBon, *Evolution of Matter*, p. 70.

[99] *Ibid.,* p. 92.

[100] *Ibid.,* pp. 194–195.

[101] *Ibid.,* p. 314.

[102] *Evolution of Matter,* like the later *Evolution of Forces,* was published in the series LeBon edited, the "Bibliothèque de Philosophie scientifique." Émile Picard wrote LeBon that he regretted not having any sympathy for the phrases "philosophy of science" and "scientific philosophy," yet he did concede the popular appeal and educational value of scientific philosophy to the general populace. In this connection he alluded to LeBon as "one of the most brilliant minds of our time." (Letter from Picard to LeBon, 19 October 1911 [Caillon Collection].)

antimaterialism and stress on action in nature were an appropriate philosophical stance, one likely to find a receptive audience.

LeBon fully participated in the embittered fin-de-siècle reaction against the so-called temple of positivistic science. He, like many others, referred to principles such as the conservation of energy and the second law of thermodynamics as dogmas or divinities. "Gods and dogmas do not perish in a single day,"[103] he lamented. In a period when many scientists and mathematicians were subjecting their disciplines and theories to scrutinizing appraisal, LeBon pictured himself as the most zealous of iconoclasts. His iconoclastic public image is reflected in the observation in a 1903 French newspaper that "Poincaré and LeBon fearlessly undermine the old scientific dogmas. They do not fear saying that these cannot fulfill and satisfy the human spirit. . . . [W]e recognize along with these teachers the insufficiency—let us use Brunetière's word . . . —the bankruptcy of science."[104]

It was not simply because of the new disillusionment with scientism that LeBon had wide appeal. His application of evolutionary ideas to the world of matter was equally responsible. He considered himself to be working within the tradition of Lamarck's *transformisme* and of evolutionary thought in general. He claimed that his theory of the dematerialization of matter showed "that the law of evolution applicable to living beings is also applicable to simple bodies; chemical species are no more invariable than are living species."[105] He believed that even as anthropoid apes form a link between the inferior animals and man, so the various forms of energy constitute intermediate stages between matter and ether.[106] LeBon's evolutionary ideas may account, for example, for d'Arsonval's initial interest in his experiments and his willingness to present LeBon's papers at the Academy. As early as 1882, d'Arsonval had written of the participation of light, electricity, and the whole inorganic world in a universal evolution: "the laws of evolution rule inorganic matter as well as living beings. A perpetual effort of nature towards improvement is universal and is applied to material forces even as to living beings."[107] The chemist Armand Gautier spoke to LeBon in the same breath of the variation of matter and the variation of

103 LeBon, *Evolution of Matter*, p. 3.

104 Jules Mercier, "L'Anarchie dans la Science," *Le Bien Public* (Dijon), 13 July 1903, Supplement to No. 171, p. 1.

105 LeBon, *Evolution of Matter*, p. 9.

106 *Ibid.*, pp. 83–84.

107 Arsène D'Arsonval, "Utilisation des forces naturelles par l'électricité," *Revue scientifique*, 3rd Ser., 2 (1881), 550–556, 603; quoted in Chauvois, p. 204.

species and races,[108] and the philosopher Jules Sageret in his 1905 review of *Evolution of Matter* assessed that "Gustave LeBon should be given the same place in the physical sciences that Darwin occupies in natural history."[109] This is not to suggest that the application of the word "evolution" to physical processes was LeBon's alone or even uncommon; e.g., in his 1903 textbook on the principles of physical chemistry, Jean Perrin wrote that he and Paul Langevin understood the second law of thermodynamics as a "principle of evolution."[110]

LeBon's emphasis on the dematerialization of matter[111] accounts for much of the appeal of his scientific philosophy. The evolution of matter through intermediate forms of energy conformed to the tenets of the intuitionist and action-oriented philosophies. LeBon's view of matter as a stable state of energy or of "force" seemed synonymous with the Bergsonian statement that there are no things, that "all is becoming." Science as well as philosophy reinforced the view that there are no things, only actions.[112]

LeBon's dematerialization of matter was interpreted as a support for psychic phenomena and for religion. Although LeBon himself was hostile to spiritualism, he was cited favorably in Hereward Carrington's spiritualist *The Coming Science;*[113] and many spiritualists believed that Blondlot's N rays and LeBon's dissociation of matter furnished arguments for psychic phenomena.[114] LeBon's cosmology—one which located the origin of the

[108]Letter from Armand Gautier to LeBon, 26 October 1902 (Carnot Collection).

[109]Jules Sageret's book review in *Revue philosophique, 60* (1905), 538.

[110]Jean Perrin, *Traité de Chimie Physique. Les Principes* (Paris, 1903), pp. 142–143.

[111]It should be noted that LeBon regarded his conception of a new cycle of "materialization" as a hypothesis, while he regarded "dematerialization" as a fact. He thought that perhaps the final vanishing of radiations into the ether "is followed, in the course of ages, by a new cycle of evolution, without it being possible to assign an end to these probably eternal destructions and recommencements" (*Évolution des Forces,* p. 96).

[112]See Sageret, *La Révolution philosophique et la science,* pp. 9, 10, 31.

[113]Hereward Carrington, *The Coming Science* (London, 1909); cited in a clipping from *The Church Times,* 11 June 1909 (Carnot Collection).

[114]When Charpentier announced that the human body emits N rays, the discovery was immediately seen by spiritualists as a confirmation of the existence of mental telepathy and general psychic phenomena (a clipping from *Illustration,* 23 January 1904, Carnot Collection). D'Arsonval was a good friend of Charpentier and was one of the few Academicians who thought he had seen N rays at Nancy. Along with the philosopher Émile Boutroux and the physiologist Charles Richet, d'Arsonval was also one of the eminent French men of letters and science who were interested in table-rapping (clippings from "The Recrudescence of Spirit Rapping," *Pall Mall Gazette,* 21 April 1910 and 3 May 1910; and "The Reply of the Table Rappers," *ibid.,* 17 June 1910; Carnot Collection).

universe in clouds of ether and prophesied its inevitable if gradual dissipation back into the ether—easily lent itself to religious interpretation. As early as 1901 *The Christian World* spoke of "matter, on its way to dissolution" taking intermediate electrical forms and ultimately passing into "that imponderable ether filling the universe, out of which, in [LeBon's] view, all matter originally came and into which it will finally return."[115] To take another example, Jules Mercier, in asserting that LeBon was boldly undermining scientific dogma, applauded him for furthering our belief "in the indemonstrable certitudes of religion."[116]

LeBon's conception of matter even penetrated politics. Jean Jaurès, whose idealistic socialism was somewhat rare among socialists, saw in LeBon's notion of the dematerialization of matter a theoretical vindication of his views and a basis for rapprochement between Catholicism, science, democracy, and social justice. In a speech to the Chamber of Deputies in 1906 he said:

> Your scientists are affirming the law of evolution, but in the measure that they analyze it more profoundly, they discover that each moment of evolution brings something new, that, under the apparent continuity of this evolution on the surface, there is a perpetual force of creation, of revelation, of revolution; your science supports the world on the opaque brutality of matter, and now this very science demonstrates today that matter is going to vanish and to be idealized; that the old opposition between imponderable ether and heavy matter is resolved in the unity of universal energy, and that this energy, by its prodigious condensations, symbolizes and announces *volonté*, by its radiating power, symbolizes and announces the force of thought and of mind. (Applause to the left.)[117]

Although Jean Perrin and other scientists scorned LeBon for his imprecision in scientific terminology—for his continual confusion of the terms "energy" and "force"[118]—this very imprecision had the effect LeBon intended. It made his scientific ideas more readily assimilable to nonscientific thought; the energies of electricity, heat, and light became symbols of "the force of thought and mind."

[115]Clipping from *Christian World,* 23 May 1901 (Carnot Collection).
[116]Mercier, *loc. cit.*
[117]Jean Jaurès, *Journal Officiel de la Chambre des Députés,* séance of 13 November 1906.
[118]See Jean Perrin, "Sur 'L'Évolution des Forces,'" *Revue du Mois, 4* (1907), 607; and George M. Minchin, "The Latest Conception of Matter," *The Nation, 4* July 1908, p. 489.

Although socialists and communists could interpret LeBon's "demateri-alization" of matter as a confirmation of Marx and Engels—Engels said that "movement is the mode of existence of matter"[119]—it was conserva-tive French political philosophy that adopted LeBon's ideas as its own, even as that philosophy adopted his psychology of crowds. Most of LeBon's friends in the political as well as the scientific community were conservative or right-center, and a few were Boulangists and Royalists; none was socialist or belonged to the left in any way. Political conserva-tism also characterized the majority of LeBon's guests at the "déjeuners." Among LeBon's scientific and philosophical friends who did not belong to the dining group, Armand Gautier, Édouard Branly,[120] d'Arsonval, Richet, Boutroux, and Bergson were also conservative. Henri Poincaré ex-pressed his opinion of the left to LeBon after reading his *Psychology of Socialism:* "if all the socialist leaders were 'apostles' as you say, we would be lost; happily, most of them are just shrewd hoaxers. Anyway let us hope so."[121]

Among politicians, Gabriel Hanotaux, who was foreign minister in the 1880's and 1890's, spoke of LeBon as a great physicist who had "destroyed matter." The parliamentarian Denys Cochin, having read LeBon's books and Rutherford's *Radioactive Transformations,* wrote to LeBon that "it seems to me that in the future you will be taken for a Lavoisier and Ruth-erford for a Stahl."[122] The ultraconservative newspaper *La Libre Parole,* edited by Edouard Drumont, praised LeBon as one who does not "put rationalism before reason":

LeBon's experiments indicate a fundamental process; "the *dematerializa-tion,* or if you prefer, the *disappearance of matter*". . . . That which is

[119]"Things are as Engels said. All is history; nature is dominated by the dialectic law of movement." (J. Diner-Dènes, "Le Marxisme et la plus récentes révolution dans les sciences naturelles," clipping from *Socialiste,* 24 November 1901, Carnot Collection.)

[120]Branly, whom Marconi recognized as a co-discoverer of wireless telegraphy, held a chair of physics at the Catholic Institute. In the Caillon manuscript collection there are numerous letters from Branly professing affection and friendship for LeBon. The two published a paper together in 1899 and corresponded about electrical experi-ments as well as about Paris gossip. Branly narrowly defeated Marie Curie for a chair at the Academy in 1911. See M. Boisseau, "Un Grand Savant Français Qui Fait Hon-neur à la Montagne Sainte-Geneviève: Édouard Branly," *La Montagne Sainte Geneviève* (1950), pp. 1–8; also Jeanne Terrat-Branly, *Mon Père Édouard Branly* (Paris, 1941), pp. 260–261.

[121]Letter from Henri Poincaré to LeBon, undated (Carnot Collection).

[122]Letter from Gabriel Hanotaux to LeBon, 24 September 1911; letter from Denys Cochin to LeBon, 12 March [no year] (Carnot Collection).

certain is that after a phase of obscurity, spiritualism is everywhere regaining a little honor. I mean here by spiritualism . . . the conception at once winged [*ailée*] and precise, liberal and respectful . . . maintaining that one breathes better to the extent that one is raised up. . . . [S]piritualism ascends from sensation to idea, by way of sentiment, while materialism follows the inverse path, which explains the high by the low and morality by instinct.[123]

LeBon's scientific views were seen by conservatives as a blow for religion against science, as a philosophical statement against the dialectical materialism of the Marxist political movement, and as a reassertion of mind and morality over mechanical and deterministic materialism.

The admiration LeBon most avidly sought through his science, however, was not that of the general intellectual and political communities. Rather it was the admiration of contemporary scientists,[124] and this escaped him in the end. To be sure, the *English Mechanic and World of Science* granted him the "merit of first having shown that there is a dissociation of matter; Madame Curie of having shown that the products of dissociation are not identical";[125] and a number of lesser known scientific journals carried reports of his contributions.[126] In the influential *Revue des Deux Mondes*, the physiologist Albert Dastre wrote that it was LeBon who first grasped the universality and other principal features of radioactivity. Lucien Poincaré cited LeBon's work in summaries of current research in physics.[127] And when the scientific editor of *La Patrie* asked the chemist Henri Mois-

---

[123]Léon Daudet, "La Fin du Matérialisme," *La Libre Parole,* 3 September 1905, p. 1.

[124]Although LeBon's writings in the social sciences qualified him for election to the section of "sciences morales et politiques" in the French Academy of Sciences, he concentrated on gaining election to the section of physical sciences. In early 1921 LeBon was proposed with the support of Émile Picard and Charles Richet, but he was not elected. A second attempt in 1923 also failed; Picard and Richet no longer voted for him. Henri Deslandres wrote LeBon in 1926 that his and Daniel Berthelot's efforts had failed to elect him that year (R. Nye, *op. cit.* [note 32], pp. 38–39).

[125]D.A. Pio, in *The English Mechanic and World of Science, 79* (1904), 214.

[126]See, e.g., Georges Somerhausen, "Une Révolution Scientifique," *Bullétin Technique (Association des Ingénieurs sortis de l'École Polytechnique de Bruxelles),* No. 1 (1903), 30 pp.; and H.J. Proumen, "La découverte de la désintégration atomique," *Bullétin Trimestriel de l'Association des Élèves et Ingénieurs Diplomés de l'École supérieure des Textile Verviers, 8* (1910), 351–362.

[127]Albert Dastre, "Les Nouvelles Radiations," *Revue des Deux Mondes, 5ᵉ Période, 6* (1901), 682–702. Lucien Poincaré wrote that LeBon was one of the first to think that radioactivity is a general phenomenon of nature (L. Poincaré, "Régions neuves de la Physique," *Revue générale des sciences, 14* [1903], 28–44).

san in 1906 for his views on the constitution of matter, Moissan replied:
"Here, sir, allow me not to answer you but to urge you to read the works
of Doctor Gustave LeBon, who is specialized in this order of questions."
To the editor's reply "Are we entering then into the imponderable?" Moissan observed: "You have said the word, and in that case, matter would
only be condensed energy."[128] Moissan wrote LeBon of his willingness to
see him and of his conviction that LeBon possessed the "courage of an im-
placable logic."[129] The chemist Henri LeChatelier later wrote LeBon that
he was well aware that most of his colleagues deplored the qualitative,
rather than quantitative, nature of LeBon's experiments: "But Dalton
scarcely made more experiments; he had an idea and expressed it with
force."[130]

But most chemists and physicists had nothing to do with LeBon or his
ideas after about 1900, and even the few sympathetic ones were critical.
The Belgian physicist Henri Lorent expressed his general admiration for
LeBon's thesis on the nature and generality of radioactivity, but marshaled
a number of questions LeBon had failed to answer. What did he mean by
the "ether"? After all, it had been diversely defined by Fresnel, Maxwell,
Kelvin, Thomson, Larmor, and Lorentz. How *exactly* did he reconcile the
"vanishing" of electron vibrations into the ether with Abraham's and
Kaufmann's views on the electron? What precisely did he mean by a chemical species when he spoke of its variability? And how did he explain the
electrical neutrality of the atom?[131]

Robert Campbell cautioned the readers of the *Athenaeum* that they
must not imagine that LeBon's writings were examples of accepted scientific procedure; Campbell later informed the public that recent research
had destroyed earlier conceptions—including his own—of the generality of
radioactivity. He said that LeBon's studies actually concerned the photoelectric effect and were not to be confused with radioactivity.[132] After
two favorable articles on LeBon had appeared in *The Yorkshire Daily Observer*, J. Arthur Hill submitted a letter on the subject from Oliver Lodge.

[128]Clipping from *La Patrie*, 31 August 1906 (Carnot Collection).
[129]Letter from Henri Moissan to LeBon, 11 April 1906 (Carnot Collection).
[130]Letter from Henry LeChatelier to LeBon, 31 May 1911 (Carnot Collection).
[131]Henri Lorent, "Les théories du docteur G. LeBon sur l'évolution de la matière," *Bullétin de la Société chimique de Belgique, 20* (1906), reprint of 27 pp., on pp. 13–19, 20, 25.
[132]Robert Campbell, "Dr. LeBon's Theories of Matter," *Athenaeum*, 17 February 1906, pp. 202–203; and Campbell, "The Physics of M. Gustave LeBon," *The New Quarterly, 2* (1909), 233–234.

In it Lodge said that LeBon's "claim to have discovered most of the phenomena referred to (whereas they are mostly the outcome of investigations at Cambridge) makes him unpardonable."[133] The British Medical Journal recommended to its readers only those portions of LeBon's books dealing with phosphorescence.[134]

Perhaps the authoritative statement from the younger French scientists was made by Jean Perrin in a series of articles in the Revue du Mois following LeBon's publication of Evolution of Forces. By this time LeBon had become rather savage in his claims for priority on the nature and generality of radioactivity,[135] and Perrin, who was an intimate friend of the Curies, had been infuriated. In the first place, LeBon's definition of radioactivity was unacceptable; LeBon said that any body that could be made to emit electric charges was radioactive, whereas the accepted criterion for radioactivity was the complete spontaneity of the radiations and the impossibility of inhibiting them by any ordinary physical or chemical process. In the second place, in claiming priorities for numerous specific researches LeBon consistently failed to cite researches by others; and he failed to realize that a majority of his experiments were discussed in school manuals and performed routinely by students for the baccalaureate. LeBon's statement prior to the work of Rutherford or the Curies[136] that matter can "disintegrate" was not scientific:

133Clipping from The Yorkshire Daily Observer, 11 June 1908 (Carnot Collection).
134Clipping from The British Medical Journal, 25 July 1908 (Carnot Collection).
135LeBon castigated the "part played, even in laboratories, by suggestion and illusions, and . . . the preponderant influence of prestige considered as a principal element of demonstration." (LeBon, Evolution of Matter, p. 19.) This and other diatribes earned LeBon private warnings; e.g., the philosopher Gaston Milhaud wrote to him in 1910 that his "reproaches" addressed to the university scientists had made him quite a number of enemies (letter from Milhaud to LeBon, 23 July 1910 [Carnot Collection]). Several writers supported LeBon's claims for priority in the "discovery" of the nature of radioactivity; e.g., Henri Lorent, loc. cit., wrote that the Academy of Belgium would not take part in the Parisian conspiracy of silence against the importance of LeBon's discoveries. Le Journal published remarks on 21 October 1903 about the recognition due LeBon only shortly after the Curies and Becquerel received their Nobel Prize. The Petit Journal likewise suggested on 12 January 1904 that LeBon deserved more credit than he had received. A brochure devoted to this theme was circulated by P. De Heen, a member of the Royal Academy of Belgium and physics professor at the University of Liége (P. De Heen, Quel est L'Auteur de la Découverte des Phénomènes dits Radioactifs? [La Meuse, 1901], 13 pp.).
136It was in 1902, after he had plotted decay and recovery curves for thorium, that Rutherford first specifically wrote of radioactivity as a subatomic phenomenon. Rutherford reported that "all the most prominent workers in this subject are agreed in considering radioactivity an atomic phenomenon," and that the Curies had stated

Before Berthelot, several intelligent men thought and said that organic bodies could be formed outside of the living being, without, however, indicating the means of making the slightest effective progress in this direction. Had any of them the right to complain that Berthelot did not remember to cite them when he realized the synthesis of solid fats? . . . These claims, which would be unjustified even if they were supported on precise words, refer generally to statements so vague that one can understand them in many different senses, and the language of LeBon is at times of an unimaginable imprecision.[137]

The justness of Perrin's criticisms may have escaped LeBon; in any case a number of LeBon's good friends attempted to make him better understand Perrin's position. Henri Poincaré, the mathematician Émile Picard, and the chemist Armand Gautier—all members of the Academy—were in regular correspondence with LeBon on this point. Poincaré continued after 1900 to indicate glaring weaknesses in LeBon's arguments, bringing to his attention, for example, the paradox that LeBon's combination of subatomic particles must be an endothermic process, one inconsistent with the subsequent actual stability of the atom. If LeBon were to insist upon his view, he should at least recognize the difficulties.[138] In a later letter, in response to LeBon's complaint that partisans of differing opinions fall prey to personal belief and sentiment, Poincaré replied that LeBon had failed to grasp that "there is no reasoning which can go to the root of things."[139]

In an early letter, Armand Gautier agreed with LeBon that "they have not sufficiently done you justice—and it is for B [Becquerel] that they beat the drum!" But Gautier himself later had a taste of LeBon's mania for priorities and was miffed at LeBon's statement in *Evolution of Matter* that some of Gautier's ideas on the storing up of oscillatory energy in atoms were due to LeBon's researches. Gautier protested: "I published these ideas in my first volume of the *Cours de Chimie* in 1888."[140] Like Poin-

---

in 1902 that this idea underlay their work from its origin. "Since, therefore, radioactivity is at once an atomic phenomenon and accompanied by chemical changes in which new types of matter are produced, these changes must be occurring within the atom, and the radioactive elements must be undergoing spontaneous transformation." (Rutherford and Frederick Soddy, "The Cause and Nature of Radioactivity," *Philosophical Magazine, 4* [1902], 370–396, on p. 395.)

[137]Jean Perrin, "À propos de 'L'Évolution des Forces,'" *Revue du Mois, 4* (1907), 606–608, on p. 607.

[138]Letter from Henri Poincaré to LeBon, undated (Carnot Collection).

[139]Letter from Henri Poincaré to LeBon, 26 November 1911 (Carnot Collection).

[140]Letters from Armand Gautier to LeBon, 26 October 1902 and 19 June 1905 (Carnot Collection).

caré, Gautier offered LeBon friendly advice, this time on the unwillingness of the scientific community to plunge into a full-scale conceptual revolution until all other alternatives had been exhausted.

It is not abhorrent to me to allow the view of the instability of parts of matter or of the ether. But is it necessary to shut off hope for some other solution before quitting them? Moreover, doesn't *official science,* which is obliged to take some responsibilities to separate ideas from generalities, always show a little fear? But this very fear keeps it healthy by keeping it on its guard. Those who question it do so at their own risk and peril.[141]

Perhaps the best counsel—counsel which LeBon did not heed—came from Émile Picard. Having read most of LeBon's articles in the *Revue scientifique* as well as *Evolution of Matter,* Picard wrote LeBon thanking him for a copy of the latter book:[142] "You know that—in regard to interpretations—nothing affronts me, and what is not understood is called ether or electron. The concern everywhere is that the idea should be susceptible of a precise enough form to be translated into a mathematical form; this, at least, is the point of view of an obscure algebraist."[143] Later, after reading LeBon's *Evolution of Forces* with its theory of the disappearance of matter into the ether and of its reemergence from the ether, Picard remarked on the new "monism" and reiterated Gautier's advice:

As to the unique principle of things, it can be seen historically in many aspects. The sages of Ionia opened the way with Thales and Anaximander. The idea of a unique principle is of strong interest for the philosopher who searches the enigmas of the Universe, but science has scarcely taken part until now in these views, which are as general as they are vague. Without going, with certain pragmatists, to the point of seeing in science only recipes for action, it is clear that current principles are to be abandoned only when their fertility has been exhausted, and above all when new views *will have escaped vagueness* and will have led to *precise rules* permitting predictions sufficiently close in well-determined cases. After having cut, it is necessary to re-sew; if not, we have only done philosophy, which is very interesting for you and for me, but which a lot of people disdain.[144]

[141] Letter from Armand Gautier to LeBon, 14 October 1903 (Carnot Collection).
[142] Other letters acknowledging receipts of copies of LeBon's articles and books include ones from J.J. Thomson (16 June 1905), G.E. Crawford (7 September 1906), Ernst Mach (2 December 1902), and Pierre Duhem (undated) (Carnot Collection).
[143] Letter from Émile Picard to LeBon, 22 June 1905 (Carnot Collection).
[144] Letter from Émile Picard to LeBon, 17 October 1907 (Carnot Collection).

Later Picard again differentiated between science and philosophy: "Without doubt it is amusing to make gigantic extrapolations, but it is only scientific poetry which, of course, cannot be without its charms."[145]

Some scientists and mathematicians were willing to concede the value of LeBon's work, particularly the *Evolution of Matter,* as "scientific poetry" and popularization. Paul Painlevé, the Sorbonne mathematician and minister of education, counseled his colleagues that it was dangerous for science to be subdivided into a multitude of specialized branches, each strange and incomprehensible to the majority of scientists and laymen. LeBon's imprecision and adventurous generalizations were a small price to pay for the benefits they brought to the scientific community.[146] The philosopher of science Abel Rey made the same point about the importance of popularization in his doctoral thesis of 1907, describing science as a product of psychological and social factors. Science, he wrote, can thrive only in a society that is interested in its results.[147] Painlevé, in fact, deemed LeBon's *Evolution of Matter* "the work which has most contributed to attracting the attention of the French public to the philosophical problems underlying the study of radioactivity." He suggested that it was not in vain that LeBon had studied the mind of crowds: LeBon "knows the art of brief and striking phrases which force their way into the memory."[148] LeBon's use of such terms as the "dissociation," "vanishing," and "evolution" of matter is illustrative of his art of finding the striking phrase. University scientists studying radioactivity in 1900 generally used more cautious language. It was reported that when Frederick Soddy suggested that the relationships of thorium and thorium emanation were a sort of "transmutation" of matter, Rutherford cautioned him against using the term with "they'll have our heads off."[149]

The history of LeBon's black light and dematerialization of matter is clearly complex. In a period characterized by ease of experimentation and by a profusion of claims for new radiations, LeBon's experimental work was discussed and criticized with the view that it might prove of scientific value. His extrascientific friendship with certain members of the French

[145]Letter from Émile Picard to LeBon, 15 June 1930 (Carnot Collection).

[146]Paul Painlevé, "Les principes de la physique et les phénomènes de radioactivité. Réflexions à propos de la théorie de l'Évolution de la matière, de Gustave LeBon," *Revue scientifique,* 5 (1906), 97–100.

[147]Abel Rey, *L'Energétique et le mécanisme au point de vue des conditions de la connaissance* (Paris, 1907), p. 80.

[148]Painlevé, *loc. cit.*

[149]Muriel Howorth, *Pioneer Research on the Atom* (New York, 1958), p. 84.

Academy facilitated the publication of his experiments. Even when his experiments met with telling criticisms, his ideas still appealed to some scientists and members of the intellectual and political elite and, above all, to the general public.

Painlevé correctly identified the source of LeBon's greatest appeal when he applauded LeBon for attracting the scientific-minded public to the philosophical problems underlying the new experimental physics. And although Picard doubted the truth of LeBon's "scientific philosophy"—or, as he called it, "scientific poetry"—he nevertheless admired LeBon's ability to reach the public.[150]

LeBon's interpretation of the various new radiations—and particularly of the phenomenon of radioactivity—appealed to the temper of his time; it was in agreement with the widespread critical attitude towards science, with the evolutionary approach to history and society, and with the prevailing antimaterialistic bias. He attacked the unpopular "dogmas" of science such as the conservation of matter and the deterministic laws of mechanics and thermodynamics. He associated himself with the fashionable view of the centrality of process and evolution in nature and of the centrality of force and action in a nonmaterialistic universe where man's spontaneous and subjective role was reaffirmed. In LeBon's work, physics meshed with philosophy; and although he never gained the reputation he coveted as a founder of modern science, he nevertheless played a notable role in the intellectual and social history of science of his time.

[150]See note 102.

# Nonclassical Science and the Philosophy of Optimism[1]

## BY BORIS KUZNETSOV*

### 1. COGNOSCEMUS!

Never before has the history of science, and particularly the history of physics, illuminated so clearly the historical fate of human civilization. In our time the very existence of civilization depends to a degree on the evolution and application of physics. The beginning of the atomic age recalls the old legend of the hero who paused before the inscription: "go right . . . go left," with opposite predictions for the two variants of choice. Today, one side of the inscription threatens atomic war and the destruction of civilization, while the other promises an unheard-of blossoming of production, science, and culture. The threat has been propagated in many novels that depict the burnt-out space of the earth, over which the last remnants of its population wander in anticipation of their own inevitable and rapid death. The second side of the inscription contains the economic curves, technological diagrams, flight plans of space voyages, and physical formulas. When one looks at the components of the optimistic prediction, one sees as their most important and common base a belief in the infinite power of reason, in the unlimited comprehensibility of the world.

In our day, epistemological optimism has become not only a result but a condition of and a factor in the acceleration of scientific, technical, economic, and social progress. Such a role is currently played by *dynamic* epistemological optimism; namely, the idea of infinite knowledge, of transformation, clarification, and particularization of valid concepts of the world.

In classical science, the transformation of fundamental principles was sporadic; it was rarely repeated within a single generation, and conclusions concerning the unlimited development of science could be drawn only on a very high level of abstraction. The science of the twentieth century—nonclassical science—is developing otherwise. In it, a reexamination of funda-

*Institute for the History of Science, Academy of Sciences, U.S.S.R., Staropanski, p. 1/5, Moscow.

[1] This article was translated from the Russian by Allen M. Hegland with the assistance of Russell McCormmach.

197

mental principles becomes a condition and a component of the continuous progress of comprehending the world and transforming civilization on the basis of new concepts. This fundamental dynamism of knowledge, this decisive meaning of differential criteria—the speed and the acceleration of science—which replaces the illusion of the realized and completed epistemological ideal is the source of the dynamic effect of contemporary nonclassical science on civilization and the basis of scientific-technical and economic optimism.

In classical science, the ideal of complete knowledge often appeared as the goal. Now the ideal of science is *infinite knowledge,* knowledge that infinitely approaches objective truth. From the contemporary standpoint, the classical illusion of complete knowledge seems a pessimistic conception, a negative statement. Here we encounter an extremely curious castling of the concepts of pessimism and optimism. It consists in the following: for a dogmatic explanation—let us say, for the understanding of science—the source of optimism is the achievement of an ultimate explanation or the hope of such an achievement. For a dynamic explanation—for the reason of science—the prospect of an ultimate solution, where questions of "why" cease, where the questioning, restless line of science disappears, will be a pessimistic one, a pessimistic prognosis. On the other hand, restlessness, incompletion, and the prospect of an infinite series of new questions are the source of optimism.

Why are the terms "understanding" and "reason" of science appropriate here? The traditional separation of understanding and reason ascribes to the understanding knowledge of the finite, to reason that of the infinite. The actual progress of science is impossible without the synthesis of laws of *understanding,* explaining a given phenomenon, and *reason's* presumption of further and potentially infinite knowledge of the world. Although in the nonclassical epoch, the questioning "reason" accompanying the "understanding," accompanying the soothing, positive melody of scientific progress is loud, it does not drown out the positive melody, but merges with it. Today *every* partial answer is simultaneously a question addressed to the entire chain of scientific explanations. We recall Einstein's answer to the question posed by optical experiments; namely, his explanation of the paradox that the velocity of light is the same with respect to different systems moving relatively to one another. Einstein's answer—the theory of relativity—consisted in appealing to very general principles, to the nature of space and time, to that which seemed original and not subject to further analysis, to that which Kant considered to be a priori. But Einstein's conception denied space and time an a priori character, denying it even to the geometric axioms. In the general theory of relativity, the transition from Euclidean geometry to non-Euclidean geometry depends on physical conditions, on the gravitational field. Thus, the geometric axioms themselves are mediated and the physical explanation of the geometry of the world leads to an infinite series of increasingly new physical statements of fact. In the theory of relativity, the infinity of knowledge is present in each concrete, local, finite link, in the explanation of the results of experiment.

Such a style of thought creates in science a continuous line of questions addressed to the future, creates unresolved conflicts, prognoses, and expectations. This line is evident with particular distinctness in contemporary nonclassical science. By its very character, it is closely related to the emotional component of science and, particularly, to optimism in its psychological aspects, to a certain complex of moods and feelings. This optimism, related to the questioning and infinity-seeking component of scientific creativity, is in no way rectilinear and monochromatic; it includes regret for the classical values being dethroned. The regret is not tragic, as it was with Lorentz, who regretted that he had not died before classical physics was wrecked, but a reconciled, lyric regret. It also includes satisfaction with the indestructibility of the classical values, and the joyful perception of the ever-present youth of science, its nonrepetitiveness, its dynamism.

The absolutes of classical science—the invariance of absolute space and absolute time, the uniformity and invariance of atoms, the uniformity, universality, and invariance of the eternal laws of existence that Newton's axioms of motion appeared to be—were the basis of Victorian static optimism, the peaceful and joyful belief that science would soon, if it had not already done so, pass into a haven of knowledge, perfect in its foundations. This feeling of haven is characteristic of Victorian optimism, just as the perception of the departure from the haven and of the boundlessness of the open sea of science is characteristic of contemporary epistemological optimism.

In relation to optimism permeated with the feeling of haven, the term "Victorian" is more suitable than the term "classical." Classical science and the contents and style of the cultural features and social psychology of the nineteenth century that depended on it were not at all unitary. The questioning, dynamic tradition addressed to the future—the necessary component of the development of science—was never interrupted. But it, if one may use such a remote analogy here, did not occupy in the parliament of science the bench of the ruling party and rather was in the opposition, expressing itself in the assertion of contradictions, antinomies, and the logical incompleteness of contemporary science. Such assertions supported in particular the relativistic critique of Newtonian mechanics in the nineteenth century. Sometimes the antinomies were called "catastrophes" (e.g., the "ultraviolet catastrophe," which physics was led out of at the turn of the century by the idea of the quantum emission of radiation). "Victorian" was applied to the illusion of constant prosperity prevalent during the long years of the reign of Queen Victoria. Victorian optimism in science was based not so much on the absence as on the ignorance of contradictions and logical inconsistencies in the classical absolutes.

During the classical period, the criticism of absolutes was related to a very high level of abstraction. When one thought of the infinity of the universe, paradoxes arose of infinite forces acting on each body in the gravitational field of the infinite universe or of the uniformly illuminated vault of the night sky owing to an infinite multitude of stars.

The genesis of nonclassical science was related to another situation. Paradoxes arose out of experiments; science could not develop (and, too, could not then find application) without the resolution of paradoxes. Einstein spoke of the "flight from paradoxes"; i.e., the transfer of the halo of paradoxicalness from experimental results to the general axioms of science, accompanied by a reexamination of the axioms. The infinite variability of the axioms, the fundamental infinity of scientific progress, became a characteristic of each large local episode in the development of science.

The illusion of complete knowledge, by conflicting with its constant, real incompleteness, occasionally led scholars to agnosticism, to the fiction of an absolute limit to the comprehensibility of the world. Toward the end of the nineteenth century, DuBois-Reymond in his famous speech on the limits of knowledge uttered the pessimistic formula: *ignorabimus!* (we will never know!). Nonclassical science makes this formula archaic and clearly not in conformance with reality. The failure to achieve ultimate perfect knowledge does not indicate a limit of science but rather its lack of limits. Presently the slogan of science is *cognoscemus!* (we will know!). Let us find out every secret of nature and let us not stop with this: ahead is the infinite field of knowing reason, and man infinitely approaches the inexhaustible truth, the inexhaustible complexity of existence.

There exists yet another form of the limitation of knowledge, of epistemological pessimism. It is not concealed under the statically optimistic illusion of complete knowledge, but involves the boundary between subjective perceptions and the objective world. Does knowledge pass through this boundary, does it reach the objective truth? Here one postulates not a complete, exhaustive knowledge of substance, but not even an incipient authentic knowledge of substance. This is the most difficult form of agnosticism to overcome, the most fundamental and the most tormenting for human thought. It is directed against the basic presumption of knowledge, against the *believable existence* of a knowable world. What can guarantee the reliability of sensory impressions, the credibility of that which registers in the consciousness through the sense organs? Is the world a dream? Does that which we see and touch exist? Are perhaps the concepts of the objective causes of our perceptions illusory? Here extending before human thought is the shadow of a more general and terrible *ignorabimus* than that threatened by DuBois-Reymond. But this shadow also is only a phantom. In the history of philosophy, science, and technology there are convincing arguments in favor of objective existence; namely, in the historical conclusions to which the picture of the genesis and transformation of the concepts of the world and of the methods of changing the world leads.

Agnosticism, which is related to the existence of an external world, is connected to the concept of a number of self-generating images and statements of fact. Consciousness here plays a passive role. It is precisely for this reason that it cannot penetrate the impermeable membrane of perceptions and can say nothing of whether or not anything exists on the other side of this membrane. But, in fact, everything takes place otherwise. Consciousness possesses an active function; it becomes objective; man acts on nature and confirms his conclusions, including those void of direct empirical roots. He does this in experiments and in industry. The coincidence of observable phenomena with those calculated from theory imparts a valid character to these phenomena. Man himself is included in the causal chain and cannot doubt the subordination of the phenomena to causes. He discovers these causes; after all, the result observed was predetermined by the component of material processes realized in an experiment or in industry.

The epistemological effect of science is demonstrated even more distinctly when experimental results do not coincide with those stemming from theory; i.e., in the case of *paradoxical* results, so characteristic of the genesis and development of nonclassical science. Nonclassical science, with its paradoxical experimental results that, within the span of a generation, find rational explanation in a new theory, does the same as classical science, but it does it quickly so that its result becomes not only belief in the credibility of existence but also the optimistic perception of continuously leaving the haven. Such a psychological tone is characteristic of sharp and decisive turns of science when science actually leaves its haven. For non-classical science, such turns are the core of its being; its constant and continuous development is always changing its fundamental principles or preparing for their change.

## 2. ENTROPY, NOÖZONES, AND MAXWELL'S DEMON

When we speak of epistemological optimism, we are concerned with the causes of phenomena, knowledge of the causal *ratio* of the world. But why is knowledge of causes accompanied by emotional uplift, by the perception of the realization of some drive or goal? This perception is a characteristic feature of optimism: the latter is related to prognosis, the prediction of such a course of objective processes that coincide with a prior plan. Optimism could be defined as the coefficient of correlation between prognosis and goal. A goal is a fundamental limit or boundary separating nature without man from man in nature. The goal of man does not flow out of intrinsically natural processes, but it is realized by an expedient grouping, by an organization, of such processes. Among such processes are those creating the possibility of expedient grouping, processes whose course may be predicted. Prediction is based on the dependence of certain local events on other local events and on the mutual dependence of local events and macroscopic processes encompassing large ensembles of local events.

In mechanics, a local event is the existence of a particle at a given instant at a given point in space. A macroscopic process in this case will be the motion of the particle, its trajectory, or, in four-dimensional space, its world line. Classical analytical mechanics stems from the assumption that if we know one of the events, namely, the state of motion of a particle in the assigned force field at the given point at the given moment, then the following events are thereby defined: the states of motion of the particle at other points and at other moments. But the fields themselves depend on the positions and velocities of particles, from which Laplace's conclusion follows: if at a certain moment the coordinates and velocities of all particles of the universe were known, then it would be possible to predict the future of the universe. The dependence of subsequent events on preceding ones is expressed by differential equations; individual events are governed by differential laws. They are the basis of prognosis, in analytical mechanics of the prognosis of future states of motion of a material point. Other more complex differential laws serve as the basis for prognosis in other branches of science where prognosis bears, as it does in mechanics, a metrical character and may, in principle, be represented by motion in some multidimensional space.

In analytical mechanics, however, other equations figure that express other laws, laws that are not differential but integral. Here the starting point for analogy and generalization is the law of least action. In the formulation of this law there enters an integral whose least, or greatest, value distinguishes the real trajectory (in four-dimensional representation, the world line) from all others; the real trajectory (or world line) is then determined by methods of the variational calculus. The direct determination of some local state, some event, some world point at which the event takes place is no longer involved; rather the process of variation of state, the dynamics, motion, and world line are directly determined. Each local event is defined by an integral result, a prolonged process encompassing the entire behavior of the particle; the behavior necessarily corresponds totally to a certain extreme, e.g., least, value of the integral. Already it is not the future that depends on the present but, to some degree, the present that depends on the future. Local events are determined not by other local events, but by an integral evolution extending from past to future and by the character and type of the evolution.

Similar processes allow themselves to be grouped in such a manner that the goal is reached, that a situation previously defined is realized. The expedient grouping of the forces of nature does not give man the right to see in external nature any kind of conscious goal, but it does allow him to view nature as a totality of possible objects of expedient human activity. Can we in this case distinguish in nature "better" and "worse," not only "more" and "less"?

Let us begin with the law of conservation of energy. At first glance it would seem to have nothing to do with "better" and "worse," but only with "more" and "less." The law of conservation of energy establishes a quantitative commensurability of different forms of energy. Energy can be greater or smaller, but in transitions from one form into another, an increase is excluded as well as a decrease; there can be neither "more" nor "less." The law of conservation of energy denies quantitative changes during qualitative transitions, but this is a comparatively simple version of the law. The qualitative and positive content of the law of conservation of energy consists in the assertion that energy, though it cannot be quantitatively created or destroyed, passes into qualitatively different forms. Similar transitions depend on differences such as those between the temperature of steam in a boiler and in a condenser or between the potential of water in upper and lower millraces.

The measure of the equalization of heat, of the obliteration of temperature gradients, is "entropy." It is the measure of the disorder of molecular motion. The same magnitude, but with a minus sign, is the measure of macroscopic ordering, of nonuniformity in the distribution of heat, of differences in temperature; it is "negentropy" (negative entropy). The concepts of entropy and negentropy can be generalized; for this, certain preliminary explanations are required. The concept of Sadi Carnot, i.e., that heat can pass from a hot body to a cold one, but cannot pass in the reverse direction, became the basis for the idea of the irreversible evolution of the world. In any process of heat transfer, the difference in temperature decreases. If it is possible in the given local system to increase the difference in the temperature, to increase the negentropy, then it can only be done at the cost of a compensating increase in entropy in the environment or in other systems or, generally, in the world. Thus, the world is threatened with the equalization of temperature. The transition of heat into mechanical energy is possible in the case of the existence of temperature gradients, but when mechanical energy passes into heat, in the total balance of nature the reverse transition becomes increasingly smaller, since temperature gradients are obliterated. The entropy of the world steadily increases. The heat death of the world is predicated on the transformation of all energy into heat, in the equalization of heat distribution, in the disappearance of temperature gradients, in the disappearance of energy transformations, in the disappearance of macroscopic gradients and macroscopic structure, and in the conservation only of chaotic molecular motion. Classical science brought forward weighty arguments against the idea of the heat death. Contemporary science—the theory of relativity and relativistic cosmology and, in no less degree, quantum mechanics—forces us to interpret the thermodynamics of the universe from new standpoints that eliminate the inevitability of heat death, although they still do not offer any concrete and unambiguous concept of the cosmic mechanism opposing it.

Presently the concepts of entropy and negentropy have taken on an extremely generalized character. In the theory of information and in modern probability theory, entropy is the name given to the measure of uncertainty, to the proximity of the probability values of different events. If all events possess the same probability, the entropy is maximal. If the probability of one event is equal to unity and that of the others is zero, then the uncertainty is transformed into certainty, and the entropy is zero and the negentropy is maximal. The disappearance of uncertainty is information; the entropy that has disappeared expresses it.

Thus, entropy is a measure of macroscopic equilibrium, uniformity, structurelessness, the chaos of microprocesses, their liberation from macroscopic ordering. Negentropy is a measure of such ordering, of the subordination of microevents to the macroscopic and, within limits, to the cosmic order. If we examine nature from the negentropy aspect, we see in local processes the growth of negentropy and in the inclusive system the growth of entropy. Such local processes transform chaos into cosmos, and apparently this process of ordering, of increasing the structure of the world, is not limited by the heat death.

Why has the picture of the formation of local negentropy caused an optimistic reaction in man? It is precisely because negentropic processes represent the basis for the expedient activity of man, and here in the analysis of such processes the objective establishment of fact and the objective prognosis become the source of subjective perception, of optimistic evaluation of the future.

In classical mechanics, the laws of motion themselves do not define unambiguously the forthcoming motion of a body without assigned *initial conditions*. The elliptical orbits of the planets may be cited as an example of the necessity of initial conditions for the determination of the motion of bodies. Why do the planets move precisely in such orbits and not otherwise? The answer is sought in the prehistory of the solar system, in cosmology. The situation is similar in the other physical properties:[2] the laws of thermodynamics determine the direction and intensity of heat fluxes, but only if the initial temperature gradients are given. An understanding of the initial conditions is essential outside physics also: for the evolution of species, for the direction of phylogeny, the initial conditions are the nature of the external environment, the living conditions of the populations.

Serving also as initial conditions is that most plastic region of the processes of nature where the transition to the expedient intervention of man began. The dam creates a new correlation of water levels; the steam engine, its fire box, boiler, and condenser create a new temperature gradient. Man creates zones of expediently ordered initial conditions and thereby controls the objective processes of nature.

V. I. Vernadski at the beginning of this century introduced the concept

[2] Max Born, "The Conceptual Situation in Physics and the Prospects of Its Future Development," *Proc. London Phys. Soc., 66* (1953), 501–513.

of the "noösphere." Beside the lithosphere, hydrosphere, and atmosphere of the earth, he designated a sphere whose structure was subordinated to human reason, to the goals of man. The noösphere is the sphere of reason, the sphere created by labor, by the expedient activity of man. The evolution of labor, the evolution of man in his relationship to nature included on the one hand consecutive miniaturization and on the other the expansion of the spatio-temporal regions that figure in those ideal predictable schemes that become the goals of labor. At present in the field of atomic energy such schemes already reach to the order of $10^{-12}$ cm; and in the long-term planning of the exploitation of fossils, in climate control, and in the conservation of nature, they reach to the lithosphere, hydrosphere, and the atmosphere of the earth.

It is here then that the separation of prediction and goal begins. Prediction in its classical form is based on the laws of motion and on their more or less complicated modifications; prediction is determined by these laws. The goal, however, does not depend on them. The goal itself determines not the ultimate course of events, unambiguously defined by the stated laws, but the choice of *initial conditions* independent of these laws. Naturally, the initial conditions in their evolution or spatial dislocation and even the goals themselves are subordinated to certain laws, but such laws are frequently found outside the limits of the given type of motion. The fact that in labor, which is considered to be an expedient activity, a goal is represented begins itself to figure as a causally defined result as soon as we pass into the region of social laws. Man, setting for himself a certain technical goal, is subordinated thereby to the social division of labor and to the totality of social relationships growing out of the division of labor. The erection of a dam on a river, which changes the initial conditions of motion of the water at the given point, is a goal in technology and, from the standpoint of the laws of the distribution of labor, funds, and industry, it is a consequence.

The concept of the noösphere can be generalized to a significant degree; there emerge zones of expediently ordered nuclear processes, quantum-electronic emissions, and structures of molecules of living matter. The concept now involves *ordered* structures, differences in water level, temperature gradients between boiler and condenser, cotton fibers that have lost their original chaotic interspersing and have become fabric, and electrons that have accumulated in the outer orbits so that the atom can emit coherent waves. It involves the *expedient* ordering of existence, the result of labor, the result of the intervention of human reason in processes of nature. Nonclassical science, particularly nonclassical physics, in its applications represents an unprecedented expansion of the noözone, a real generalization of the concept of the noösphere. We can speak of the noözone of emissions in quantum electronics, the noözone of nuclear processes in atomic energy, and the noözone of the hereditary code in molecular biology and radiation genetics; in each of these cases, there is an increase in negentropy, due to its reduction in other systems. The labor of man, which is based on his reason and which leads to the expansion and deepening of the noözones, is an analogue of the Maxwellian demon who, operating a barrier, admits rapid molecules into one side of a container and slow molecules into the other, thus reducing entropy and increasing temperature gradients, negentropy, and the ordering of existence.

## 3. PREDICTION AND PLANNING IN SCIENCE

Let us now switch from nature, the object of science, to science itself, from the phenomena of nature to the process of their causal explanation. This process is an objective, historical one, and here objective prediction is possible. Prediction, according to the place that this concept occupies in the theory of science, is analogous to a differential equation: by knowing the state of science at the present instant, one may predict its future state. Of course, the predictions are not unequivocal; one may not with certainty assert that some prospect will be realized, nor may one say that a given prospect is more probable than another. By the same token, a prediction that is related not to the future local state but to the dynamics of science in the course of time is analogous to an integral equation. Differential and integral laws allow the future to be predicted if the initial conditions are selected, and in the present case the role of such conditions is played by the structure of science, by the distribution of intellectual and material forces among the regions of investigation and coexisting theoretical and experimental problems. In nonclassical science, which is based on studies of the ultramicroscopic world and of the megaworld, fundamental investigations require significant funding and become a noticeable component of the national-economic balance; the creation of "initial conditions" is found to be an element not only of the planning of science but also of national economic planning.

Within the limits of such planning the selection of initial conditions of scientific development also takes place, conditions determining, to the degree that the concept of determination is applicable here, the attainment of the goal of science. The determination belongs to the *theory* of science; for in science itself, in natural science and in fields subject to natural-scientific analysis, i.e., in nature-minus-man, there is no such choice.

But on what then is this expedient, free choice causally dependent? What is it a *result* of? What is the nature of the regularities that determine the goals that man places above science? The regularities are those of social development. In a static approximation, it may be said that natural science is a monologue of nature and the social sciences a monologue of man, whereas history and the theory of natural science are a dialogue between man and nature.

In the planning of science, the initial conditions figure as predictional variants. In essence, discoveries are not planned results, but research directions, and in contrast with results, research directions are an unequivocal function of the "initial conditions." However, the unequivocal prediction of discoveries and "instantaneous" situations in general in science is a necessary condition for its planning. Ideal schemes for making discoveries allow a more concrete conception of certain tendencies of science; e.g., in contemporary theoretical physics, an important tendency is to explain the characteristic features of certain types of particles not by grouping subparticles of smaller mass within these particles but, on the contrary, by combining particles of larger mass that have lost a significant portion of their mass in the form of particle bonding energy. Such a tendency is seen in a more concrete form in the construction of hypothetical models; e.g., in the hypothesis of quarks and, accordingly, in the limits of predictions of the experimental discovery of quarks. Such partial prognoses may merge in a certain general ideal scheme; the unified field theory, the contemporary fundamental ideal of science, belongs among such schemes.

## 4. THE METRICS OF SCIENCE

In science an optimistic prediction is one that coincides in maximum degree with the goal posed for science; i.e., it defines the optimal combination of initial conditions. The combination will be optimal if a certain result of science or industry acquires its maximum value. Since a fundamentally metrical result is involved, the goal of science itself must be a metrical concept, and the concepts which express the effect of scientific research must be metrical.

Technical and economic progress includes consistent liberation of man from the power of the blind laws of nature. The liberation consists in the increasing possibility of compounding the forces of nature consciously, and the measure of such liberation, which is the measure and the technical and economical basis of the progress of civilization, is the growth of the productivity of labor. To the degree that the productivity of labor is a function of technical progress, it is proportional to the measure of expediently grouped forces of nature. Accordingly, it is directly dependent on the sum of the reliable data, verified in experiment and in labor, concerning nature, which itself is not a measurable value.

Thus, we come to the concept of a certain metrical equivalent of the level of science. Is it possible to find the metrical equivalent of the *goals* of science? Evidently, such an equivalent must be an expression characterizing the dynamics of science, corresponding to the dynamic goal of science. Contemporary nonclassical science obtains its impetus from dynamic ideals; it continues to manifest the dynamic tendencies of classical science. In the kinetic picture of the world of the seventeenth century, the measure of motion, now liberated from Aristotelian "natural places," was not the distance from natural places, but velocity; similarly, differential determinations have become characteristic of continuously advancing science, of the "world line" of science.

The dynamic effect of science is the metrical equivalent of such characteristics. By the term "economic effect of science," we should understand something specifically dependent on science, something arising only when industry becomes applied science, something quantitatively dependent on the intensity of scientific progress. To understand the economic effect of science, we must look at the *dynamics* of economic development, at the dynamics of the varying productivity of labor and of the structure of industry, at the "world line" of economics. If $P$ is the productivity of labor, $P'$ the first derivative of $P$ with respect to time, and $P''$ the acceleration of the growth of productivity of labor, the economic effect of science may be expressed functionally as $\Omega = f(P,P',P'')$. A given productivity of social labor is maintained at a constant level by controlling the technical parameters. Technological and constructional operations guarantee practically continuous variation in these parameters, and with them a nonzero first time derivative of the productivity of labor. The operations consist in the steady improvement in the realization of certain ideal physical and chemical cycles. The variation in the cycles themselves is the result of scientific research, which, when sufficiently developed, guarantees a nonzero second time derivative of the productivity of labor.

## 5. THE INTEGRAL GOAL OF SCIENCE

The *metrical* goals of science are those that can be expressed in integral, measureable magnitudes. It is precisely the economic effect of science that is such an integral and measureable goal. Addressed to science as a whole, the question "what for?" is a practical question, a question of the integral goal of science; it includes a quantitative question, which is, why does society devote a certain portion of its material and intellectual resources to scientific research? It includes as well the question: precisely what portion of its material and intellectual resources should society spend on scientific research? As soon as such a question arises, as soon as the concept of the *structure* of the resources expended by society appears, namely, the ratio of different expenditures, as soon as science stands before us as a part of a general and expedient social activity, science enters into the balance of social labor; and the determination of the social goal of science becomes an economic problem, a problem of the integral economic effect of science.

I will approach this problem by first making several remarks on the effect of modern science on the subject of labor, namely, man himself, on the character of labor and its content, and on the nature both of the object of labor and the totality of material processes that labor groups in an expedient manner. The volume and capacity of such processes controlled by man are the measure of the distance covered by man since he separated himself from nature, since human civilization appeared on the earth. Is it possible to find an economic index corresponding to this measure, to the level of civilization, to the degree of liberation of man from elemental forces and their subordination to man?

The productivity of social labor and its derivatives are the natural measure of expediently grouped forces and objects of nature. Labor consists of such a grouping. In science, regarded as a reflection of nature, man emerges primarily as *Homo sentiens;* man possesses organs of sensation, possesses historically developing means for the sensory attainment of the world. In science, regarded as a form of social consciousness, man emerges as *Homo cognoscens;* he possesses developing logical methods for the attainment of the world. In science, regarded as an expedient activity, man emerges as *Homo construens,* as creative man who changes the natural grouping of the forces of nature, who realizes his goals, who selects in advance the predictable results of objective processes and, accordingly, the initial conditions of these processes.

The contemporary integral goal of science, which can be realized in national-economic planning and which includes and is essentially based on the planning of science, is related to man himself, to his labor, and to natural resources. To the degree that man himself can be separated from labor, the goal of science consists in lengthening life, eliminating disease, and increasing consumption. With respect to the character of labor, the goal of science consists in continuously transforming the chief content of labor into increasingly more dynamic functions: from the maintenance of established processes to the regulation of alternating loads and regimes, then to the radical change of technological processes, and beyond to the change of increasingly more fundamental principles that have been incarnated in technology and construction. With respect to natural resources, the struggle for their profitable exploitation and the protection of nature from exhaustion and pollution are the beginnings of a general and far-reaching tendency. The ensemble of natural objects under man's control includes the spectrum from the subnuclear world to the entire lithosphere, hydrosphere, and atmosphere of the earth, and even beyond (as in such consciously evoked expedient processes as space flights and the propagation of extremely remote radar signals). Presently the entire lithosphere, hydrosphere, and atmosphere are becoming the noösphere, a structure essentially defined by human activity. In addition the time scale of the processes being regulated is increasing: human labor in its scale and effect on the subsequent dynamics of production predetermines not only planetary changes in space, but also changes encompassing decades and even centuries. Therefore, labor cannot presently fail to involve a peculiar planetary-secular calculation; in his labor, man emerges as an initiator and controller of planetary and secular processes in nature.

## 6. THE "IS" AND THE "OUGHT TO BE"

The theory of relativity, quantum mechanics, and the scientific-technical revolution that grew out of these developments have radically changed the old conflict of knowledge and action, truth and morality, what is and what ought to be. Now the answers to the question concerning the structure of space-time regions of the order of $10^{-13}$ cm and $10^{-25}$ sec and to the related question of the structure of the metagalaxy require inspiring national-economic actions. In their turn, the results of investigations of the microworld impel men to actions of vital importance for the fate of civilization and for the ecological conditions of human existence: naturally the conflict of what is and what ought to be changes at this time.

In his article "La morale et la science," Henri Poincaré says that morals and science, what should be and what is, cannot be combined through the logical deduction of one from the other, since science deals with the *indicative* mood and morals with the *imperative*.[3] Declarative statements of the type, "such an object exists," "such a process occurs," "such an event did happen," as well as others of the type, "the cause of the event was . . . ," cannot be obtained from imperative statements of the type, "one should act in such a way"; nor can one proceed in the other direction, from declarative to imperative. The logical independence of scientific and moral statements seems absolute; but is it so in reality? If science is understood as the *content* of certain statements, as something stable and remote from the process of its evolution, transformation, and change, and if morals are understood as the *content* of certain norms abstracted from their genesis and realization, then science and morals are indeed independent. However, as soon as we destroy the immobility of the statements on the one hand and of the norms on the other, as soon as science and morals emerge in their concrete, varying essence, then immediately their independence of one another becomes problematic and arbitrary.

For this reason the relationship between science and morals changed during the transition from classical to nonclassical science. In classical science, the positive content of scientific statements could, to a significant degree, be separated from their negative accompaniment, from the contradictions and from the questioning line of scientific progress. In nonclassical sciences, the positive content is practically inseparable from the dynamics; the understanding of science cannot be separated from its reason. The character of morals also changes, as the center of gravity passes from norms to paths of realization; not only the norms of good but also its realization, the transformation of what should be into what is, becomes essential in the moral self-consciousness of mankind. The optimism that grows out of contemporary science is inseparable from moral self-consciousness; in this connection I want to make some remarks on the criticism of the stationary canons of morals in dialectical philosophy, in art, and in culture.

Stable morals are closely related historically to stable cultures with stationary or slowly changing conditions and norms of social life and with stationary or quasi-stationary economics. In the middle ages, morals were embodied in traditional norms; the good was that which was hallowed by tradition, the moral norms having regulated economics and, to a certain

[3]Henri Poincaré, Chapter VIII, "La morale et la science," in *Dernières pensées* (Paris, 1919), p. 225.

degree, having guaranteed its keeping with tradition. Typical of medieval concepts were "fair price," "fair profit," "fair percent." The optimistic prediction was that of an unchanged repetition of customary and therefore "fair" norms and conditions. They are compatible only with such negative and conservative optimism as "so it was, so it will be." Sometimes the traditional conceptions of good painted the moral world a single color, without hues, in the image of a uniform or homogeneous physical world without nonbeing, as it appeared in Cartesian physics. Good seemed to be uniformity of existence, penetrated by a "continuous hosannah." This term appears in *The Brothers Karamazov,* spoken by the devil who brings the thoughts of his fellow conversationalists to their logical conclusion, thoughts which seem unbearable to Ivan Karamazov himself and unbearable even to Dostoevsky, whose interpreter in the last analysis is the "certain kind of Russian gentleman with not very strong streaks of gray," the infernal guest. The devil says to Ivan: "Without criticism it would be nothing but one 'hosannah.' But nothing but hosannah is not enough for life, the hosannah must be tried in the crucible of doubt. . . ."[4]

The earthbound and emphatically banal devil of Dostoevsky says something extremely fundamental, something similar to the remark of his much more imposing, philosophically educated colleague from *Faust.* Mephistopheles identifies himself to Faust as "part of that force which desires evil and does good." "Desires evil" means destroys "hosannah," and "does good" means transforms good from a stationary canon into something historically realizable and developing. Like Karamazov's devil, Mephistopheles expresses thoughts and personifies aspects of the psyche of his companion and fellow conversationalist and, in the final analysis, his creator as well. Faust departs from science because the elusiveness of thought that identifies existence and makes it uniform does not satisfy him; and in the lines of *Faust,* the anti-Newtonian, sensualistic, and emotional tendency of Goethe comes through. Science as the sum of ultimate and eternal results, as the kingdom of pure thought, uncomplicated by contradictions, impressions, and emotions, is the "hosannah" to knowledge. In the same manner, the philosophy of known, uniform good is the "hosannah" to morals. Faust departs from reason, from science, from good, and concludes a bargain with the spirit of evil; but the reason, science, and good that he rejects are uniform and immovable, lifeless and elusive. Faust wishes evil, and he pursues it not so much under the control of the spirit of evil as by

[4] Fyodor Dostoevsky, *The Brothers Karamazov,* in *Great Books of the Western World* (Chicago, 1952), *52,* 341.

its technical support. This is the dialogue of good and evil, and it ends when Faust demands of the moment, "Stop, you are beautiful!" It is absolute victory, the identity of each successive moment with the foregoing one, the cessation of existence, death. It is the absolute victory of good. But Faust overcomes death in labor, in creation, i.e., in a process that cannot be stopped. The finale of *Faust* is the apotheosis of good that does not exclude evil but struggles with it, the apotheosis of the dynamic moral ideal.

## 7. NONCLASSICAL SCIENCE AND IMMORTALITY

The optimistic mood and feeling are contrasted with the pessimistic shadow of death. Reaching maximum entropy, bereft of temperature gradients, nature approaches heat death, and with it the death of knowledge and the death of man. Is the shadow of the death of man driven away by contemporary science? Science has saved nature from the spectre of inevitable heat death; its starting point is the inexhaustibility of knowledge from the infinite evolution of fundamental principles; but does it disperse the pessimistic shadow of the death of man himself?

Recall the formula of Epicurus that counters the fear of death: "when we exist, death is not present, and when death is present, we do not exist." Why has this logically irreproachable formula not saved mankind from the fear of death? I want to call attention to the negative and static character of the formula. Everything good and bad according to Epicurus consists in perception, and death is the absence of perception. In essence, such a formula is in no way optimistic, but only antipessimistic. The pessimistic perception of life, the perception of its perishability and the fear of nonexistence, is not contrasted here by an active, optimistic perception that could not only logically discredit the fear of death but also remove it from consciousness. An optimistic perception that could free man from the fear of nonexistence is the perception of the fullness of existence.

In the philosophy of Epicurus, man is liberated from fear of future nonexistence. He must not think of that which seems threatening to his local existence. Death does not in fact threaten man; he lives now, in the organic time limits of his existence. Nonexistence does not frighten him because it is beyond the limits of local individual existence: where there is death, there we do not exist, and this "we" and this "exist" do not extend to the infinite future. The solitude in infinite space and time that induced such chilling horror into the soul of Pascal seemed a refuge to Epicurus. Man is confined to the "here" of the limits of the earth and to the "now" that encompasses his short life. But this is a *logical* refutation of the fear of death, and evidently even in ancient times it was not psychologically active. The contemporaries of Epicurus perhaps rather felt not so much liberation from the fear of death as the transformation of this fear into the quiet, reconciled sadness that permeates the *Odyssey*.

For Pascal, the concept of infinite space and infinite time, the imagined departure from the limits of local existence, transformed life into an instant, transformed finite existence into nothing. Pascal writes: "I know not who put me into the world, nor what the world is, nor what I myself am. I am in terrible ignorance of everything. I know not what my body is, nor my sense, nor my soul, not even that part of me which thinks what I say, which reflects on all and on itself, and knows itself no more than the rest."[5] Pascal mourns inevitable death and the finiteness of human existence in infinite space and infinite time: "I see those frightful spaces of the universe which surround me, and I find myself tied to one corner of this vast expanse, without knowing why I am put in this place rather than another, nor why the short time which is given me to live is assigned to me at this point rather than at another of the whole eternity which was before me or which shall come after me. I see nothing but infinites on all sides, which surround me as an atom and as a shadow which endures only for an instant and returns no more. All I know is that I must soon die, but what I know least is this very death which I cannot escape."[6]

Pascal's is not so much fear of death as fear of the infinity of space and time, of the infinite universe unconcerned with man and his infinitely short life and infinitely small sensual experience. His is a feeling of being lost in infinity and of the insignificance of life in the face of infinity. The feeling derives not only from the infinity of time that remains after death, but also from the infinity of past time. The pessimism of the seventeenth century feared both directions of infinity. This was not even fear, but a melancholy feeling of the impossibility of comprehending infinity. The fundamental tendency peculiar to the sixteenth and seventeenth centuries of striving to extend rational thought to infinite nature underlies the pessimistic outlook; the tendency is the tragedy of classical rationalism. The quattrocento saw in art, and precisely in art, the overcoming of solitude, of the nothingness and mortality of man. Beauty unites man with the infinite world; it personifies infinite existence in the finite and limited. The cinquecento in the person of Giordano Bruno felt *heroic furor,* an emo-

---

[5] Pascal, *Pensées,* in *Great Books of the Western World* (Chicago, 1952), *33,* 207.
[6] *Ibid.*

tional and intellectual rush toward the infinite world, toward its rational and comprehensible essence. In the seventeenth century, yet another component of pessimism was added to the feeling of solitude and death; in Pascal one hears above all the tragic perception of the incomprehensibility of the infinite world to human reason. The tragic perception expresses not only a pessimistic judgment, but also a rush toward the comprehension of the infinite world.

In the optimistic conceptions of the Renaissance and the Baroque, infinity did not lie beyond the limits of individual, local, and finite existence. The future, to the degree that it complemented the present, became a component of existence; man could not exclude himself from the future. If knowledge and activity directed at the infinite future became the content of human existence, then that content was not interrupted by death. A new concept of immortality arose; man perceived in the infinite activity and knowledge of mankind the immortality of his personality.

In the seventeenth century, Spinoza added a very important new element to the optimistic conception. In saying that the "free man thinks of nothing less than of death and his wisdom is not a meditation upon death but upon life,"[7] he made freedom a necessary component of being, and it is precisely that which liberated man from the fear of death. For Spinoza, the infinite world was not a threat, since the content of mortal life reflected an infinite process. The behavior of man, like that of every particle, was not the compulsory result of sudden acts but the manifestation of an internal, immanent essence, and this was what Spinoza understood by freedom. The same immanent essence reflected the harmony of the whole, the cosmic harmony of the infinite world. Spinoza did not know the reverse process; namely, the action of a finite, individual mortal on the surrounding infinite world. The idea not only of infinite knowledge of the world but also of infinite transformation of the world goes beyond the framework of seventeenth century philosophy and, further, beyond the framework of the classical philosophy of the eighteenth and nineteenth centuries.

Nonclassical science signifies not only the possibility but also the necessity of continuous reflection on infinite knowledge of the world and infinite action upon the world. The perception of immortality is the perception of the unlimitedness of that which man does, thinks, feels, and strives for. In nonclassical science and in the scientific-technical revolution evoked by it, epistemological optimism—it is not only epistemological, as

[7]Spinoza, *Ethics*, in *Great Books of the Western World* (Chicago, 1952), *31*, 444.

it includes the prospect of unlimited transformation of the world—becomes the basis for conquering the darkest, seemingly most fundamental and inevitable spectres of nonexistence. When each local element, each "here and now" of human existence, is complemented by merging with something wider and fundamentally unlimited, then Feuerbach's words are realized: "each second you drink up the cup of immortality which replenishes itself like the goblet of Oberon."

## 8. NONCLASSICAL SCIENCE AND THE "OLD AGE OF HOMER"

Contemporary science and the character of the related dynamics of labor and production fill the "goblet of Oberon" with the nectar of immortality. Does this nectar dry up, or does modern science preserve it in the process of the aging of the organism? Is the active, transforming function of man preserved in old age? Does the traditional concept of old age change in the conditions of the new science? It does; old age begins significantly later. Furthermore, old age is almost totally void of its traditional definition as a period of irreversible degradation. The relationship between the change in the concept of old age and contemporary science is seen distinctly in the liquidation of a number of diseases that shorten life and reduce man's capacity to work. Less distinct is the connection between modern science and the rationalization and amelioration of ecological conditions. Today the negative side of the problem is on the agenda—the need for protecting forests, water bodies, and air—but this is only a part, only the beginning of the radical rationalization of the ecological environment of man as a condition of the radical increase in the duration and fullness of life.

The two terms, "duration" and "fullness," the extensive and intensive increase in human life, characterize the change in the nature and content of labor. The application of nonclassical science signifies a change of labor into a new, dynamic, increasingly more general and fundamental function that reconstructs industry. Such an evolution of labor is inseparable from the evolution of science, in which increasingly more fundamental principles become plastic, variable, and dependent on experimental and industrial experience.

In such a transformation of the nature and content of labor is the source of their specific action on old age under the conditions of the scientific-technical revolution, action which combines with the immediate physiological and ecological effects of science. Such a distribution of functions among coexisting and collaborating generations, when "fathers" preserve the existing order and "sons" emerge as the bearers of a new one, is represented as classical. The conflict of "fathers" and "sons" usually also expresses the break between the two components of labor and knowledge: the maintenance of tradition and its transformation. Such a break is the basis of the traditionalism of old age and the nihilism of youth.

In the third century, the Greek philosopher Longinus ascribed the *Iliad* with its heat of passions to the young Homer and the *Odyssey* permeated with quiet thought to the old age of the poet. The *Odyssey* in Longinus' words suggests the sun as it is about to set; it preserves its colossal dimensions, but it no longer blazes. If the explosion of constructive thought is associated with the sun at its zenith, with youthful passion and temperament, and the peaceful development of a new principle with the *Odyssey,* with the sun at the horizon, then such an analogy does not hold for contemporary scientific creativity. In modern industry the development of technical principles (at one time one could say "peaceful development") and the revolutionary transformation of these principles are combined.

On the whole, nonclassical science and its application approach those characteristic features of creativity that were associated with the stages of aging. The concept "acme," which the Greeks used to designate the higher blooming of the creative powers of man, changes; it already is not a narrow peak on the graph but a curve extended along the time axis. It reaches a maximum comparatively early and retains a value comparatively close to the maximum nearly until death. Therefore, the struggle for longevity in the sense of improving the conditions of life, particularly improving the ecological environment, and of increasing the efficiency of medicine corresponds to the requirements and possibilities of modern science and industry. Demographic fears resulting from the increasing percentage of the elderly in the make-up of the population and the resulting decrease in the labor potential of society are connected with a naive numerical fetishism in the determination of age; in fact, the lengthening of the average duration of life signifies a sharp reduction in the portion of invalids in the working population and a sharp increase in the maximum creative working capacity. Thus, gerontological optimism is closely related to epistemological, scientific-technical, and economic optimism.

However, one should not think that gerontological problems flow out of economic problems. Man, the subject of labor, and his interests are the goal, the starting point that determines the plans for the reconstruction of the character, the tools, and the objects of labor. The interests of man are the extensive and intensive enlargement of life; they are to lengthen life and to fill it maximally with the active transformation of the world.

## 9. THE YEAR 2000

The relation of modern optimistic predictions, encompassing the duration and fullness of human life and the style of thought and feeling, with extremely exotic, paradoxical, seemingly remote-from-life details of physical experiments is characteristic. The theory of relativity and the experiments that led to it are a case in point: could one direction or another of a ray passing through a cabin, one or another slope of the loads suspended in the cabin, and tens of other analogical, imaginary, or actual experiments really have evoked radical changes in the style of man's thought and the power of man over nature? The answer is yes, and that it was accomplished with the aid of innumerable schemes of mirrors, screens, lanterns, clocks, and rulers is all the more surprising. But it is not more surprising than the radical changes in life evoked by Galileo's cabin where butterflies flew, where water ran into a vessel placed below it, and where everything took place in the same way regardless of whether the ship were stationary or moving. (This description is found in Galileo's *Dialogue,* a book which led to a trial in 1633, a prolonged reaction throughout the entire Catholic world, and a multitude of other historical events.) And it is no more surprising than the effect on life of experiments described in Newton's *Mathematical Principles of Natural Philosophy,* from which lines of historical relationship stretch to the French Revolution and the English Industrial Revolution.

At present the lines of historical relationship are proceeding toward those scientific-technical, economical, and cultural shifts that contribute to the predictions pertaining to the end of our millennium, to the year 2000. It is clear to everyone that 2000 is a conventional date. It is not, however, arbitrary, since it indicates the order of magnitude of a term during which the modern tendencies of scientific and scientific-technical progress are realized. Perhaps such realization will occupy not thirty but twenty or forty years, but it involves some definite order of magnitude of the term. The date 2000 conceals in itself the thought of some single complex of shifts related to one another. This complex consists in the integral realization of nonclassical science, above all in the realization of those physical ideas that matured in the middle of the century in nuclear physics, in quantum electronics, in cybernetics, and in molecular biology.

Why is it that precisely now in the 1970's the shifts have taken on a distinctiveness that is incomparable with the shifts of the past? Why do the end of the 1960's and beginning of the 1970's allow the curtain of the future to be lifted? It is, above all, precisely in these years that atomic power plants have become capable of competing with thermal, coal-burning plants. The fact that the costs of a kilowatt-hour from atomic and coal-burning plants have drawn closer creates the possibility of a prolonged, encompassing decade of transition to predominantly atomic-electrical energy production. Naturally, the speed of the transition depends essentially on the degree to which the proximity of these costs is replaced by a difference in favor of the atomic plants. But now we are passing the point of intersection of the curves of kilowatt-hour costs. A number of circumstances allow us to think that the cost of a kilowatt-hour from atomic power plants will decrease more rapidly than the cost from thermal power plants and allow us to predict a consistent increase in the difference in favor of atomic plants. The predictions of the future role of atomic energy stem from the fact that it has already proven possible to efficiently switch over to the new energy-balance structure. One may even count on acceleration of the transition, since the problem of reactors that produce more nuclear fuel than they consume has been solved physically and technically. For the beginning of the 1970's, it is also characteristic that the new technology based on electronics has approached the basic industrial processes. In this same period, cybernetics, after successes of great importance for the future in the fields of communication, processing and storage of information, and control, has approached purely industrial problems. The three basic developments—atomic energy, electronics, and cybernetics—have now reached their own, if one may put it this way, economic maturity. They also represent the scientific-technical basis for a new prediction that fleshes out nonclassical science.

In connection with the revolution brought about by atomic energy, one may consider a certain complex of interrelated shifts in technology, the character of labor, the character of the raw-material base, culture, and science as the content of this particular period. One may call the transformation of atomic power plants into the predominant source of electrical production, the automation resulting from electronic computers and controlling machines, and the liberation of industry from the threat of the exhaustion of resources the completion of the characteristic process of the period. One should emphasize the nonclassical, paradoxical character of the processes lying at the heart of the new developments. Quantum electronics, the most important component of the atomic age for technology (no less important, anyway, than nuclear processes for energy production), is based on Bohr's quantum model of the atom and on Einstein's prediction of the electronic transitions within the atom. In 1916, Einstein published an article, "Emission and Absorption of Radiation in the Quantum Theory," in which he discussed a system of particles that emits and absorbs quanta of radiant energy by changing its structure. As a concrete example of such a quantum system, one may take an atom consisting of a nucleus and electrons and possessing two energy levels. These levels may be represented as two electron orbits, the lower level corresponding to an orbit close to the nucleus and the upper level to one farther away. Of course, it is possible to take instead of an atom a molecule which, in one configuration of atoms, has a higher and in another a lower energy. According to Einstein the electron transitions from one level to the other can be spontaneous, but they can also be evoked by the action of radiation, i.e., by a flux of photons. The interaction of atoms with radiation is twofold: in one case, the photon is simply absorbed by the atom, and in the other, the atom emits a new photon. In 1927, Dirac noted that the new photon cannot be distinguished from the old one; it possesses the same energy and the same direction. If many electrons are at the upper level, they all synchronously jump to the lower level, and the atom emits photons of the same energy and the same direction; but there will be more of such photons than in the external radiation inducing the electronic transitions. Thus, the possibility is created of intensifying radiation through the induced emission of quantum systems. Such a possibility is realized in lasers.

One of the most important tendencies of technical progress in the last quarter of the twentieth century will be the spread of lasers into industrial technology. Mechanical methods of working metals and other materials are giving way to methods employing laser rays. A thin, monochromatic, and, at the same time, powerful laser ray allows the accuracy of the sizes and dimensions of shaped products to be brought within several microns. Quantum electronics is discovering, moreover, the possibility of a deep regrouping of molecules in crystal lattices and of atoms in molecules. Since such a regrouping may yield products with superhard surfaces, the perfection of lasers is the source of a broad reconstruction of all of the basic technological branches. Quantum electronics is only seeing the beginning of the engineering realization of the ideal physical scheme that Einstein developed in 1916 and that took on concrete form in the middle of the century. One may imagine that in the decades remaining until the end of the century, lasers will be developed that transform the energy of the most widely dispersed sources into energy concentrated into directed streams of coherent electromagnetic waves as powerful as desired. The band width of laser emissions will expand so that they can operate in the infrared and ultraviolet regions. Perhaps laser rays will replace metal wires for the transmission of electrical energy in the future.

The elements of molecular biology that are most important for technology, economics, and culture are also nonclassical. A significant, even predominant, portion of biological and biochemical processes can be described without taking into consideration either the behavior of the individual electrons and the wave properties related to them or the specific features of the emissions related to their corpuscular nature. In particular, the processes of chromosome splitting, RNA synthesis, and the synthesis of protein molecules on RNA matrixes are not quantum processes. However, there are biological processes that cannot be explained and, correspondingly, cannot be reproduced in an experiment without quantum concepts. These processes hold great interest for prediction. Such a process is the change in the genetic code in chromosomes evoked by quanta of short-wavelength radiation.

One might think that the modern application of radiation in agriculture and medicine is still very remote both in scale and in nature from that which will take place in the last quarter of this century. Here one should remember quantum electronics; it is not out of the question that by the end of the twentieth century mankind will have made further advances along the paths of a radical increase in food resources, of the treatment of cancer, and of a substantial lengthening of human life with the aid of quantum electronics and molecular biology.

For the character of labor, the application of nonclassical processes in electronic computing and controlling devices has the greatest value. Cybernetics is far removed from its historical antecedents, the ancient mechanical imitations of animals and humans; it is removed not only by the complexity of its mechanisms, not only by its physical-technical bases, but also by its function. It sees as its main task not the imitation of the biological functions of organisms, but the task that contains the predictions conventionally bound to the year 2000. The task consists in the programming not only of self-reproducing mechanisms but also of their consistent evolution toward new parameters. Such dynamic programming fundamentally differs from biological phylogeny, which is based on statistical laws of selection. The laws of the phylogeny of technical progress, of change in the technical level in each new generation of machines, are different. Technical progress leads man out from under the power of the statistical regularities of natural selection. The highest expression of the programming of technical progress will be a series of consecutive generations of machines capable of creating plans more perfect than those realized in themselves. Such a replacement of man in his dynamic, reconstructing function is the apotheosis of man in his intrinsically human essence.

Cybernetics is the most important condition for the *acceleration* of scientific-technical and economic progress. The basis of the acceleration is the appearance of an increasing number of new physical and chemical plans that become new ideals, purposive canons for construction engineers and technologists who create new machines and technological processes. In the contemporary mathematization of nearly all branches of science, the path leading from a certain theoretical conception to the conclusions that may become the subject of experimental testing and constructive realization includes in the majority of cases long series of calculations. Machines perform such calculations in the course of minutes. The application of computer technology is one of the bases for projecting to the last decades of the twentieth century a practically continuous flow of new physical and chemical schemes that will be at the same time purposive schemes of technical progress.

I want to return again to the derivatives with respect to time of the productivity of labor as the metrical expression of the effect of science. There exists a distinct connection between the degree of totality, of depth and nonutilitarian focus of scientific investigations, and of the uncertainty of their economic effect. An increasingly more intensive and simultaneously more uncertain and unexpected effect results from control measurements, constructive-technological operations, truly scientific investigation along already laid-out fundamental channels, and, finally, fundamental research. A reasonably accurate and universal law is: the higher the order of a derivative on whose magnitude the result of research acts, the more uncertain and profound is the economic effect of this result. Accordingly, economic theory must include uncertainty as a fundamental concept. Economics has become such an accurate science that it must share the common fate of the exact sciences and operate with the fundamental concept of uncertainty.

## 10. POST-ATOMIC CIVILIZATION

Atomic energy, quantum electronics, cybernetics, and radiation genetics are directions of nonclassical science that characterize the atomic age; they are directly or obliquely related to atomic and nuclear physics and to the fundamental principles of the theory of relativity and quantum mechanics. But atomic physics gives an impulse to research that goes beyond its limits, penetrating into the subnuclear region and preparing a new, post-atomic civilization. Such research is devoted to the theory of elementary particles and to the problems of astrophysics related to it. It is based on a new astronomical revolution, on the observation of the sky from the planets of the terrestrial group and from orbits near them and on the study of a series of emissions other than the optical ones. It is based also on exceptionally powerful particle accelerators, on high energy physics. In contrast to the classical ideal of science, which consisted in explaining the properties of the universe by the arrangement and motion of discrete, indivisible, and indestructible bodies and their mutual forces, the new research is striving for a new ideal of science. The theories of relativity and quantum mechanics, in the form in which they were given early in the century, have introduced substantial changes into the classical ideal: the mass of discrete bodies depends on their velocity; they themselves are foci of fields; and they are subordinate to probability laws. But the basic problems in the world picture associated with relativity and quantum mechanics are related to the behavior of particles, to their position, velocity, and acceleration, to older concepts that are carried over with certain reservations and limitations. By contrast, the new ideal of science shifts the center of gravity of the problem from the *behavior* of self-identical particles to their *existence;* science is striving to explain the very existence of particles, their origin and decay, their transition from one to another type. Processes that take place in very small space-time regions of the order of $10^{-13}$ cm and $10^{-24}$ sec are irreducible to the regrouping of some kind of subparticles and, in general, are irreducible to behavior, i.e., to the position, motion, and interaction of self-identical objects.

We can note, or rather guess with some probability, the fluctuating, interrupted contours of the effect of subnuclear and cosmic research on civilization. Evidently, the processes of the transformation of the elementary particles of one type into particles of another type and the annihilation and creation of particles will find broad application after the atomic age. Such application will mean that no longer events in the atom and the nucleus but transmutations and interactions of the elementary particles are the object of rationalizing organization. What can industry gain from the transmutation of particles, from the formation and subsequent annihilation of the "particle-antiparticle" pair? It is known of such reactions that they cannot become the source of energy, since the production of antiparticles requires greater energy than is formed during their annihilation. But perhaps it will be possible to accumulate energy by isolating antimatter from matter, and then to obtain energy in an extremely concentrated form; the energy will be a hundred times greater than that given off by a thermonuclear reaction with the same quantity of matter. Such accumulators will expand several-fold the possibilities of space travel. Perhaps an even greater effect on civilization will be exerted by the miniaturization of energy devices; complex and powerful generators and motors such as those imitating muscle fibers give tens of thousands of kilowatt-hours in volumes of the order of a cubic millimeter and require no recharging for decades. Elementary particle research today is already exerting an effect on the pace of technical and economic development, *raising the intellectual potential of science.* We should expect not only radical changes in construction and technological processes that are the embodiment of ideal physical schemes, but also changes in the fundamental principles of science that become initial impulses for the broad elevation and creation of new ideal schemes in all fields.

## 11. PROGNOSES OF UNDERSTANDING AND PROGNOSES OF REASON

The change in the fundamental principles of science, the change in style, logic, and initial concepts, cannot be excluded from contemporary predictions, and at the same time they cannot be predicted in the way that the concrete physical cycles and the technical constructions embodying them can. In the case of technical constructions, prediction stems from an established physical scheme; in the case of a change in the scheme involving an established fundamental principle, the change of such a principle can be based only on very general epistemological premises. Changes of the latter sort encompass *infinite* multitudes of schemes, schemes that are not yet realized. Here are those components of knowledge that classical philosophy ascribed not to *understanding* but to *reason*.

According to the traditional duality, understanding comprehends regularity in the world, whereas reason is capable of seeing and predicting the necessity of switching to a new order. Such a switch is a function of reason, which is inseparable from the function of understanding: in order to switch to a new regularity and law, a concept of regularity and law is necessary, a concept of that which Hegel called the "peaceful" aspect of knowledge. In short, the functions of the understanding are necessary.

Classical science in the eighteenth century already showed how *reason* passes from one understandable ordering of the world to another. The harmony of the universe in Aristotle corresponded to the invariability of the *positions* of bodies that occupy "natural places." In Galileo's *Dialogue* and in the concept of inertia on the whole, the harmony corresponded to the constancy and invariability of *velocities,* the first derivatives of positions with respect to time. In Galileo's *Discourses* and Newton's *Principles,* the harmony corresponded to the constancy and invariability of *accelerations,* the second derivatives of positions with respect to time. These invariabilities are confirmed by understanding, and reason forces the transition from one invariability of understanding to the other.

In nonclassical science, reason was not limited to the sporadic translation of intellect to another stage; e.g., from positions to velocities, from velocities to accelerations. It was constantly lying in wait for understanding and was constantly capable of transforming established peaceful laws of understanding into paradoxical, new ones. Such a relationship between understanding and reason is typical not only of nonclassical science but also of the scientific, scientific-technical, and economic predictions related to it.

Radical shifts related to new physical and chemical schemes not only lead to acceleration in one branch of industry but also evoke acceleration in the growth of productivity of labor in other branches, an acceleration that cannot be predicted by extrapolating from the past tempo. The effect of one branch on another gives it the right to the title of "leading," which is sometimes expressed in a fundamentally new development of the branch being led. Reason continuously intervenes in the transition from an established intellectual line of development to a new line predicted by extrapolation, assuring the continuous possibility of such a transition. Such is the effect of nonclassical science, and the highest form of "leading." A hierarchy of the branches of industry exists according to their proximity to nonclassical science and according to the character of "leading." In planning the national economy of the Soviet Union, the title "leading branch" was originally applied to energetics, to the production of energy. The utilization of cheap energy opens the road to electrical industries and to the automation of labor, causing deep reconstructive shifts in all branches of industry.

For the following concentric group of branches the concept of "leading branch" has a somewhat different sense. It is still dynamic, but dynamic in a higher order. The leading branch of this higher order of leading acts on the other branches through new technical schemes that serve in the other branches as a source of new constructions or new technological prescriptions on a *nonclassical basis*. The leader is atomic energy and electronics in the broad sense, including the production of computers and laser devices. Not only engineering solutions but fundamental physical schemes are rapidly changing (fast neutron reactors, semiconductor instruments, and fundamentally new types of lasers). The change occurs in all branches that clothe the new fundamental scheme in concrete forms. It is not difficult to show that the groups of branches must possess varying speeds of expansion. If energetics not only ensures the expansion of industry among consumers but also stimulates the transition to a new, more electrified technology, it must develop more rapidly than the volume of production in the consuming branches. If a nonclassical branch, e.g., electronics, reconstructs energetics itself, then it must ensure not only the rapid development of energetics but in addition the "capacity" of energetics to grow together with the tempo of development, with the growing consumption under the new plans. The expansion of fundamental research not only has an effect on the growing industry, but the effect itself becomes more powerful.

## 12. MATHEMATICS, THE SYNTHESIS OF SCIENCE, AND MODERN OPTIMISM

For modern optimism, a deep faith in the inevitability of radical transformations of the world picture and in the positive effect of such transformations on the tempo of technical, economic, and cultural progress is characteristic. This effect is inseparable from the synthesis of science, from the formulation and reformulation of the most general first principles uniting science. The modern epoch in science is the epoch of *practical synthesis:* scientific data do not lead simply to one general synthetic scheme or another; for the scheme influences the structure and its planning.

What role does mathematics play in such a synthesis of science? In the seventeenth and eighteenth centuries, mathematics possessed only one direct physical equivalent, mechanics; but the synthesis of science consisted precisely in the subordination of the universe to mechanics, in the explanation of all processes by central forces. The echo of this tendency was Kant's formula: in every science there is as much scientific as there is mathematical. This formula seems close to the contemporary role of mathematics, but, in fact, the modern significance of mathematics for science (and not only for science) finds few analogies with its significance for the mechanical natural science of the seventeenth and eighteenth centuries.

In the nineteenth century, the scheme of the continuous movement of bodies preserved its role as the most simple and fundamental scheme of the universe. The complex laws of higher forms of motion did not allow the explanation of the processes of nature to be reduced to this simple scheme. Accordingly, mathematics could not pretend to a substantial role in the explanation of chemical processes, still less to a substantial role in biology, in the social sciences, and in the applications of these sciences; this fact in no way deprived these sciences of their scientific character. In the twentieth century, all of this has radically changed. First, simple mechanical motion, the displacement of a self-identical object in space and time, has been shown to be a most complex process. The laws of such motion include the optical constant, the speed of light, and under certain conditions they lead to the transmutation of the moving object; i.e., they destroy its self-identity, that which makes mechanical movement "simple." Second, mathematics is no longer limited, as it was in the nineteenth century, to universal applicability in mechanics, complex and limited applicability in physics, and sporadic and insignificant applicability in chemistry and no applicability in biology. In the second half of the twentieth century, mathematics pretends to applicability not only in the enumerated fields, but also in the analysis of processes more complex than biological ones; namely, in those of higher nervous activity, human psychology, and human economic and social life.

The synthesizing function of mathematics is presently based not on the immobility but on the variability of its most general axioms, which alone may serve as the foundation of a universal synthesis. Mathematical axioms have become dynamic, mobile, dependent on physical experiments and thus on all the basic empirical sources of knowledge. The famous definition of Russell, namely, that mathematics is a science that does not know what it speaks about and does not know if what it says is true, a logical independence that has allowed mathematics to grow into a powerful tool of modern science, now becomes somewhat archaic: mathematics, including its most general and fundamental branches, speaks of the world and says something that can be confirmed, refuted, or modified by experimental knowledge of existence. The physical content of mathematical concepts makes mathematics not only the tool of theoretical synthesis; the mathematization of science is the basis for the transformation of the world, for the creation of noözones. The transforming effect of applied mathematics on civilization includes the transformation of the character of labor: the combination of the mathematization of science and control with the application of electronic devices allows the content of labor to be changed, its creative, reorganizing potentials to be increased. Mathematization lies in that path of modern science that leads to the realization of the integral goal of science: the transformation of the subject, content, and object of labor.

Thus, applied mathematics becomes the axis of economic prognoses, of optimistic prognoses, of prognoses related to society's goal of rendering its activity expedient. But then the goal itself must possess some metric coefficient; furthermore, optimism, faith in the achievement of the goal, must possess some metric coefficient expressing the probability of realizing the goal. Here is a small setback. Is it possible in general to express emotion (and optimism, whatever epistemological, scientific-prognostic, economic, and econometrical sense we ascribe it, remains an emotion) in quantitative parameters? Is this question not related to an observation of Salieri's to the effect that music is reduced to algebra, and even then it is not music but that which is expressed by music and cannot be expressed otherwise, e.g., by words?

Saint-Exupéry observes that, to the child, the interests of adults seem strange. Adults are interested in quantitative definitions: they must know how old someone is, how much he earns, and the like. These matters are of no importance to the child. Science, and not only science, requires some approximation to "childish" interests. Einstein acknowledged this in the case of science; outside science it is expressed by Christ's formula: "If you do not be as children . . . ." Children, as *Alice in Wonderland* has shown, do not actually dislike counting; only counting for them must be paradoxical. Precisely such a transition from the traditional mathematical correlations to the paradoxical was realized in the theory that Einstein considered the result of "childish" interests. (He said that he had arrived at the theory of relativity because he had retained a childish interest in fundamental problems until he was old enough to do something about solving them.)

The transition to paradoxical, non-Euclidean correlations from the traditional Euclidean ones, which is considered as a physical transition, the non-Euclidean character of the metric of space being identified with the gravitational field, lies at the basis of the general theory of relativity. Such a transition was not the dissolution of music into algebra; it was rather the transformation of algebra into music, analogous in a somewhat metaphoric sense to Kepler's "music of the spheres."

The emotional content of optimism is inseparable from its metrical expression. Faith in the forthcoming realization of a goal is impossible without quantitative calculation and, since the structure of industry is involved, without metrics.

## 13. THE CURVATURE OF THE SPACE OF ECONOMIC STRUCTURES

Metrics, i.e., all methods of determining distances by the differences of the coordinates, applies to phenomena that may be represented by points in a certain abstract $n$-dimensional space. In particular, metrics applies to the structure of industry. If, for instance, fifty branches ($n = 50$) of industry are involved, then the point corresponding to the given structure is a point in 50-dimensional structure space, defined by fifty coordinates, each of which measures, e.g., investment or production in one of the branches of industry. The transition from one structure to another is measured by the vector connecting two such points, and the curve of the dynamics of the structure of industry is made up from such vectors. The structural changes evoked by scientific and technical discoveries are the basic economic effects that must be measured in order to know the optimal dynamics of the structure of industry, assuring that the productivity of labor and its derivatives, velocity and the acceleration of its level, are on the whole greatest.

I will not discuss in detail the geometrical methods for representing not only the changes in this curve, expressing the prognoses of understanding, but also the changes related to fundamental discoveries, expressing the prognoses of reason. Briefly speaking, in these more radical prognoses, the very dependence of economic dynamics on the increase in the coordinates, on the variation of the structure, is changing. The formula connecting each infinitely small increment of the vector in $n$-space to the infinitely small increments of the coordinates changes. Such a change in metrics can be represented as a curvature not of the world line in $n$-space but of the space itself.[8] These concepts were introduced into science in connection with the general theory of relativity, in which the gravitational field is identified with the curvature of space (4-dimensional space-time). The change in the direction of a vector caused by gravitation is not a change within *space,* but a change *together with space;* the gravitational field acts uniformly on all bodies, so it is as though the properties of space itself and not the behavior of bodies in space were changing. The gravitational field goes, so to speak, beyond the limits of that which occurs in a given space. Similarly, radical turns in science, which act as a rule not only on the separate branches of industry but on industry as a whole, change the curvature of the space of economic structures, making it non-Euclidean.

[8] Boris Kuznetsov, "The Economic Effect of Nonclassical Science and Methods of Economic Forecasting," in *Problems of the Science of Science* (Warsaw, 1971), pp. 63–75.

# Note on Contributors

ROBERT FOX is Senior Lecturer in the History of Science at the University of Lancaster. He is the author of *The Caloric Theory of Gases from Lavoisier to Regnault* (1971) and has a special interest in the work of Sadi Carnot.

ROBERT E. KOHLER is a member of the Department of History and Sociology of Science at the University of Pennsylvania. His special interests include the history of physical chemistry, biochemistry, and the relations of science and technology.

BORIS KUZNETSOV is Professor and Director of Studies in the Institute for the History of Science of the Academy of Sciences of the U.S.S.R., Moscow. His writings are devoted to problems of philosophy, theoretical physics, and the history and economic effect of science.

MARY JO NYE teaches part time in the history of science at the University of Oklahoma. Her book *Molecular Reality. A Perspective on the Scientific Work of Jean Perrin* appeared in 1972, and she is now engaged in a study of the French chemist and educator Paul Sabatier.

ROBERT H. SILLIMAN is Assistant Professor of History at Emory University. His research interests are the history of the physical sciences, especially in France, in the eighteenth and early nineteenth centuries.

# IN MEMORIAM:
## Charles A. Culotta (1938–1974)

Before he could see his article in print, Charles Culotta died tragically at the age of thirty-five. He leaves his wife, Rosemary, and three children.

The measure of Culotta lay in the grandeur of his vision of the history of science. Through teaching and scholarly investigation, he sought to encompass the entire spectrum of human understanding in the history of natural knowledge. He was widely recognized as a generalist at a time when exacting standards have made it increasingly difficult to master even a small area in the history of science.

To his colleagues and students, Culotta was a scholar who never feared transcending slight themes. His robust spirit was willing to grapple with the most profound problems in the history of science. As his article in this volume indicates, he sought consistently to redefine the history of science by careful analysis and penetrating synthesis.

The appearance of his doctoral dissertation, an exhaustive study of eighteenth and nineteenth century respiratory physiology, marked the beginning of research that led to three important papers on the subject. These papers demonstrate a deep understanding of historical methodology and a desire to treat broad questions in the history of science.

Particularly remarkable was the breadth of Culotta's scholarly interests. With enthusiasm and ability he studied the history of medical, biological, and physical sciences from antiquity to the twentieth century. In all of his work, he was extraordinarily sensitive to philosophical issues in the history of science, and in the last years he had become increasingly sympathetic to the social history of science. These themes were evident in his unfinished accomplishments: at the time of his death, he was completing manuscripts on Renaissance science, on networks of scientific correspondence in the seventeenth century, on science and politics in nineteenth century, and on Darwin.

Culotta will be remembered above all as a teacher. It seemed that at any hour of the night he would be available to help a student clarify an embryonic idea, make a critical comment, or transform a faltering theme into a magnificent one. Culotta demanded of his students the same rigor and universality he sought in his own work, but those who were close to him realized quickly that he was a sympathetic teacher.

Culotta sometimes admonished his students, "Don't promise more than you can deliver." Culotta promised, and he delivered. When he died he was formulating yet a deeper understanding of the broad picture of the history of science he so dearly sought. Tragically, he had only begun to realize his great potential.

As with any remarkable individual, death cannot take away that part of Charles Culotta that lives on in his ideas and in the work of his colleagues, students, and friends.

Lewis Pyenson
*21 February 1974*